Movie Greats

Movie Greats
A Critical Study of Classic Cinema

Philip Gillett

Oxford • New York

English edition
First published in 2008 by
Berg
Editorial offices:
First Floor, Angel Court, 81 St Clements Street, Oxford OX4 1AW, UK
175 Fifth Avenue, New York, NY 10010, USA

Berg is the imprint of Oxford International Publishers Ltd.

Library of Congress Cataloging-in-Publication Data

Gillett, Philip (Philip John)
Movie greats : a critical study of classic cinema / Philip Gillett.
p. cm.
Includes bibliographical references and index.
ISBN-13: 978-1-84520-652-9 (cloth)
ISBN-10: 1-84520-652-5 (cloth)
ISBN-13: 978-1-84520-653-6 (pbk.)
ISBN-10: 1-84520-653-3 (pbk.)
1. Motion pictures. I. Title.
PN1994.G533 2008
791.43—dc22 2008027331

British Library Cataloguing-in-Publication Data
A catalogue record for this book is available from the British Library.

ISBN 978 1 84520 652 9 (Cloth)
978 1 84520 653 6 (Paper)

Typeset by Apex CoVantage
Printed in the United Kingdom by Biddles Ltd, King's Lynn

www.bergpublishers.com

For Roz, with love

Contents

Acknowledgements

My thanks go to the library staff at Torbay, Bradford, Leeds, Manchester and the University of Exeter. They endured my pleas for help. Roz Ellis and Graham Derrick commented on early drafts. I am grateful to them and to Brian McFarlane and Keith Withall who readily answered my queries. Eric Fenwick identified scriptural references and Archie Montgomery gave me an insight into morality in nineteenth-century Scotland. Needless to say, any errors are mine. Particular thanks go to Tristan Palmer of Berg Publishers for his encouragement when this book was just a bright idea.

Introduction

How do films achieve eminence? The question has troubled me ever since a friend admitted that he found *Citizen Kane* boring. My guilty secret was that I shared his feelings. This was sufficient reason for reappraising the film canon. Reputations once achieved are apt to be taken for granted even in academic circles. Who would admit that a work on every film student's curriculum is unworthy of study?

A related issue is how we look at films. Film-makers know instinctively that emotions come first. As Ingmar Bergman put it: 'Both film and music bypass the intellect and assail the emotions. Both film and music are rhythm, breathing—that is what I have learnt.'[1] Film-makers seek to move audiences, eliciting tears, fear or laughter. Academics follow in their wake, assessing and justifying, with the emotional response relegated to being a shabby adjunct which does not easily fit within the critical apparatus. One consequence is a mismatch between what the public likes and what it should like. Horror films seem condemned to remain marginal despite their popularity. This phenomenon is not peculiar to film: crime novels and fantasy fiction have a reputation for failing to win major literary prizes. The arts are judged by status as much as quality.

This book seeks to reassess a selection of canonic films more subjectively than usual. Some proved popular with the public; others did not. The opening chapter looks at how greatness is assessed in the arts and the usefulness of concepts such as the sublime, myth, ambiguity and the collective unconscious in understanding the phenomenon. A more subjective approach is introduced which foregrounds the emotions. The second chapter examines the film canon and seeks to apply the subjective approach to film. Each of the following fourteen chapters focuses on a film which has garnered critical adulation and which disappoints me, the final two being speculative entrants to the canon. Accolades can drown out dissenting voices, but the number of heretics is surprising. It is reassuring not to be in a minority of one. The final chapter returns to the question of how some films achieve prestige at the expense of others and the implications this has for our culture.

Credits are transcribed from the films, supplemented by information from the International Movie Database (IMDb) (http://imdb.com), the British Film Institute's (BFI) Film and TV Database (http://www.bfi.org.uk/filmtvinfo/ftvdb), Film Reference (http://www.filmreference.com) and AGP (http://www.agpfilms.com/defaut.asp). Names become anglicized or shortened, so spellings may vary. Release dates are as given in the IMDb. Useful sources not cited in the notes are listed as further reading. These fall into three categories: neglected works, seminal works applicable to my approach and relevant new material. Extensive use is made of internet sources. Quality is variable, but this applies to any medium. Changes in URLs pose a difficulty, but the information provided should allow works to be located using a search engine.

–1–

So Who Says It's Great?

Three Models of Greatness

For those who consider themselves open to new ideas, 'I know what I like,' with its implications of narrow-mindedness and inflexibility, is not a remark which springs readily to the lips. Not that 'I don't know what I like' is any better, with its tacit admission of an inability to discriminate. The acceptable response lies somewhere between these extremes, assuming the whiff of compromise can be negotiated.

We might keep quiet about what we like, but there is no shortage of voices eager to fill the silence. The media abound with recommendations for what we should see, read and hear. And we take heed. Art lovers worship at the shrine of the *Mona Lisa*. Musicians revere Bach's unaccompanied violin works and the operas of Mozart, just as lovers of literature venerate Cervantes and Proust. Most of us recognize the pinnacles of our culture, if only by repute. We may have no liking for them: of those who embark on reading Proust, how many reach the final page? And who would admit to preferring Stephen King?

Just as recommendations are plentiful, so are study guides and critical analyses which help us to appreciate the works of Beethoven, Conrad, Ibsen, Turner, and so on. It is axiomatic that these figures are great. A consistent if partisan concern with how such judgements are made has troubled art critics from John Ruskin onwards. This concern has not been matched in the other arts. Such neglect is unsurprising given the arcane processes involved in elevating a work to greatness, which make choosing a pope seem a model of transparency. Three ways of attempting to cast light on how greatness emerges are the market model, the consensus model and the time model. If none provides a sure route to greatness, at least the journey should encourage caution about applying labels.

The market model is precise but limited in its scope: CDs of Beethoven symphonies sell better than those of Havergal Brian; therefore Beethoven is the greater composer. This approach becomes problematic when Dan Brown is revealed as our greatest writer, with Agatha Christie taking the laurels in the longer term. Putting a monetary value on art means living with such anomalies, but at least it makes greatness quantifiable. The market model can be seen operating in its purest form when collectors bid for works of art. If Jackson Pollock's paintings command higher prices than those of Seurat, then Pollock is the greater painter. The snag is that when the public supports its preferences with cash, popularity becomes a term of disdain rather than a signifier of greatness. Reproductions of Constable's paintings on tea towels have not enhanced his reputation, while Vladimir Tretchikoff and Jack Vetrianno remain beyond the critical pale despite their popularity, indicating how power is wielded in the art establishment. This tension between art and commerce has a long history. At the first Impressionist exhibition in 1874, Courbet rejected the usual practice of exhibits being chosen by judges in favour of asking artists to pay a modest fee. Was this a triumph for democracy or commerce? The music world is more democratic, or shows more commercial acumen, with figures such as Brian Eno and Frank Zappa probing the boundary zone between serious and popular music without losing their audiences. But playing classical music to deter teenagers from congregating in such semipublic places as shopping malls and railway stations should prompt speculation beyond the psychological mechanisms involved to the values of a society which uses art in this way.

The appropriateness of the market model varies across the arts. It reigns supreme in the visual arts, where most works are unique. Limitless copies of a book, film or CD can be produced, meaning that a work has to take its place in a wider and more competitive arena. Producing and marketing multiple copies requires a complex organization, so that the work of the creator becomes but one stage in this process. The symbiotic relationship of art and commerce is a source of recurring tension.

The consensus model rejected by Courbet focuses attention on how power is exercised. A work is great if it is deemed to be great or, more accurately, when people with influence arrive at this conclusion. If a little-known painting by one of Rembrandt's followers is reattributed to the master, its value soars and queues form outside the gallery. Provenance counts for a lot, and not only in the fine arts. A reliance on experts as arbiters of quality poses obvious dangers. Does a coterie somehow distil a range of opinions, or is it dictating what the public should like? Would exhibitions by Young British Artists attract crowds and rich buyers in the absence of endorsements by curators, critics and agents? These activities would be deemed insider dealing in the stock market. And just when things are getting cosy, every coterie spawns its mavericks. Dissident but influential critics including Kenneth Tynan and Harold Hobson championed new dramatists in the 1950s. Would Samuel Beckett or John Osborne have achieved fame without them?

However exciting the lure of the new, there is still a large audience for traditional art forms, often bequeathed to us by yesterday's rebels. Beethoven's star has not waned, Ibsen is still being staged, and George Eliot's novels remain in print. Yet tradition is itself the product of selection, and sometimes advocacy is needed to overcome a neglect of the past. Mendelssohn championed Bach, while Schumann reawakened interest in Schubert. Proselytizers are not always successful in their endeavours, as the number of contenders for the Great American Novel demonstrates. A divide can open between an elite and the public, allowing experimental work to take place away from the public gaze, but sooner or later bridges must be built if art is to find an audience and not become self-serving. The rationale for establishing the

Arts Council of Great Britain in 1946 was to bridge this divide; the paradox is that it did so by putting power and money in the hands of coteries. This is more than an issue of quality. It involves the power to adjudicate on what constitutes good art, and the rebellion of Courbet and others who disagree. At least received opinions can get reappraised in the maelstrom. And there is always room for people to change sides.

Art needs an audience if it is to be judged great, which is easy for the *Mona Lisa* or a Shakespeare play, but harder for Petrarch or James Joyce, whose work is more often revered at a distance. Popularity is not a necessary criterion for greatness, given that pronouncing on works of art is likely to remain a minority pastime. The metropolitan elite is alive and well and always up for such a task, though whether it should be left to this group is another matter.

The consensus model intuitively feels more acceptable if an elite is not involved, but then it risks becoming amorphous. How do judgements on quality arise from the aesthetic equivalent of the primordial soup? It can be shown how such judgements are disseminated formally through the curriculum of schools and universities, and informally by media recommendation and word of mouth. Harder to explain are why critics differ wildly in their judgements, the implications of this plurality and how cult works capture the public imagination in the absence of advocacy. The process of consensus-building is nothing if not haphazard, with a range of competing ideas vying for attention in the artistic marketplace. One implication is that the market model should not be discarded so readily. If it is reformulated in terms of a market for ideas, it becomes more useful and more acceptable. Pierre Bourdieu has built an elegant model based on treating culture as a commodity.[1]

The time model also relies on impersonal forces, with greatness being seen as the product of a filtering process. Like panning for gold, the attrition of time winnows away lesser works, so what is left deserves to be revered. There are four flaws in this approach:

1. It assumes that time will somehow produce the right decision about quality. It may simply leave an inheritance whose culturally acceptability has endured. The Nazis banished degenerate art; in turn we have banished Nazi art. Quality becomes irrelevant in the world of cultural politics.
2. The time model ignores the vagaries of survival which skew our interpretation of the past. War, natural disasters, the processes of decay and the enthusiasms of archivists all affect what has come down to us. Classical Greek drama is judged by the few plays which have survived. What the Assyrians laughed at is not on record, for comedy is apt to be subversive and subversive traditions are not written down, however good the jokes. Gerard Manley Hopkins and Brahms were too self-critical for posterity's good, destroying works which failed to meet their own exacting standards, while ignorance or design may lead to works being destroyed or dispersed on their creator's death. The attrition of time does not just affect the inferior; it can sweep away everything.

3. The length of time needed to ensure greatness is hazy. Dante has had seven hundred years, which should be long enough; go back any further and survival becomes increasingly problematic. But what is the minimum period needed? Can Britten's *Peter Grimes* join the pantheon after sixty years? And where does this leave living artists? Are they condemned to a cultural limbo until later generations arbitrate on their work? For Andy Goldsworthy and others who work with ephemeral materials, posterity will not be in a position to judge. And as the dissemination of ideas becomes easier, is the period necessary to qualify for greatness shortening?

4. Such arbitrary factors as advocacy and changing technology can determine what is considered important. The death of F. R. Leavis, that champion of D. H. Lawrence and detractor of Dickens, led to a reversal of the writers' reputations, so that today, Lawrence is hard to find in any university syllabus, while Dickens fills our television screens. Mahler's music remained almost forgotten for half a century after his death; since the advent of the long-playing record, he has become one of the most frequently performed and recorded of composers. The plays of George Bernard Shaw have largely fallen from the repertoire, along with those of Christopher Fry, John Whiting and Jean Anouilh. Victorian painting was reviled for much of the twentieth century. There is no logic to these changes of fortune. Nor is there any point in waiting for time to put things right. Fashions sometimes come around again, but they may consign an artist and his work to permanent oblivion.

The passage of time weeds out the modish, but it encourages conservatism if we always fall back on the tried and trusted. Exasperation shines through the words of choreographer Alan Carter: 'Do let's experience the already tried experience. No experiments please. Nice clean drama that won't upset Gran. Nice clean jokes that Grandad can laugh at again.... Forget all the scandalous experiments of the past and keep only the successes. Please no failures, no attempts, no defections, deflections. No change only success.'[2]

Michael Thompson's rubbish model brings together the time, consensus and market models: 'Those people near the top have the power to make things durable and make things transient, so they can ensure that their own objects are always durable and those of others always transient.'[3] For 'things', read 'art'. Critics are among those who wield aesthetic power, controlling the transfer between categories. The process involves consensus building, with culture being seen as a rule book of what the right people agree is important. Being at the summit of the cultural hierarchy can be displayed by having the market power to buy a painting or a seat at the opera. At the bottom of the hierarchy comes rubbish, which is anything we cannot see, or conspire not to see. Graffiti and pavement art are disposable and come into this category. As well as embracing the market and consensus, the rubbish model has a temporal dimension, with fixed assumptions being accepted about the distant past and the present. By contrast, the recent past is negotiable and potentially disposable.[4] The nineteenth-century industrialist chose not to see the polluted town where his money was made, demonstrating his power and wealth and keeping to the cultural rule book by settling in the country and employing artists to decorate his home. Charles Foster Kane in *Citizen Kane* (Orson Welles, US, 1941) is his cinematic exemplar. Today, the industrialist's furniture is unsalable, while his family portraits languish in the basement of a provincial art gallery. These items belong to the recent past, whereas his collection of old masters has retained its value. Today's norms are fashionable, meaning that we accept them unthinkingly, while we recognize an old master when we see one. Our assumptions are fixed in both cases. By contrast, the values of the industrialist's era—the recent past—are open to negotiation. Thompson misses the significance of technological change in a movement such as the Bauhaus school, or the political role of art: a performance of Auber's opera *La muette de Portici* sparked the Belgian Revolution of 1830. Despite these blemishes, Thompson's model offers a way of understanding how cultural values become dominant and persistent.

The Sublime, Ambiguity and Myth

Teasing out the meaning of greatness in art is not a new preoccupation; only the terminology varies. A key work is *On the Sublime,* attributed to the third-century Greek poet Longinus. This relies on the consensus model, with cultivated intellects agreeing on what is sublime. Not that the intellect is dominant. Passion may not be all, but it counts for a lot in our recognition of the sublime. We are taken out of ourselves, 'for, as if instinctively, our soul is lifted by the true sublime, it takes proud flight, and is filled with joy and vaunting, as though it had itself produced what it had heard.'[5] The concept was taken up by Edmund Burke, whose *Philosophical Enquiry into the Sublime and Beautiful* (1757) influenced the romantic movement by aligning the sublime with horror. Both overwhelm the senses, leaving the mind paralysed, the Gothic novel being a product of this marriage. In contrast to the formality and regularity of beauty, the sublime elicits strong emotions, making it unpredictable and unforgettable. It draws on the world of the senses rather than formal analysis. We are able to experience the thrill of recognition because the emotions portrayed are the same as ours. The sublime remains just out of reach, as in a dream, creating a dual consciousness of the self and something outside oneself.[6] Later commentators have characterized the process in different ways—Walter Benjamin refers to the shock of sensation, Martin Heidegger to the moment of vision and Walter Pater to the sublime moment—but all stress its fleeting nature and its unexpectedness.[7] Monika Fludernik contends that elements of discontinuity and the bizarre have been appropriated by the postmodern movement, but she is surely too pessimistic in seeing awe, transcendence and elevation of spirit as being lost in the process of appropriation, with even beauty becoming obsolete.[8] Art becomes no more than a source of transient pleasure by this reading: a safe alternative to drugs and casual sex. The enduring appeal of art suggests that something deeper is being experienced.

One mark of greatness is ambiguity. A work which never completely yields its secrets can be endlessly reinterpreted and remains an object of fascination. This gives it durability. In Umberto Eco's words, 'Ambiguity is what forces the addressee to approach the message in a different fashion, not to use it as a mere vehicle, but rather as a constant source of continually shifting meanings.'[9] The lure of the *Mona Lisa* is that enigmatic smile. Composers as diverse as Bach, Schumann and Berg incorporated ciphers into their works; if we do not always recognize the messages, we sense that a discourse is taking place under the melodic surface. Conversely, the limitation of the whodunit is that its secret is revealed in one reading. Ambiguity increases a work's complexity, enhancing its power. This appeals to romantics and the avant-garde, though, as David Cohen cautions, ambiguity can be found in poor art.[10] What matters is how it is used.

The conjunction of comedy and ambiguity is of particular interest. Longinus was dismissive of comedy, comparing its low style unfavourably with the high style of tragedy.[11] Serious drama is still accorded more respect: how many actors aspire to be stand-up comics? The movement is always in the other direction. Yet the best comedy refuses to be confined by the straitjacket of genre. Alan Ayckbourn's farces teeter on the brink of tragedy. We laugh, but we wait for somebody to fall. Igor Yevin stresses the ambiguity at the heart of comedy, which is often based on abrupt changes of status (Eliza in Shaw's *Pygmalion*), or has dialogue replete with double meanings (anything involving Frankie Howerd).[12] To appreciate the full gamut of devices entails visiting a traditional British pantomime, where rags to riches, double entendres and gender reversals are the order of the day. But kick yourself afterwards as a reminder that this is not great art.

A function of art is the reformulation and retelling of myths for a new generation. Norse legends and Greek gods made sense of those twists of fate which brought death, disaster and occasional good fortune to our ancestors. Now we have science to explain the processes involved, but in the view of Herbert Read, it has not replaced the symbolic functions of art.[13] Because dance is not limited by words or notation, it can present human existence in its starkest terms, from fertility (Kenneth Macmillan's *The Rite of Spring* and Peter Darrell's *Sun into Darkness*), to the death of children (Antony Tudor's *Dark Elegies*) and sexual attraction (Peter Darrell's *Jeux* and Kenneth Macmillan's *Las Hermanas*). These works touch what Burke would call the sublime by harking back to mythic themes. Yet the inherent conservatism of myth is its limitation. Movements including Cubism and Futurism arose as a response to dilemmas of the machine age which were beyond the scope of myth to explain. In Fludernik's terms, one consequence of this emphasis on discontinuity and the bizarre was a lack of agreement on how to assess quality in art.[14] In Thompson's terms, it is easier to recognize greatness from the distant past rather than yesterday: the status of Marcel Duchamp's urinal is still being negotiated, while that of Michelangelo's *David* is secure. A harbinger of this tension was the championing of tradition by John Ruskin and William Morris. Theirs was a rearguard action, but their spiritual heirs continue the war undaunted.

Jung and the Collective Unconscious

Carl Gustav Jung's essays provide a way of linking the sublime, ambiguity and myth. He reveals his awareness of the sublime by citing Immanuel Kant, whose *Critique of Judgement* (1790) derived from Longinus.[15] For Jung, there is a dual consciousness of the self and the other. The latter he terms the collective unconscious, which is inherited and carries societal ideas in the form of archetypes. These have existed since earliest times and are expressed in myths, fairy tales and rites.[16] Such ideas are not new: Duns Scotus (d. 1308) proposed the notion of man having a common as well as a particular nature. A key archetype for Jung is the anima, the mystical, conservative and female part of the collective unconscious epitomized by Helen of Troy. Everything she touches becomes taboo, dangerous or magical.[17] This is the realm of the emotions (the sublime), where ideas often present as contradictions (ambiguity) which have to be reconciled. Such notions pervade religious philosophy: yin and yang, the virgin mother and the human but divine character of Jesus. Jung's ideas on the importance of dreams, the inherited nature of the collective unconscious and the almost mystical role of the woman are open to question, but he touches on our need to make sense of hopes and experiences through art, and how such ideas take particular forms. Puccini's *Turandot* explores from a male perspective the dangerous and magical in women; so in their different ways do Shakespeare's *Macbeth,* Henri Alain-Fournier's *Le Grand Meaulnes* (1913) and film noir pieces such as *Double Indemnity* (Billy Wilder, US, 1944). These examples may be 'treasure in the realm of shadowy thoughts' in Kant's terms, but force a work to fit Jung's construct and the usefulness of his approach can vanish as though a beam of light has been turned on those shadows.[18] Analysis of any art work is only useful insofar as it aids understanding. It must be appropriate and it must be used sensitively.

Classics and the Canon

Labelling works as classics can be contentious. Mark Twain's dictum that 'classics are books people praise and don't read' is too often true.[19] The title of Holly Koelling's book *Classic Connections: Turning Teens on to Great Literature* serves to emphasize that classics need special pleading.[20] One problem is finding a definition which does not amount to the time model by any other name. To define classics as works which have withstood the test of time fails by this criterion. The time element means that classics are inherently conservative: if works not only survive, but ascend to the pantheon of greatness, then the weight of tradition helps to keep them there. Yet displaced they are as the attrition of time continues and each generation seeks different qualities from their great works. This is the rationale for the Ex-Classics Web site, which includes works by such neglected figures as Samuel Butler and the Reverend Richard H. Barham among its offerings.[21] A more dynamic definition of classics is needed, such as that proposed by Charles Augustin Sainte-Beuve, who saw them as 'works that are contemporary with every age.'[22] His approach catches the freshness of classics rather than their fustiness. In previewing a classic film festival, Julie Phillips· manages to pre-empt a panel discussion on the topic by offering a succinct definition of a classic as 'a part of our history, our cultural understanding of ourselves'.[23] This shifts attention from a work's inherent qualities to its function. The classic contributes to social cohesion by introducing each generation to the values of its predecessors—the favourite book a parent reads to a child—and to shared traditions, from the annual visit to the pantomime to the film which is screened on television every Christmas.

According to John Guillory, just when everybody understood the meaning of classic, the term was displaced by the canon in academic circles.[24] This can be seen as one way in which an elite seeks to maintain its exclusiveness. The term classic has gained widespread currency, for example classic cars, with canon taking on a more restricted meaning. For the purposes of this discussion, what is considered important and worth preserving in the arts is enshrined in the canon, which embodies the aesthetic values of an era and a social group.

A staunch defender of the canon in recent times is Harold Bloom, for whom, 'Aesthetic value emanates from the struggle between texts: in the reader, in language, in the classroom, in arguments within society.'[25] This catches the fluid nature of canons, though Bloom confuses the issue by declaring: 'Writers, artists, composers, themselves determine canons, by bridging between strong precursors and strong successors.'[26] Not only does this shift the principal role in canon formation to the producers of art, but it risks making the process teleological, with the artist becoming a link in a chain which can only be appreciated in retrospect. Bloom selects authors by their sublimity, but the inclusion of Ronald Firbank suggests that personal taste counts for more than he acknowledges.[27]

A warning comes from Eco: 'The difference between critical sensibility and snobbery is minimal.'[28] For Matthew Arnold and T. S. Eliot, the difference sometimes appears nonexistent, and Bloom follows in their footsteps when he sees aesthetics as producing anxiety in the working class.[29] Herbert Read begins in crusading style: 'Art ... is eternally disturbing, permanently revolutionary. It is because the artist ... always confronts the unknown, and what he brings back from that confrontation is a novelty, a new symbol, a new vision of life, the outer image of inward things.'[30] Then the tone changes: 'The signals he sends back are often unintelligible to the multitude, but then come the philosophers and critics to interpret his message.'[31] Thompson's notion of critics as cultural arbitrators is not far away. Pop art has no place in the rarefied world of Read or Bloom, where the very notion of a Nobel Prize for Pearl S. Buck is likely to rankle.

The values and assumptions embodied in canons have as much to do with power and status as aesthetics. Fully appreciating the canon's riches may require specialized knowledge of a foreign language, musical form, or the principles behind such movements as Surrealism. Not knowing or appreciating such works is to demonstrate ignorance and lack of taste. The converse is that canons confer status not only on the artwork, but on those who appreciate it. If you know the great works, you are cultured. Canons are also inherently conservative. Change comes as the elite changes, or as canon formation is democratized, but the process can be slow and there will be a rearguard action, the battle being played out publicly (the Turner Prize), or behind closed doors (drawing up the examination syllabus).

Canons demand veneration, so that art galleries packed with old masters attract more visitors and money than more modest collections. This is not to imply that a Rembrandt painting is unworthy of such attention, but should a gallery purchase it for a price which would buy the entire works of a lesser-known artist? By implication, what is outside the canon is less worthy of attention, irrespective of its popularity. Critics disparage Beryl Cook's paintings, their absence from the canon preserving its exclusivity. In Thompson's terms, if you are in a position to define what is good, you can also define what is rubbish. You are also making an implicit judgement about people who enjoy rubbish.

Clement Greenberg offers an approach which gets away from Bloom's reliance on rigid aesthetic standards: 'But the ultimate values which the cultural spectator derives from Picasso are derived at a second remove, as a result of reflection upon the immediate impression left by plastic values. It is only then that the recognizable, the miraculous and the sympathetic enter.'[32] By distinguishing immediate and secondary responses, Greenberg prefigures a model proposed by the philosopher Jenefer Robinson, which departs from established approaches to criticism. Robinson seeks a synthesis of ideas drawn from psychology, neuroscience and the arts, her contention being that in confronting an art object, there is a primitive and speedy primary stage of affective appraisal (emotion) triggering physiological and behavioural changes. This is followed by cognitive appraisal (reflection), drawing on rational thought processes. The viewer gains an emotional education from the experience. Crucially, the emotional response is a form of understanding in itself, however difficult to articulate, and a source of data for interpreting the work.[33] In short, it colours the rational appraisal. An example cited by Ivan Gaskell is how art historians' responses to Rembrandt's *Jeremiah Lamenting the Destruction of Jerusalem* (1630) are influenced by their first encounters with the painting.[34] Four elements of Robinson's model deserve particular attention. Taking literature as an example:

1. The reader can bridge gaps in the text by making inferences.[35] The process of film editing also relies on this: we infer from a sequence of a child stepping into the road, a driver's horrified expression and a foot stamping on a pedal that the child has stepped in front of a car and the driver is trying to brake. Inferences allow us to make sense of the narrative, the enhanced knowledge drawn from interests and experience meaning that a mother, a racing driver and an accident victim will fill the gaps in different ways.

2. The reader gains a sense of how the author wants us to react, and hence, of the implied author, who functions as intermediary. Writers from Jonathan Swift to Vladimir Nabokov have used the implied author as an extra character.[36] Each reader's notion of the implied author yields a unique reading, though too much authorial intrusion leaves the reader feeling manipulated. In Noël Carroll's terms, the author prefocuses the text, guiding the reader towards a desired response like the voice-over in a film.[37]

3. The immediate response to a book is no different from the emotional understanding needed in everyday life.[38] We respond to the story of an intruder in the same way as we respond to an intruder in our home, the difference being a matter of degree. The implication is that we use stories to rehearse situations encountered in everyday life, while bringing experience of everyday life to stories.

4. Emotions focus attention and provide a means of judging a work. A comic character will not be appreciated unless he or she can raise a smile. Humour has to be experienced somatically: being told that the character is funny is not enough. Once the comedic element is appreciated, the world of the book can be experienced through the prism of the emotion.[39]

Robinson's model is relevant to a work's reception. It says nothing about a work's creation, where a similar complex of affective and cognitive factors apply, but mediated by technique. An incidental virtue of the model is that it helps us to understand why revisiting a book or a film never recaptures the impact of the first encounter: the emotional response will differ the second time around. A limitation of the approach is that causal inferences provide a way of understanding narrative; move away from narrative form and the model becomes less useful. Robinson acknowledges this, citing the works of Italo Calvino and Robert Coover, which deliberately prevent the reader from becoming emotionally involved.[40] Her model is distinct from academic approaches favouring a quasi-dispassionate analysis. In this she is returning to something akin to traditional literary criticism: F. R. Leavis could hardly quibble with her response to Edith Wharton's novel *The Reef*.[41] Nor is there any reason why emotion should not be incorporated successfully into academic teaching, as Natalie Friedman demonstrates.[42] A contrary view is that art which can be appreciated at first sight is superficial, while serious art requires a more considered response.[43] Without denying that understanding can be enriched by objective study, this ignores the first impression which even a complex work has to make. Using terms like *superficial* and *serious* leads to the dichotomy between high and popular art which bedevilled culture in the twentieth century. By making her feelings explicit, Robinson provides the springboard for a wider spectrum of responses than is normally seen in academic work. Liking a work does not become secondary to its formal qualities: canons need scrutinizing with this in mind. At least questioning the adulation given to the few might allow others to share the limelight.

–2–

The Celluloid Canon

Defining the Canon

Film in Britain lies outside the remit of the Arts Councils, which sums up its anomalous position among the arts. Should this shadowy treasure be called an art at all? Janet Staiger in her seminal paper sees this as the question which exercised the first generation of film theorists.[1] Aesthetic purists can dismiss film as an upstart and a bastardized one at that in its evolution from a fairground attraction. The British Film Institute might have been established to encourage the art of film, but it has had an uphill struggle given that film production, distribution and exhibition are controlled by commercial interests. This does not preclude artistic merit, but the emphasis on box-office returns skews priorities. The problem for the cinema industry is the high cost per film and the low return per customer. Film demands collaborative effort and elaborate technology, both of which are expensive. A large paying audience is needed to recoup the outlay, but attracting such an audience requires star names and an elaborate publicity machine, both of which ratchet up costs. To complicate matters, only a minority of films become commercial successes, so that the few have to subsidize the many. Of the 505 films released in the UK and the Republic of Ireland during 2006 and which ran for a week or more, 48 per cent of total box-office receipts came from the top 20 films (a decline from 61 per cent in 2002), while 11 per cent came from the bottom 405.[2] This ignores the many films which never reach the screen. The cinema remains a high-stakes game, even if the dependence on a handful of blockbusters is reducing, possibly because an emphasis on box-office returns over the first weekend has resulted in a higher turnover of films which have shorter runs.

Now that high-definition video cameras, digital projection, DVDs and the internet allow films to be shot and distributed at lower cost, old assumptions are being challenged; the dogma manitesto with its return to basic sets, lighting and sound being a philosophical celebration of changed times. The cinema release has become a way of attracting publicity for DVD sales, reversing the situation which existed in the early days of prerecorded videos. Attempts to trim costs by introducing new technology are not new: Rank toyed with Independent Frame (a sophisticated back-projection system) in the late 1940s, while *Secrets* (Philip Saville, GB, 1971) was an early instance of shooting a feature film in 16mm. What distinguishes digital technology from these earlier efforts is the enthusiasm with which it has been embraced by film-makers. If the Hollywood blockbuster still dominates multiplexes, at least it keeps open production facilities and networks for the distribution and exhibition of film, benefiting makers who attract smaller audiences.

In common with the other arts, gatekeepers control access to film. Production companies, distributors and exhibitors determine what appears on screen; critics then attempt to influence public opinion about which films to see. Academics and prestigious film-makers such as Martin Scorsese give considered but equally partisan views on what they consider to be significant. By contrast, the public is amorphous and unpredictable, capable of turning a film which is excoriated by the experts into a box-office success, or ignoring films deemed significant. Despite this unpredictability, public interest has to reach a critical mass to ensure that a film remains in circulation or is worth reviving. The alternative is being relegated to an academic footnote.

The cinema might be an expensive upstart, but it has accrued its share of masterworks which are enshrined in canons. The trouble is the multiplicity of canons. Adrian Martin distinguishes three types.[3] The popular canon characterized by *Star Wars* (George Lucas, US, 1977) he considers of no interest. The old masters canon is promoted by critics and academics who have the power to influence public opinion through the media or by determining which films are worthy of study. This canon risks becoming self-perpetuating as each generation passes on to its successors what is deemed to be great. Martin's third and favoured canon is eclectic and more anarchic, which prompts the question why he dismisses the popular canon so cursorily. Ava Preacher Collins plays down the influence of academics and takes a more sympathetic view of popular film in her quest for the political and social influences which are brought to bear.[4] Though she finds some form of canon inevitable, she follows Martin in looking forward to a more inclusive approach. But is the canon inevitable, and what is its purpose?

Ian Christie follows Frank Kermode in viewing the canon as a consensus on what is worth interpreting and reinterpreting, though he skates over who contributes to this collective decision.[5] As older works are re-released, new films enter the market and film-makers are reassessed, established values and opinions are challenged. Change is slow in Martin's old masters canon. The popular canon is evanescent, which makes it difficult to study: by the time a film is written about, it will already be displaced, making the very notion of a market-led canon problematic. Its virtue is that it reveals what people watch rather than what they ought to watch.

Attempts to defend the old masters canon as an imprimatur of quality steer a perilous course between relativism and dogma. Aesthetic, social and political values can all be wielded as proponents and opponents battle for dominance. These shifting sands undermine the notion of a canon as a standard to which film-makers can aspire and against which films are assessed. As an instance of the methodological problems encountered, a distinguishing characteristic of the popular canon is accessibility, but does the fact that a work can be appreciated at first viewing exclude it from the old masters canon? Conversely, is the old masters canon kept sacred by obscurantism, the inclusion of foreign language films being an obvious example? One response is that the old masters canon represents liberation from the need to be immediately comprehensible. The paradox is that this freedom comes at the cost of excluding a large segment of the potential audience. This dilemma is not unique to the cinema: it faces literary fiction and classical music, both of which are minority tastes for increasingly older age groups. It is questionable whether such protectionism really constitutes freedom.

Which Are the Best Films?

Sight and Sound has published a list of the best films every decade since 1952. This selection by critics, writers, academics and directors is a coterie consensus view which has the virtue of revealing changes over time. *Bicycle Thieves* (Vittorio de Sica, Italy, 1948) heads the 1952 list, followed by *City Lights* (Charles Chaplin, US, 1931), *The Gold Rush* (Charles Chaplin, US, 1925), *The Battleship Potemkin* (Sergei Eisenstein, USSR, 1925), *Intolerance* (D. W. Griffith, US, 1916), *Louisiana Story* (Robert Flaherty, US, 1948), *Greed* (Erich von Stroheim, US, 1924), *Le Jour se lève* (Marcel Carné, France, 1939), *The Passion of Joan of Arc* (Carl Dreyer, France, 1928), *Brief Encounter* (David Lean, GB, 1945), *Le Million* (René Clair, France, 1931) and *La Règle du jeu* (Jean Renoir, France, 1939).[6] Separate lists for critics and directors were introduced in 1992, but the choices of both groups are similar. The top ten films chosen by 145 critics in the 2002 poll are *Citizen Kane, Vertigo* (Alfred Hitchcock, US, 1958), *La Règle du jeu, The Godfather* (Francis Ford Coppola, US, 1972), *The Godfather Part II* (Francis Ford Coppola, US, 1974), *Tokyo Story* (Yasujiro Ozu, Japan, 1953), *2001: A Space Odyssey* (Stanley Kubrick, GB/US, 1968), *The Battleship Potemkin, Sunrise* (F. W. Murnau, US, 1927), *8½* (Federico Fellini, Italy/France, 1963) and *Singin' in the Rain* (Gene Kelly and Stanley Donen, US, 1952).[7] Only *The Battleship Potemkin* and *La Règle du jeu* survive from the first list. Comedy has fallen from favour, with Chaplin being the principal victim. Being the best means being serious, though *The General* (Buster Keaton, US, 1927) and *Singin' in the Rain* have made intermittent appearances through the decades. Antonioni and Bergman came and went, while *Citizen Kane* has topped every list since 1962.

Few of the films selected are likely to be screened commercially, so these selections have nothing to do with popularity. What makes them intriguing is how notions of quality change, with older films like *Sunrise* suddenly assuming importance. Restorations and availability on new formats are contributory factors, though silent films have not retained their cachet. As snapshots of elite taste—overwhelmingly male taste—over fifty years, the *Sight and Sound* listings are unrivalled. From one viewpoint, the recurrence of titles like *Citizen Kane* decade after decade demonstrates a reassuring consistency of values; from another, it betrays critical sclerosis, with the more thought-provoking selections coming from critics and directors who break ranks.[8] The charge of conservatism was widespread enough to prompt a further poll in 2002, when fifty critics and writers chose the best films from the previous twenty-five years. *Apocalypse Now* (Frances Ford Coppola, US, 1979) heads the list, followed by *Raging Bull* (Martin Scorsese, US, 1980), *Fanny and Alexander* (Ingmar Bergman, Sweden/France/W. Germany, 1982), *Goodfellas* (Martin Scorsese, US, 1990), *Blue Velvet* (David Lynch, US, 1986), *Do the Right Thing* (Spike Lee, US, 1989), *Blade Runner* (Ridley Scott, US, 1982), *Chungking Express* (Wong Kar-Wai, HK, 1994), *Distant Voices, Still Lives* (Terence Davies, GB, 1988), *Once upon a Time in America* (Sergio Leone, Italy/US, 1984) and *Yi Yi (A One and a Two ...)* (Edward Yang, Taiwan/Japan, 2000).[9] This mixture of the epic and the intimate invites several questions, including whether interest has been sustained since 2002 and what prevents these films from appearing in the decennial listings. Is there a feeling that they need time to prove themselves? The American bias might reflect market dominance, more innovation in American films as the studio system foundered, or a mellowing of British critics' wariness towards all things American.

Sight and Sound is not alone in trying to pick the best of the best. In 1998, the American Film Institute (AFI) unveiled its list of the hundred greatest American films. Any qualms *Sight and Sound* editors might feel about using the word *great* are absent here, while the definition of American film is elastic: English-language films is a more accurate description. Topping the list are *Citizen Kane, Casablanca* (Michael Curtiz, US, 1942), *The Godfather, Gone with the Wind* (Victor Fleming, George Cukor and Sam Wood, US, 1939), *Lawrence of Arabia* (David Lean, GB, 1962), *The Wizard of Oz* (Victor Fleming, US, 1939), *The Graduate* (Mike Nichols, US, 1967), *On the Waterfront* (Elia Kazan, US, 1954), *Schindler's List* (Steven Spielberg, US, 1993) and *Singin' in the Rain.*[10] The exercise was criticized by Jonathan Rosenbaum, who accused the AFI of recycling product which was already over-touted. This may be true, but exposure is the concomitant of greatness, however much this makes critics uneasy. Rosenbaum's alternative listing is alphabetical and could never be called bland, ranging from *Ace in the Hole* (Billy Wilder, US, 1951) to *Zabriskie Point* (Michelangelo Antonioni, US, 1970).[11] His selection belongs among Martin's eclectic canons, though where the AFI's choices fit in Martin's scheme of things is less clear, with four of the top ten regularly appearing in critics' lists. Rosenbaum argues for the canon in *Essential Cinema.*[12] This appears contradictory, but he has made clear that his objection to the AFI's listing is the absence of explicit criteria, though the AFI is hardly alone in this.[13] Rosenbaum's views will be considered further in the final chapter.

In what is destined to be a decennial event, the AFI held another poll in 2007, when 1,500 people from the film community made their choices from among 400 nominated films. With a nod to the time model, these had to be made before 1997. The result is a reordering of the earlier list, the only new entrants to the top ten being *Raging Bull* in fourth position and *Vertigo* in ninth, displacing *The Graduate* and

On the Waterfront.[14] Whether the changes are attributable to advocacy, accessibility or the political climate is an intriguing question which must remain open.

New York's *Village Voice* unveiled its choice of the hundred best movies in 2000, though not without expressing reservations about the exercise in a preamble. The selection was made by fifty critics, including Jonathan Rosenbaum. *Citizen Kane* heads the list, followed by *La Règle du jeu, Vertigo, The Searchers* (John Ford, US, 1956), *The Man with a Movie Camera* (Dziga Vertov, USSR, 1929)*, Sunrise, L'Atalante* (Jean Vigo, France, 1934)*, The Passion of Joan of Arc, Balthazar* (Robert Bresson, France, 1966) and *Rashomon* (Akira Kurosawa, Japan, 1950).[15] This is an intriguing selection which makes no concession to popular appeal, with seven of the top ten films being either silent or in languages other than English. The taste on display is that of a metropolitan elite having access to some offbeat material and parading a wide range of cinematic references.

Leaving aside the AFI's selection, a core of old masters provides the mainstay for these lists, revealing a broad consensus about what is deemed great or best. Critics, academics and film-makers may participate in several polls, contributing to the sameness of the results. This can make the choices appear safe at first sight, yet they are adventurous in spanning the history of film and a range of cultures. Notable changes are the assimilation of Japan into the world community—the first Japanese film appeared in the 1962 *Sight and Sound* list—the reappraisal of older works such as *Sunrise* and the championing of *Vertigo,* which came back into circulation after several years and is indicative of Hitchcock's enhanced status.

The public has its own polls. More precisely, television viewers, magazine readers and internet users are polled, creating a bias towards the taste of particular groups. This skews the results from a market model to what might be called an enthusiasts' consensus. In Martin's terms, this is the popular model fused with the eclectic.

With over fifty million visitors a month, IMDb is the probably the most heavily used internet film site. The 250 films which have received the highest ratings are listed, along with the number of votes. A Bayesian estimate yields an ongoing listing which is updated daily, though in practice voters' selections are remarkably stable. The top-rated films on 27 December 2007 were *The Godfather, The Shawshank Redemption* (Frank Darabont, US, 1994), *The Godfather Part II, The Good, the Bad and the Ugly* (Sergio Leone, Italy/France, 1966)*, Pulp Fiction* (Quentin Tarantino, US, 1994)*, Schindler's List, Star Wars Episode V—The Empire Strikes Back* (Irvin Kershner, US, 1980)*, Casablanca, One Flew Over the Cuckoo's Nest* (Milos Forman, US, 1975)*, The Seven Samurai* (Akira Kurosawa, Japan, 1954)*, The Lord of the Rings: The Return of the King* (Peter Jackson, US/NZ/Germany, 2003) and *Star Wars.*[16] Restricting participation to regular users and weighting the ratings minimizes the risk of tactical voting but restricts the number of potential voters. The mixture of the classic and the popular points up the varied reasons why people visit the site: for study purposes, to read a film review, to lobby for a favourite film or to see how other people have voted. This makes drawing conclusions difficult, but what distinguishes the IMDb poll is the demographic analysis of voters. There is an inevitable bias towards keen internet users. Young males have predominated, but as they are also the most enthusiastic cinema-goers, such a skewing is not necessarily a problem. Demographic shifts and changing patterns of internet usage may alter voting patterns in the future. It is notable that *The Godfather* was released in 1972, before most voters in the 18–29 age group were born (a few will have graduated to the next age group since voting). Males in this group comprise 47 per cent of the quarter of a million voters for the film, their mean rating being 9.3 out of 10.[17] This popularity may not be maintained as the cohort ages and other films jostle for attention. An alternative possibility is that this first generation to grow up with the internet may continue to exercise its voting power in support of a cherished film which is regularly watched on DVD.

Although 57 per cent of voters for *The Godfather* award the maximum rating of 10, suggesting uncritical adulation, 6 per cent give it the lowest rating of 1.[18] Dissenting voices are drowned out in other polls, but their views deserve to be taken seriously. They are a corrective to the critical myopia displayed towards the obvious favourites. The emphasis in the IMDb top ten is on blockbusters and newer releases, with more violence than comedy on display. It would find a place among Martin's popular canons, except that the high placing for films a quarter of a century old confounds glib generalizations about a passion for the new. This is one of several polls which reveal a fondness for fantasy epics such as the *Star Wars* and *Lord of the Rings* sagas.[19] Kevin Maher concurs with Pauline Kael in discerning a nostalgia for childhood in the appeal of these works, which is an intriguing aspect of how films are evaluated.[20]

The films with the largest international box-office grosses are also listed on the IMDb site, the top ten being *Titanic* (James Cameron, US, 1997), *The Lord of the Rings: The Return of the King, Pirates of the Caribbean: Dead Man's Chest* (Gore Verbinski, US, 2006), *Harry Potter and the Sorcerer's Stone* (Chris Columbus, GB/US, 2001), *Pirates of the Caribbean: At World's End* (Gore Verbinski, US, 2007), *Harry Potter and the Order of the Phoenix* (David Yates, GB/US, 2007), *Star Wars: Episode 1—The Phantom Menace* (George Lucas, US, 1999), *The Lord of the Rings: The Two Towers* (Peter Jackson, US/NZ, 2002), *Jurassic Park* (Steven Spielberg, US, 1993), and *Harry Potter and the Goblet of Fire* (Mike Newell, GB/US, 2005).[21] The list demonstrates the industry's success in attracting audiences who cannot wait for the DVD to be released. With the exception of *The Lord of the Rings: The Return of the King,* there is no overlap with the top ten in the voters' poll. On this evidence, achieving box-office records is not the same as providing audiences with memorable films. Popularity is a more complicated phenomenon than it appears at first sight.

The BFI has compiled a list of the most popular films in the United Kingdom based on audience figures. This exercise yields markedly different results, the top films being *Gone with the Wind, The Sound of Music* (Robert Wise, US, 1965), *Snow White and the Seven Dwarfs* (David Hand, US, 1937), *Star Wars, Spring in Park*

Lane (Herbert Wilcox, GB, 1948), *The Best Years of Our Lives* (William Wyler, US, 1946), *The Jungle Book* (Wolfgang Reitherman, US, 1967), *Titanic, The Wicked Lady* (Leslie Arliss, GB, 1945) and *The Seventh Veil* (Compton Bennett, GB, 1945).[22] Here the emphasis is on films from the heyday of cinema-going. Record-breaking attendances could be built up in the 1940s, even if a film's popularity was ephemeral. The list demonstrates the time model in operation, but in a way that might upset critics.

The popularity of the Hollywood narrative-driven product is evident in audiences' choices and may be one reason why Martin disparages the popular canon. Critics' lists are more varied, with offerings such as *Distant Voices, Still Lives* departing from the Hollywood style. Yet the ubiquity of *The Godfather* and the presence of *The Seven Samurai* in the IMDb poll give the lie to facile judgements.

The flurry of polls has abated as celebrations for a hundred years of cinema and the end of the twentieth century pass into history. Critics, film students and enthusiasts still find niches in the media for their personal selections. Both official and unofficial listings have been collated for avid collectors.[23] Beyond Britain and the United States, film polls seem less popular. The Brussels-based International Federation of Film Archives (FIAF) nominated its choice of the best films, but a list which begins with *Citizen Kane* offers few surprises.[24] There is no reason why one list should be more authoritative than another, however august the institution producing it. The invidious question many commentators gloss over is whether disparate works should be ranked at all. Films need advocacy rather than listings, which is a case for selections made by individuals rather than lists compiled from audience polls. Derek Malcolm has the luxury of being able to give reasons for his personal best selection, and he bucks convention by heading his list with *Tokyo Story* and omitting *Citizen Kane*.[25]

An argument in favour of listings ordered by popularity is that voting provides a quantifiable measure; an objection is that publicity machines would be failing if the new and the novel did not generate more enthusiasm than yesterday's blockbuster. Reassuringly, new films do not have it all their own way, while the limitations of publicity are all too evident in the prestigious films which never make the lists. Cinema history is littered with commercial flops, though few have caused as much soul-searching among studio bosses as Michael Cimino's *Heaven's Gate* (US, 1980).

The Godfather fascinates in how it manages to survive the insistent clamour of the new and straddle the divide between the popular and the great. Do audiences and critics perceive the same qualities? Are critics influenced by sustained public support for a film, so that *The Shawshank Redemption* is destined to enter the pantheon of greatness despite current critical antipathy? Alternatively, do the public follow influential critics who lauded *The Godfather?* This less attractive possibility demonstrates the pernicious power of list-makers rather than the enduring qualities of the film. It would require a detailed study of poll participants to reveal whether either option is correct.

Why bother to select the greatest films? The cynical answer is that it increases DVD sales, which is not something to be despised if it reawakens interest in neglected masterpieces. Rosenbaum takes the more aspirational view that making a choice rouses us from our boredom and stupor.[26] Undeniably his own selection encourages debate, but another list headed by *Citizen Kane* is apt to induce stupor rather than dispel it. For Tim Dirks (who succumbs to the lure of compiling his own list but follows Rosenbaum in presenting it alphabetically), 'They are films almost every educated person with a solid knowledge of film history and cinema would be expected to know and to be literate about. These crucial film selections provide a common goal and foundation for the study of film.'[27] The aim is worthy, but worthiness can be dull, and Dirks's justification begs too many questions. Nor can any list compiler fail to be influenced by previous selections, making quality vie with status. This reifies a canon which becomes an unthinking consensus rather than a celebration of quality. Ty Burr writing in the *Boston Globe* takes a radically different line, stressing the implications of demography:

> The canon has been changing over the last decade, and what makes a classic of cinema is now drastically different to discerning young moviegoers than it has been to their teachers or to the critics or to Leonard Maltin. The implications of the new canon are vast, much bigger than the specific films themselves, and they speak to the ways in which a new generation perceives history, reality and even perception itself.[28]

The vulnerability of a list which sometimes seems cast in stone is exemplified by the high status of *Citizen Kane* in *Sight and Sound* listings, which contrasts with its lower ranking in popular polls. Critics and academics might judge it a great film, but its popularity among younger viewers is less secure. Only 35 per cent of the 98,057 votes cast for the film in the IMDb poll come from males in the 18–29 age group. This is a lower percentage than for recent works achieving higher placings. Less than 2 per cent of all voters for the film are under 18.[29] It may be that, like fine wine, *Citizen Kane* is appreciated increasingly with age. An alternative interpretation is that the young approach film (and wine) without the preconceptions and pretensions of their elders. If this is the case, interest in *Citizen Kane* may dwindle further as a new generation of cinema-goers becomes increasingly distanced from an elderly black and white film.

Seeking the Great Films

What makes a film good or even great? Charlie Keil of the University of Toronto defines a great film as one which makes a contribution to the medium, has lasting importance and influence, and 'must strike a chord with viewers no matter how much time has passed since it was made', which is an emotional response by any other name.[30] It can be argued that Keil's first two criteria are the results of greatness rather than preconditions. The inclusion of any film in a canon can be contested, with Keil's fellow academic Kay Armitage braving the wrath of the film community by disputing that *Citizen Kane* was influential.[31] This is a reminder that received opinions need reassessing from time to time.

Do canonized films have anything in common? Among frequent entrants to the *Sight and Sound* listings, *Citizen Kane* flourishes among its credentials technical bravura and innovation. Good acting is to be expected, but only *Singin' in the Rain* is remembered primarily for the performances. The story may be strong, as in *The Passion of Joan of Arc* or *Citizen Kane,* but the story in *L'Avventura* (Michelangelo Antonioni, Italy/France, 1960), which made the *Sight and Sound* top ten in 1962 and 1972, is little more than a device for allowing characters to interact, while the mystery which launches the film gets left behind. *Tokyo Story* has an intimacy of scale missing from *The Battleship Potemkin.* What these films have in common is that they offer distinctive visions of the world which go beyond plot and characterization. This has echoes of the director as auteur, that seductive way of defining authorship in the cinema. The weakness of this approach is that the director may work with the same writer, designer and cinematographer over several films, so that style becomes the result of collaboration, Michael Powell's work with Emeric Pressburger, Alfred Junge, Hein Heckroth and Erwin Hillier being a case in point. A production company may also impose a unified style on its films, Hammer horror and the James Bond brand being obvious examples. In spite of such caveats, directors like Bergman, Passolini and Buñuel are among that select company whose style and subject matter are distinctive. The 2002 *Sight and Sound* poll is helpful in listing the best directors as well as the best films. Critics' choices are Welles, Hitchcock, Godard, Renoir, Kubrick, Kurosawa, Fellini, Ford, Eisenstein, Coppola and Ozu.[32] Directors opt for Welles, Fellini, Kurosawa, Coppola, Hitchcock, Kubrick, Wilder, Bergman, Scorsese, Lean and Renoir.[33] Whatever quibbles might be made about the choices or their ordering, these are directors who have produced consistent bodies of work. But what of chameleons like Carol Reed or Robert Altman? Are they condemned to be also-rans, forever being edged out of polls because of their sheer versatility?

A related question is whether a film can hold a fascination for cognoscenti and public alike, not because of its intrinsic quality, but because of external factors such as the prestige of its director or star, or the advocacy of its distributor. Such external factors might be expected to become less important with the passage of time, but when circumstances conspire against a film, quality may never get a chance. Delays, disagreements and financial difficulties during production and post production, followed by lacklustre distribution, can make the difference between a film which is widely seen and talked about and one which remains on the shelf, or is released in a cut form so that it cannot be properly judged. Orson Welles's career suffered from all of these problems and exemplifies the highs and lows of film-making.

Once released, a film faces the vagaries of physical survival, fashion and accessibility. Film stock has a short life compared with printed material or an artist's canvas. Neglect and inferior materials worsen this situation, with colour prints from the 1970s already deteriorating. Films have survived from the silent era more through luck than because they were deemed worth keeping. Nobody thought it worth preserving the work of D. W. Griffith or Michael Powell until they were established as significant film-makers. This puts the onus on archivists to act as gatekeepers for what future generations can see.[34] The loss of so much TV footage from the 1960s reveals how the criteria for preservation can change over a generation. As well as *Vertigo*, *A Clockwork Orange* (Stanley Kubrick, GB, 1971), *The Passenger* (Michelangelo Antonioni, Italy/France/Spain, 1975) and *Paris, Texas* (Wim Wenders, W. Germany/France, 1984) disappeared from circulation for long periods, so that several generations of film students knew them only by repute. The output of the East German DEFA studio was little known in the West and has sunk further into obscurity since German unification. A gem from the collection which shows up the superficiality of *Schindler's List* is *Stars* (Konrad Wolf, GDR, 1959), the story of a doomed romance between a German transit camp guard and a Jewish prisoner, but this work is unlikely to be widely seen. There is an element of luck in the progress of any film from bright idea to critical or popular success and finally to entry into the canon. Cost, the number of people involved, the potential for clashing egos and disputes over rights all have the potential to make the journey precarious.

Towards a Subjective Approach to Cinema

Discerning common threads among the listings is an interesting exercise, but seeking a formula for greatness is a task worthy of Casaubon (in George Eliot's *Middlemarch*) and ultimately fruitless. This bleak conclusion is not original. Donato Totaro criticizes film canons for the absence of any agreed criteria for inclusion, their vulnerability to the vagaries of availability and the bias of Western critics.[35] An alternative approach is to move from the notion of canonic works to those which in Jenefer Robinson's terms have meaning for the individual. This is the strategy advocated by Martin in his call for a canon which is polemical rather than based on consensus, and which communicates the passion and intensity of individual experience (and yes, he does offer his own choice of films).[36] The message is that however worthy a film, whatever skills and money are lavished on its production and whatever the critical reception, what ultimately matters is the response of audiences. How they respond is an individual matter, without recourse to a quasi-objective list of core values. One implication is a more varied range of choices. This was exemplified in 1995, when Milan Pavlovic, editor of the German *steadycam* magazine, took a sophisticated take on knowing what you like by inviting seventy-eight critics, directors, producers and writers to list thirty films which were not the greatest or best but were close to their hearts (*Lieblingsfilme*). Whether the resulting list should be called a canon is debatable. Joint first place in this intriguing selection goes to *The Searchers, Taxi Driver* (Martin Scorsese, US, 1976), *Vertigo* and *The Night of the Hunter* (Charles Laughton, US, 1955), followed by *Lawrence of Arabia, North by Northwest* (Alfred Hitchcock, US, 1959), *Le Samourai* (Jean-Pierre Melville, France, 1967), *To Be or Not to Be* (Ernst Lubitsch, US, 1942) and *The Last Picture Show* (Peter Bogdanovich, US, 1971).[37] Tantalizingly, the names of contributors and the reasons for their choices are not given. This has the potential for being as interesting as the list itself, with each contributor offering different justifications for inclusion of the same titles.

The criteria used in selecting my *Lieblingsfilme* are fourfold. First, a work must be absorbing enough to suspend time. The total concentration of a large audience is palpable enough to make even a cynic believe in the collective unconscious. Second, a work should offer a fresh way of looking at the familiar. Nothing can be quite the same again, and it is impossible to think of the world without it. Christopher Hitchins calls this process upturning the furniture of your mind.[38] Third, the work must linger in the memory if it is to enrich or disturb. Even when the details are forgotten, its emotional impact remains. Finally, the work has to be experienced in the gut as well as the mind. Admiration without feeling cannot touch the sublime. By these criteria, many of the films regularly appearing in polls are unimpressive. My choices include (in alphabetical order): *Annie Hall* (Woody Allen, US, 1977), *Blow-Up* (Michelangelo Antonioni, GB, 1966), *Le Boucher* (Claude Chabrol, France, 1970), *The Conformist* (Bernardo Bertolucci, Italy/France/W. Germany, 1970), *The Go-Between* (Joe Losey, GB, 1970), *The Lacemaker* (Claude Goretta, France/Switzerland/ W. Germany, 1977), *M. Hulot's Holiday* (Jacques Tati, France, 1953), *Mulholland Drive* (David Lynch, France/US, 2001), *Sons of the Desert* (William A. Seiter, US, 1933), *Stalker* (Andrei Tarkovsky, USSR, 1979), *Stars, Sunday, Bloody Sunday* (John Schlesinger, GB, 1971), *Suzhou he* (Ye Lou, Germany/China, 2000) and *Tante Zita* (Robert Enrico, France, 1968).

If these are generally intimate stories rather than social and political statements with the sweep of *The Battleship Potemkin,* they embody society's values with the precision of a Jane Austen novel. *Sunday, Bloody Sunday* transcends the everyday concerns of Jewish, middle-class London to explore friendship and love. *The Go-Between* is an unblinking account of a boy's loss of innocence, but the forensic dissection of the English class system on the eve of the First World War prevents the film from lapsing into heritage cinema. The historical accuracy of Losey's vision is secondary to conveying psychological truth. The same quality marks the little-known *Tante Zita.* Set in Paris, Enrico's film charts the relationship of a teenage student with her dying aunt. Sentimentality is kept at bay in this coming-of-age story by the rawness of the emotions. *Blow-Up* occupies more glamorous territory, catching the heady promise of swinging London, but the treatment of the multilayered mystery at the heart of the film transforms it into an exploration of fame and illusion. *Mulholland Drive* inhabits a similar unsettling hinterland, this time between dreams, ambitions and the sordid realities of Hollywood. All the films are marked by their directors' intellectual control. The characters inhabit rich emotional worlds and are willing to take emotional journeys on the wild side which may culminate in a catharsis. This is the fate of Isabelle Huppert's character in *The Lacemaker,* her breakdown giving the film the dimensions of Greek tragedy. These are works which make the soul take proud flight. The selection reveals bias, notably towards West European cinema of the 1970s, but this is inevitable. If personal taste is set aside, admiration is usurping feeling. The list is not fixed: I might discover on reacquainting myself with the films that they no longer have the same impact. As my feelings change, so does the meaning the films hold for me.

Ambiguity threads through this selection, from Jung's 'strange realm of shadowy thoughts' represented here by the photograph (*Blow-Up* and *Suzhou he*), to the moral dilemmas and compromises which arise when ideology and emotions collide (*The Conformist* and *Stars*). All the films portray relationships which are intriguing enough to merit repeated viewing. Could it be that *Schindler's List* has never made the *Sight and Sound* listings because it has no secrets to yield after one viewing?

What gives a comedy such as *Sons of the Desert* enduring appeal? Harold Lloyd's *Feet First* (US, 1930) is ingenious and funny, but ultimately it is a one-gag film. Once the gag has been enjoyed, there is not much left, which may be why few comedies figure in polls. Yet familiarity can breed fondness as well as contempt, judging by the continuing popularity of television sitcoms such as *Dad's Army* (BBC TV, 1968–77) and *Fawlty Towers* (BBC TV, 1975–9). Repeated viewing requires watching in a different way, with the gag assuming less importance. Instead, the performers endear themselves to us because we recognize the flaws and foibles of their characters. Oliver Hardy, Tony Hancock and W. C. Fields crave status which always eludes them; they fail because their means never match their aspirations. Is Chaplin's tramp less funny because he does not have so far to fall? Instead, he solicits the audience's sympathy, which is fatal to comedy and a trap avoided by Laurel and Hardy. The innocent Laurel and the ambitious Hardy bring their contrasting viewpoints to every situation. Both are logical in their own terms, the question for the audience being whose ideas will prevail. The only certainty is that the results will be disastrous and comic. Ambiguity for Jacques Tati is embodied in the lugubrious M. Hulot. A childlike delight in technology vies with nostalgia for a more traditional way of life in which relationships take precedence. Humour bubbles up when the two worlds collide. What links Tati with Laurel and Hardy is that pathos is not in their repertoire.

The cinema industry has taken myth to its heart from its earliest days, fashioning its own myths around screen goddesses, roistering consorts, tyrannical directors and philistine producers. On screen, monsters have regularly threatened the world and supermen have confronted them with the aplomb of Greek gods. The Western represents the clearest statement of myth in the cinema, a common pattern being a mysterious stranger who takes on the ills of society. After battling with dark forces he goes on his way, leaving behind a community which is transformed by his actions. This basic plot has enthralled generations of schoolboys and was memorably parodied in

Mel Brooks's *Blazing Saddles* (US, 1974). Comedies belong to the hidden, subversive tradition rather than to myth, while the episodic works of Fellini and the satire of Kubrick's *Dr Strangelove; Or, How I Learned to Stop Worrying and Love the Bomb* (GB, 1963) seem light years away. Among other films touched on in this chapter, *2001: A Space Odyssey* and *The Searchers* fit the mythic mould, while the series based on *Star Wars* and *The Lord of the Rings* aspire to be sagas of Wagnerian proportions. The *Godfather* trilogy and *Citizen Kane* also display mythic qualities, while being set in a recognizably twentieth-century America. *Stalker* is notable for attempting to refashion myth for the modern age—perhaps a post-nuclear age—the enemy being an alien landscape where a disparate group of men search for their grail.

In Jungian terms, a heroine, or the star playing her, can be seen as the anima. The 'superhuman glamour' of the mother is transferred to this love object, who is treated with 'boundless fascination, overvaluation, and infatuation'. As Jung concedes, this is a matter of psychological need, not of truth. Rational explanation achieves nothing.[39] This disposes of rational explanation, but more pertinently, is the notion of the anima useful? It provides a way of exposing a weakness in *Vertigo*. The love object (Kim Novak) provokes boundless fascination on the part of the hero (James Stewart) and the audience, but Hitchcock sacrifices her, along with ambiguity and any aspiration to psychological insight, in the interests of a neat ending which fails to ring true. Any film with a femme fatale can be approached using the concept of the anima, but what of *Some Like It Hot* (Billy Wilder, US, 1959), or the black comedy *The Anniversary* (Roy Ward Baker, GB, 1968)? These are cases where the Jungian model fails to fit.

A canon of great films justifies the medium being defined as an art form and directs attention towards important works. A new generation may accept the status of some films in today's canon, or newer works may displace the old as Burr contends, changing the nature of film culture and overturning the rubric that greatness emerges over time. Does this reveal independence of mind, or a relentless emphasis on the ephemeral? In an ideal world, a liberal education exposes us to all forms of expression and offers glimpses of their potential; then we should be free to seek works which have meaning for us, regardless of their status. A canon has value if it introduces us to works we do not know; too often it is greeted as confirmation of greatness. Accepting that some films are above criticism closes down debate as effectively as an obsessive focus on box-office returns. It concentrates power in the hands of a coterie of opinion-formers whose influence is already pernicious, with the result that some films are approached with reverence rather than any expectation of pleasure. Films speak to us across time and across cultures. Those flickering images of our lives are something societies must share, and we erect barriers against this process at our peril, handing decision-making to experts and to those who shout the loudest. This should be resisted.

The film canon may not be displaced easily, but it bears critical examination. If less attention were devoted to so-called masterworks, more eclectic tastes might prevail, making private passion central to evaluating films.

The Battleship Potemkin (USSR, 1925): The Politics of the Cinema

Production Company: Goskino
Producer: Jacob Bliokh
Director/Screenplay/Editor: Sergei Eisenstein
Scenario: Nina F. Agadzhanova-Shurko
Photography: Eduard Tisse
Art Director: Vasili Rakhals
Cast: Aleksander Antonov (Grigory Vakulinchuk—Bolshevik sailor), Vladimir
    Barsky (Commander Golikov), Grigori Alexandrov (Chief Officer Giliarovsky),
    Aleksander Liovshin (petty officer), N. Poltatseva (woman with pince-nez),
    Beatrice Vitoldi (woman with pram)

Synopsis

The crew of the battleship *Potemkin* relax in their hammocks after coming off duty
and show no support for the agitator Vakulinchuk. Their mood is different the next
morning. They complain about their diet of maggot-infested meat and raid the food
store when nothing is done. They are summoned on deck, where the commander
harangues them. Many sailors ignore orders to disperse and congregate by the
turret. Armed guards are summoned. An isolated group of sailors tries to escape
through the hatch used by the admiral, but they are beaten back. A tarpaulin is
thrown over them and orders are given to shoot them. Vakulinchuk successfully
urges the guards to rebel. The officers are thrown overboard, but Vakulinchuk is
killed in the struggle. His body is taken to the pier, where the townspeople pay
their respects. They support the sailors by taking food to the battleship. Soldiers
appear, driving people down the Odessa Steps and shooting them. The battleship
fires on the army's headquarters in retaliation. When the sailors hear that the fleet
is approaching, the battleship steams out of the harbour to confront the other ships.
The sailors on the *Potemkin* are ready to fight for their cause, but the other crews
side with them.

Cultural Context

The Battleship Potemkin was conceived as an episode of an eight-part series celebrating the failed 1905 revolution. A French magazine article about the mutiny provided the likely starting point for the film's scenario.[1] The cast was assembled from residents of Odessa, augmented by Eisenstein's colleagues, with First World War newsreel being used for shots of the fleet in the film's final section.[2]

The negative was sold to Germany in 1926 and returned to the Soviet Union in 1940, minus material excised by the German distributors. Ivor Montagu brought a print to Britain for the London Film Society's 1929 screening, while Jay Leyda took a print to the United States in 1936. Both prints came from Moscow and escaped the German cuts. The 1997 restoration by Ennio Patalas of the Munich Film Museum incorporated twelve scenes from the British print and further material from a restoration by the New York Museum of Modern Art based on Leyda's print. The Munich restoration is the nearest we have to a complete version.[3] The film was considered so politically incendiary that it was banned from public exhibition in France and Britain until the 1950s and in Italy until 1960. Private screenings by such organizations as the London Film Society provided a way to evade these restrictions.[4]

Soviet reviews on the film's initial release were mixed. For the correspondent of the Moscow evening paper, *Vecherniaia Moskva,* 'The film is an event. Just as Griffith's *Birth of a Nation* initiated the great American cinema, so this second work by Eisenstein initiates *the great Soviet cinema.*' [original italics][5] Yet the artist Alexei Gan could write: 'The work of the cameraman is good, but sentimental. The individual performers illustrate well the eclectic method of the production. *Potemkin* sows confusion in Soviet cinema. As a whole, it is a bad film.'[6]

The film's reputation in the Soviet Union was allied to that of its director. Although *Potemkin* was a celebration of people power, Eisenstein was attacked for not following the party line. After Stalin's death, dissidents including Solzhenitsyn accused Eisenstein of being an opportunist, while the authorities branded him a Stalinist. A member of a Soviet delegation visiting Hollywood in 1979 opined that Eisenstein could only be taken seriously for his editing and cinematography.[7] A review of the DVD for the Maoist Internationalist Movement in 2001 was equally dismissive, complaining of unfinished plot threads resulting from Eisenstein's concern with achieving maximum effect.[8] In the West, the initial response was mixed. The correspondent of *The Times* summed up the negative view: '*The Battleship Potemkin* disappoints most of the hopes which the censor's ban has aroused.... In particular, the massacre of the citizens of Odessa, effective enough in itself, loses all reality from the omission of any mention of the riots and arson which were its immediate cause.'[9] When the *Sight and Sound* top ten list was published in 1952, such opinions went unheard. *The Battleship Potemkin* was judged the greatest film at the Brussels World Fair in 1958 and if it has lost its pre-eminence, it regularly features in *Sight and Sound* decennial listings.[10]

The circumstances of Soviet film-going make it difficult to gauge the response of the first audiences. Richard Taylor concludes that the film was popular on the workers' film circuit in the USSR, but less so where people had to pay. In Moscow, it ran for a month in the winter of 1926; *Robin Hood* (Allan Dwan, US, 1922), starring Douglas Fairbanks, ran till the summer.[11] *Potemkin*'s commercial potential in the West was summed up by Fred Schader in *Variety:*

> It may interest a few Russians in this country, but it is utterly devoid of entertainment and box office value.
>
> The authorities need not fear that the showing of this picture will cause any unrest among the lower classes in this country, for not enough of them will see it to make any difference. Those that are out-and-out reds, and those that are inclined to socialism will undoubtedly find great things about the picture, but hardly anyone else will.[12]

Censorship ensured that the film was more talked about than seen; *Potemkin* was too dated to arouse general interest by the time it became freely available, and it does not feature in audience polls.

Subjective Impression

It is hard to approach *The Battleship Potemkin* without preconceptions. Eisenstein's daunting reputation made me expect to revere the film rather than enjoy it. Today, the propaganda seems crass, which is an added hurdle. Those early Soviet audiences must have seen things differently, making me want to know more about their responses.

A further difficulty is responding emotionally given the subject and Eisenstein's approach. The 1905 uprising is an historical curiosity which arouses no passion today. With its focus on events rather than individuals, the film comes across as a dramatized documentary with a justifiably austere reputation. If I cannot support its revolutionary ideals or empathize with the characters, I am thrown back on Eisenstein's reputation as a reason for watching. I know that I am looking at a masterwork and I should respond accordingly.

The first section, 'Men and Maggots', introduces Vakulinchuk, who tries unsuccessfully to incite his fellow seamen to rebellion. He provides a narrative link with the following section, 'Drama on the Quarterdeck', in which the crew are pushed so far that they side with him. I feel little concern for somebody whose only function is to serve the plot. He is never presented as an individual, which makes it hard to understand the townspeople's response to his death. The quarterdeck scene does have drama, though I puzzle over how such a large company of guards is assembled so quickly, or why the sailors allow themselves to be covered with a tarpaulin, given the spirit they have already shown in disobeying orders. Following a narrative depends on a logical development from one event to another rather than this disjointed approach.

The Odessa scenes conclude the second section and extend into the third, 'The Dead Man Calls for Justice', which shows citizens coming to view Vakulinchuk's body. These are the least didactic sequences of the film and contain the least action. The cinematography is consciously artistic, with sailing boats gliding past the Odessa shoreline in the early morning sun. The seemingly endless procession of citizens moves in choreographed patterns down flights of steps and along the breakwater. Here is the humanity which is missing elsewhere. There is a moment of drama when the crowd turns on a businessman who shouts 'Kill the Jews,' but this interjection remains unexplained.

The lyrical mood is shattered by the arrival of the troops in the 'Odessa Steps' section. The citizens' headlong flight down the steps creates a mood of frenzy emphasized by the staccato editing, yet I sense I am being manipulated. Why the soldiers are attacking the populace remains unexplained. The propaganda element antagonizes me, which must run counter to Eisenstein's intentions.

My DVD of the film has a musical accompaniment based, somewhat repetitively, on extracts from Shostakovich symphonies. The fifth was described enigmatically by the composer as a Soviet artist's reply to just criticism. The bombastic finale accompanies the film's final section, 'Meeting the Squadron'. Once more events take over from individuals, giving the sequence an impersonal air as sailors on the *Potemkin* await the fleet. When their colleagues side with them rather than opening fire, I sense the hollow triumphalism which Shostakovich captures in his music. We are meant to cheer, but I never feel the inclination.

Images such as the waterfront at Odessa and the citizens gathering to view Vakulinchuk's body linger in my mind, but this is not a film which moves me. Neither do I gain self-knowledge. The warmth and humanity which Eisenstein eschews are the very qualities I miss, which makes me question whether an emotional approach is the best means of appreciating the film. Now that the politics are outdated, I am not sure what should replace revolutionary zeal. Admiration for Eisenstein's technique is not enough.

Analysis

Opinions on the film cannot easily be separated from opinions about Eisenstein. David Thomson illustrates this point while voicing his disillusion: 'With Eisenstein, you confront a demonic, baroque visual theatricality, helplessly adhering to the confused theories of his writing on film.... Eisenstein's treatment of violence is always participatory and masochistic. The images alone suggest how well he might have acquitted himself in the horror genre.'[13] Dan Shaw puts the case for the defence in an internet essay.[14] Unlike a good defence lawyer, he concedes most of Thomson's points, so that differences between the two writers become matters of emphasis. The problem areas they examine are the effect of the editing, the lack of individual protagonists, stereotypes, the intrusive propaganda and the film's coldness.

Shaw summarizes the intellectual underpinnings of Eisenstein's work. The director subscribed to the teachings of Meyerhold, who equated Pavlov's experiments on conditioned reflexes in dogs with how audience responses are aroused by presenting viewers with images which stimulate basic responses and induce appropriate attitudes. The approach is evident in Eisenstein's writing: 'The first thing to remember is that there is, or rather should be, no cinema other than agit-cinema. The method of agitation through spectacle consists in the creation of a new chain of conditioned reflexes by associating selected phenomena with the unconditioned reflexes they produce.'[15] The example he gives is creating fellow feeling for the hero by surrounding him with kittens, which always elicit sympathy. The callousness of the officers on the *Potemkin* elicits sympathy for the ordinary sailors. A crescendo effect is created by the juxtaposition and accumulation of associations (montage fragments) evident in the Odessa Steps section. Yet Eisenstein fails to follow his own precepts, and even Shaw has to concede that the editing techniques have a distancing effect rather than giving rise to the intended emotional pathos. Thomson takes the same view: 'One is less moved by the Odessa massacre in *Potemkin* than excited by it: the frenzied pictorial dynamism and the pulsing montage refute the message that cruelty is destructive.'[16] An audience of Soviet workers might have responded differently. Nor is it the director's fault if newsreels of Soviet and Nazi troops have invested his images with unintended associations. Less charitably, Shaw's assumption that Eisenstein's aim was pathos rather than masochism is not certain, while bravura editing raises the suspicion that technique comes before content. As Eisenstein was eager to liberate himself from the script, he might not have objected to this judgement.[17] Or is the impression he conjures an inevitable concomitant of his method?

The accusation that *Potemkin* lacks identifiable protagonists prompts Shaw to a spirited defence. According to the tenets of Marxism, worsening economic conditions should lead to the proletariat rising against the bourgeoisie. This turns the populace into protagonists rather than the roles being assigned to particular individuals. But a feature film is not a treatise on Marxism. It has to engage an audience, which requires emotional involvement with the characters. As Shaw admits, 'Unfortunately, the writer-director was never capable of creating a believable individual character other than Vakulinchuk in *Potemkin*. Though he is granted little screen time as a common seaman who helps lead the mutiny, the sympathy generated by his death attests to the extent to which our identification with individuals is at the heart of much of our cinematic pleasure.'[18] For me, the stilted acting detracts from Vakulinchuk's death and nullifies any identification. A comparison can be made with the visit of the petty officer to the empty crew's quarters. The tables are suspended from the ceiling and sway with the movement of the ship. Their pendulum-like motion mesmerizes him. Smiling, he follows their movement, his head tilting from side to side. For a few moments, Eisenstein seems in touch with real emotions and the limitations of his actors can be forgotten, or was the actor intending to portray maliciousness?

Shaw's next point is a corollary: 'Sergei Eisenstein lampooned the bourgeoisie with naive and unconvincing stereotypes more suited to vaudeville or the circus, which soon were more likely to induce ridicule than revolutionary fervour.'[19] To promote a populist message, it is tempting to resort to stereotypes of evil and righteousness, however inconvenient the facts. Religious evangelism and melodrama are never far apart. As Shaw implies, the weakness of this strategy becomes apparent when the propaganda loses its relevance and audiences seek more sophisticated imagery. Then the hollowness of the stereotypes is revealed, making it difficult to take *Potemkin* seriously. The lack of veracity in the characters serves to point up that this is primarily a director's exercise. To accept the film's greatness requires overlooking this fault. Judging by *Potemkin*'s absence whenever the public are polled on their favourite films, they have exercised their own discrimination.

Shaw and Thomson continue to find common ground in the bludgeoning effect of propaganda. Thomson detects a paradox: 'The propagandist purpose in Eisenstein's films diminishes the human beings dressed up as authority just as uncompromisingly as the authorities are supposed to oppress the workers.'[20] Commentators handle the propaganda in different ways. The approach taken by Seymour Benjamin Chatman is to ignore it in favour of the film's compositional qualities. These include the 'golden rule' of contrasting even and uneven numbers, which is evident in the alternating groups of two and three citizens who view Vakulinchuk's body, and the arc formation of bridges and parasols.[21] The historian D. J. Wenden accepts the propaganda on the grounds that *Potemkin* was intended to appeal to unsophisticated audiences.[22] Against this pragmatic interpretation, it is clear from the care Eisenstein lavished on the composition of the shots that his aim was not merely propaganda. He faced similar problems to Shostakovich in his dealings with the authorities, but the composer's bitter humour finds no parallel here. From today's perspective, art and propaganda sit uneasily together in *Potemkin,* even if Eisenstein's insistence on agit-cinema suggests that for him the two elements were inseparable.

Shaw's final point is that Eisenstein displays the strengths and weaknesses of the Renaissance man, subjugating all the elements to the driving idea. Not only does this produce a cold epic, but humans are reduced to cogs in a revolutionary machine.[23] Thomson is more charitable, detecting in Eisenstein's paintings a self-mocking, cartoony exuberance which is absent from the films.[24] *Potemkin* is short on self-mockery, yet there is respite from coldness in the shots of citizens paying their respects to Vakulinchuk's body. It is easy to understand how such a sequence influenced John Grierson and other documentary film-makers. It shows real people, including a high proportion of women who are neither old nor asexual as Nestor Almendros contends.[25] James Goodwin can praise the film's affective structure, seeing *October* (USSR, 1928) as marking Eisenstein's shift to intellectualism, while ignoring the fact that individual protagonists become the heroes in his later work.[26] Helen Grace takes a different approach, detecting in *Potemkin* a contrast between maternal feeling and masculine virility, with the latter winning out in the film's final section.[27]

My estimation is that this does not compensate for the film's lack of humanity, even if it makes the coldness elegant.

For that well-known propagandist Joseph Goebbels writing in 1933, 'It is a fantastically well-made film and displays considerable cinematic artistry. The decisive factor is its orientation. Someone with no firm ideological convictions could be turned into a Bolshevik by this film.'[28] The irony is that Eisenstein edited a version for Goebbels.[29] Writing some sixty years later, Roger Ebert shows a similar appreciation of the work's potency:

> If today it seems more like a technically brilliant but simplistic 'cartoon' (Pauline Kael's description in a favorable review), that may be because it has worn out its element of surprise, that … it has become so familiar we cannot perceive it for what it is…. In prosperous peacetime, it is a curiosity. If it had been shown in China at the time of Tiananmen Square, I imagine it would have been inflammatory.[30]

The two strands to Ebert's criticism are overfamiliarity and the context in which the film is viewed. The element of surprise is always at risk from familiarity, even if *Un chien andalou* (Luis Buñuel and Salvador Dali, France, 1928) evades this pitfall, but is *Potemkin* familiar? The image of a pram tumbling down steps has become common cinematic currency, but familiarity comes from knowing images from the film rather than seeing it in its entirety. This is to rely on the film's reputation rather than its intrinsic quality.

The film's reception today raises other issues. It is likely to be seen at home, or in an academic setting. One is too intimate and the other too sterile for the triumphalism the director envisaged. Since the ending of the Cold War, it should be possible to view *Potemkin* from an historical perspective, yet the film's critical reputation has waned over this period. One reason may be that the left-wing revolutionary impulse has dissipated among the student generation since the 1960s. More simply, perhaps we are less willing to accept crude propaganda of whatever hue.

Irrespective of whether anybody has been converted to the Soviet cause by watching *Potemkin,* the film has a reputation for being dangerous, judging by the attitudes of censors. It fits the precepts of the Futurist *Manifesto of Social Change,* which proclaimed war as 'the only health-giver of the world'.[31] The mutiny proclaims this spirit of change, but the manifesto dates from 1910 and the First World War shattered the Futurist ideals. This gives the film its piquant flavour: the technical innovations might point forward, yet its ethos and subject matter look back a generation. The years before 1914 were marked by a frenzy of artistic experimentation in Europe, with Fauvism, Cubism and localized groupings such as Les Apaches in France and the Blue Riders in Germany. Dada, Surrealism and jazz were prominent among postwar developments. Eisenstein was a polymath: a writer, stage director, artist and designer who spoke English, French and German and was at home in this artistic firmament. His work appeared in *Documents,* the journal founded in

1929 by Georges Bataille and his circle, which carried forward many of the ideals of Futurism.[32] Russia was on the fringes of the European cultural scene before the First World War, with Impressionism remaining popular when elsewhere it had been overtaken by newer movements. The 1917 revolution increased Russia's artistic isolation. Constructivism, with its precept of using art for social purposes, was popular in post-revolutionary Moscow and pervades the film, even if the authorities were turning against the movement by 1925. There are elements of Cubism in the fractured images of fleeing crowds on the Odessa Steps, while the didactic address to the audience brings to mind Alfred Jarry and Bertolt Brecht, albeit without their irony. Like *Un chien andalou, Potemkin* is of interest because it is experimental, but this is incidental to its quality.

Eisenstein based the film on an incident during the 1905 revolution, but Wenden reveals the licence taken in the interests of propaganda. In reality, the officers were as hesitant and uncertain as the crew, who showed scant interest in the Odessa uprising. Eisenstein also ignored the ultimate failure of the crew's stand. On a point of detail, the crowd surged up the steps, their intention being to reach the fashionable shopping areas.[33] The film's reversal of this serves dramatic rather than propagandistic ends. Grace notes how the depersonalization of the soldiers on the steps is achieved by placing the camera above them, while the citizens are photographed from lower levels.[34] Photographing the crowd surging up the steps rather than down would render the camera angles less effective in portraying their panic.

One incident which stands out is the well-dressed businessman shouting 'Kill the Jews.' He is a putative member of The Black Hundred, a virulently anti-Semitic society. Jews comprised 30 per cent of Odessa's population and were unpopular for controlling 90 per cent of the export trade in grain, though the reaction of the crowd fails to make this clear. Not is there any hint that the riots had an anti-Semitic element.[35] The film is not an accurate record of the failed 1905 revolution, but a celebration of revolutionary ideals. It provides a glimpse of Russian attitudes in the 1920s, filtered through Eisenstein's internationalist sensibility and the promptings of his political masters. These conflicting demands mean that the result may not be typical of either.

The film's crude propaganda and lack of humanity remain stumbling blocks. A lesser-known film about strikers facing the militia is *Adalen 31* (Bo Widerberg, Sweden, 1969). I recall the total concentration the confrontation commanded in a crowded cinema on the film's opening British run. It is doubtful whether *Potemkin* could hold today's audiences in the same way: restlessness and sniggers are more likely responses. Yet one viewer's comment gives pause for thought. Dr William Boehart of Mölln in Germany comments: 'I had seen the film before in offside university cinemas with canned music and on tape, but I never realized what an impact the film can have. It simply blows your mind. The live music turned it into a totally different experience.'[36] Context may not be everything, but it counts for a lot.

—4—

The 39 Steps (GB, 1935):
Romance on the Run

Production company: Gaumont British
Producer: Michael Balcon
Director: Alfred Hitchcock
Source: John Buchan (novel: *The Thirty-Nine Steps*)
Screenplay: Charles Bennett, Ian Hay
Photography: Bernard Knowles
Art direction: Albert Jullion, Oscar Werndorff
Music: Hubert Bath, Jack Beaver, Charles Williams
Editor: Derek N. Twist
Cast: Robert Donat (Richard Hannay), Lucie Mannheim (Annabella Smith), John
    Laurie (Crofter), Peggy Ashcroft (Crofter's wife), Godfrey Tearle (Professor
    Jordan), Madeleine Carroll (Pamela), Wylie Watson (Mr Memory)

Synopsis

Richard Hannay is alone in London. His visit to a music hall coincides with a fight in
the auditorium. Outside, he encounters Annabella Smith, who invites herself to his
flat. There she reveals that her mission is to stop foreign agents from stealing British
military secrets and that she caused the disturbance in order to evade her enemies.
The presence of watchers in the street lends credence to her story. She mentions the
thirty-nine steps without explaining what they are and insists that she must go to
Scotland the next day to prevent the secrets from falling into the wrong hands. She
warns Hannay of a man with part of his little finger missing. Later that night she is
stabbed to death. In her hand is a map of Scotland with Alt-na-Shellach marked. The
next morning, Hannay evades the watchers and sets off to Scotland in her place. He
discovers from a newspaper headline glimpsed on the train that Annabella's body
has been found and he is wanted for her murder. To evade the police who are searching the train, he throws himself at a blonde and pretends to be locked in an embrace
before escaping on the Forth Bridge.
  Hannay travels across Scotland on foot, taking shelter with a crofter and escaping when the police close in. At Alt-na-Shellach, he seeks help from a local resident,

– 35 –

Professor Jordan. Too late he notices that part of the professor's little finger is missing. Hannay escapes after being shot, giving himself up to the local sheriff, who pretends to believe his story but alerts the police. Another escape leads Hannay to seek refuge in a public hall, where he is mistaken for the guest speaker at an election meeting. Pamela, the blonde from the train, is in the audience and has him arrested.

When the policemen insist that Pamela accompany them in the car, Hannay realizes they are impostors. Pamela is handcuffed to him while their captors clear sheep from the road. He seizes the chance to escape, dragging Pamela with him. At an inn where they share a room, she frees herself from the handcuffs while he is asleep. Before she can phone the police, she overhears the agents talking in the bar and realizes that Hannay has told the truth.

The couple return to London, where the gang are to meet at the Palladium. Pamela tells the police. Though they disbelieve her, they follow her to the theatre, where a memory act is taking place. Hannay asks from the audience what the thirty-nine steps are. When Mr Memory replies that it is a gang of spies, the professor shoots him and is chased through the theatre by the police. As Mr Memory dies in the wings, he reveals the formula for an aircraft engine, which he had been paid to memorize. Hannay and Pamela hold hands, this time without the handcuffs.

Cultural Context

The 39 Steps was made towards the end of Hitchcock's career in Britain. First reviews were favourable. Aside from carping about the crude studio sets, the *Monthly Film Bulletin* called it 'An exciting film of espionage ... very freely adapted with complete success from John Buchan's novel. The atmosphere of adventure and mystery ... is excellently maintained throughout ... First class entertainment.'[1] The reviewer for *The Times* was equally enthusiastic: 'Mr Alfred Hitchcock's treatment of the story gives us a first-rate adventure edged with comedy.... Its climax verges upon ingenuity of the kind that we resent, but by the time that it has been reached we have been much too well entertained to think of resenting it.'[2] The film proved popular with British audiences. The *Daily Mirror* hailed it as the most popular British film of the year, while by John Sedgwick's POPSTAT index of popularity it was the eighth most popular film of 1936.[3] There was sufficient commercial potential for a re-release in 1942. In America, the film proved more popular in New York and Minneapolis than elsewhere.[4] Andre Sennwald of the *New York Times* praised Hitchcock's artistry and his 'sinister delivery and urbane understatement'.[5] *The 39 Steps* is regarded as among the best of Hitchcock's British films, being ranked fourth by a thousand film professionals in the 1999 BFI poll to select the hundred best British films.[6]

Subjective Impression

Hannay is a loner. He enters the music hall alone and is thrown on his own resources when he is pursued. The way Annabella Smith invites herself to his home suggests that she is a prostitute. Later it is made clear that they sleep in separate rooms, but by then members of the audience must have drawn their own conclusions. The surprise is that the censor went along with the ploy.

Hannay is thrust into worlds he knows little about, from espionage to being a suspected murderer on the run. The safe, respectable world is that of Professor Jordan at Alt-na-Shellach, to whom Hannay turns for help. The professor's houseguests accept the newcomer in a civilized, English manner. It is only when Hannay is alone with his host that the mask drops. Even then the professor talks of the need to maintain respectability and expresses regret at what has happened. Hannay looks around helplessly for a means of escape now that his illusion of security is taken away. When the professor's wife and a maid enter, the apparent normality never wavers. The two women seem complicit in the plot, while never acknowledging it. There is genuine ambiguity here. Hannay fears for his life, yet he too is constrained by politeness. Nor does he know whom he should trust. Are the guests aware of their host's true identity? When the two men are alone again, the professor offers to let Hannay do the gentlemanly thing and shoot himself. Hannay hesitates and the professor loses patience, turning the gun on him.

Hannay learns to distrust appearances. Annabella Smith and the professor are not what they seem, and the sheriff pretends to believe him but has him arrested, while the policemen who arrest him at the public meeting are impostors. Hannay joins in the game by assuming different identities. The exceptions to this emphasis on masquerade are his relationships with women. The central relationship between Hannay and Pamela begins badly, but grows stronger. Like Hannay, Pamela has to learn about trust.

I can savour the excitement of the chase as well as appreciating Hannay's disorientation in a world where nothing is as it seems. His innocence is established early in the film, so I am on his side. I also appreciate Pamela's suspicion and feel frustrated by the misunderstandings which keep the couple apart, yet I know this is what happens in a good story.

The ensuing stage of cognitive appraisal is not just a matter of acquiring or reinforcing beliefs, but of obtaining a deeper understanding of human behaviour by seeing how the accumulation of incidents fits together. Here the film reveals its shallowness. The situations seem contrived to provide excitement. While they need not be realistic, they have to engage me. The trouble is that they lack veracity, serving the plot rather than arising from the characters' feelings or concerns. Hannay comes across as the epitome of the English upper-middle-class gentleman. His political ideas might confound the stereotype; so does his Canadian nationality. He never sounds Canadian. Pamela and Hannay are as much enigmas at the end of the film as they were at the beginning. They have enacted an adventure for my entertainment and nothing more. Holding hands in the final frames is not enough to convince me that their relationship is credible or interesting.

Two uniquely cinematic moments stay in the memory because of their humanity. One occurs when Hannay seeks shelter in an isolated croft. There is a palpable sexual tension when he encounters the crofter's wife. As the crofter says grace before their meal, his wife notices the newspaper on the table. The murder has made the headlines. She looks at Hannay and makes the connection. The crofter intercepts their glances and jumps to the wrong conclusion. He makes an excuse to go outside, from where he spies on the couple through the window. When a car is heard approaching that night, his wife realizes that he has told the police and she urges Hannay to escape. The crofter hears the couple talking and accuses them of having an affair. He accepts a bribe from Hannay but betrays him in the hope of a reward. In a few short scenes, the relationship between the jealous, hypocritical crofter and the wife who yearns for her home city of Glasgow is revealed through acting and editing. These are real people, whose marriage is laid bare for us.

The other memorable moment comes at the end of the film, when the professor shoots Mr Memory. The variety show continues as the dying performer recites the secret plans in the wings. The effect is in large part attributable to Wylie Watson's performance as Mr Memory. Memorizing the formula is his greatest achievement; he would not regard it as an act of treachery. The two leading characters are present, but it is Mr Memory who grips the attention as we come to understand what is important to him.

Analysis

Hitchcock has spawned a vast literature, as well as having a daunting influence on Western cinema.[7] This is unusual for a British film-maker, particularly one who was not taken seriously until his later years. Robert E. Capsis offers three explanations for the change of heart: the work got better as Hitchcock matured, aesthetic standards changed (Hitchcock and the notion of the auteur were promoted by Chabrol and Truffaut in the 1950s) and Hitchcock actively moulded his own image.[8] The risks of so much academic attention are twofold. First, as a film becomes an object of study, its original purpose as entertainment becomes overlooked as researchers squabble over the entrails. Secondly, it is easy to overintellectualize a director who claimed less for his films than those who write about them. Few would deny that *The 39 Steps* is an effective adventure story, but is it better than dozens of others produced in the 1930s by such directors as Maurice Elvey and Bernard Vorhaus?

Raymond Durgnat's *The Strange Case of Alfred Hitchcock* was published in 1974, on the brink of Hitchcock's elevation to the ranks of great directors. Durgnat is one of several dissenting voices among the critical adulation.[9] Though Hitchcock's supporters have kept the upper hand, four of Durgnat's criticisms deserve consideration: Hitchcock's social values, his portrayal of couples, the films' superficiality and his resort to cliché.

Though Hitchcock's world is less complacent than that of Ealing, 'All his films, up to and including *Jamaica Inn,* renounce a kind of psycho-cultural relevance which is not too much to expect from entertainment, let alone art.'[10] When crofters and London sophisticates slot unquestioningly into their class positions, it is hard to disagree that Hitchcock's conflicts are played out in safe, noncontroversial terms.[11] The upper-middle-class Professor Jordan remains a gentleman, even if he is a traitor and murderer. The duplicitous crofter seems the greater villain as he lives up to his working-class stereotype as a wife beater. Hitchcock's acquiescence to the status quo is unlikely to be the consequence of censorship, given the sexual innuendo which he slipped into the film. His world remained anachronistic and steeped in an imagined past throughout his career, the London of *Frenzy* (GB, 1972) seeming little different from that of *The 39 Steps,* when he was already showing a nostalgia for the music hall of his childhood. Entertainment can have social relevance, as the comedies made by George Formby and Gracie Fields in the 1930s demonstrate. By comparison with *The 39 Steps,* the shadow of the Depression hangs over them. Whether such relevance is always necessary is debatable, but Durgnat's judgement is justified if Hitchcock is to be ranked with directors like Renoir and Ozu.

Fascism lies at the heart of *The Lady Vanishes* (GB, 1938), which is to be expected given its date, but Hitchcock came to the project after the Launder and Gilliat script was written. The enemy in *The 39 Steps* is less clearly defined. Mark Glancy writes in his otherwise admirable study of the film: 'At nearly every stop on Hannay's cross-country journey we find complacency and venality. It is a vision of a country without confidence, unity or purpose.'[12] This is to rely on hindsight. To see Hannay as undertaking a journey of the soul is to weigh the film down with a significance inappropriate for a director not noted for his political or social commitment. Durgnat almost falls into the same trap, discerning in *The Lady Vanishes* comments about confusion and vapidity within the democratic creed. *The 39 Steps* does not measure up so well in his terms: 'It's a thousand pities that some such meaning, of unity-and-disunity, wasn't extended to the film's admirable central idea, the handcuffing of hero (Robert Donat) and heroine (Madeleine Carroll).... Each is tyrant of the other. Unity is paralysis.'[13]

This second criticism takes the argument a step further. The potential of the film's central idea with all its metaphorical resonance of how couples or allies are constrained by being yoked together is not exploited. Instead, the handcuffing is treated as an interlude of comedy romance inserted in an adventure story. Clark Gable and Claudette Colbert were paired a year earlier in *It Happened One Night* (Frank Capra, US, 1934). The relationship between Donat and Carroll in *The 39 Steps* catches something of the same quality, though it takes a while to splutter into life. Donat's pencil moustache makes him resemble Gable. Carroll had more studio experience than her co-star, who established his reputation in the theatre. Donat seems uncomfortable in the early scenes, as though he had trouble scaling down his performance for the camera, or he found Hitchcock's direction restrictive. The change occurs when the couple are handcuffed together. Melodrama dissolves into comedy, which both actors handle more successfully. The moment has been defined by John Orr as a shift from Lang's Expressionism towards American screwball comedy.[14] Hitchcock was ever responsive to what audiences wanted, which is a reason for considering him as a showman rather than an artist.

An internet essay by Tim Dirks focuses on Hannay's shifts of identity, but Dirks's introduction reprises Durgnat's concern: 'One of the film's major motifs is the confining, sexually-frustrating institution of marriage.'[15] Marriage means something different for each of the film's established couples: jealousy and violence for the crofters, good-natured companionability for the innkeepers and complicity for the professor and his wife. These relationships are contrasted with the fledgling partnership of Pamela and Hannay. Pamela's wariness at sharing a bedroom with Hannay echoes a scene in Carol Reed's *Bank Holiday* (GB, 1938), where a young couple show unease at booking into a hotel under an assumed name. In both films the point is laboured, suggesting that although the pretence of marriage was considered daring, it was a common ploy. Dirks does not pursue this theme. Nor does he address the constraining effect of playing a role, which afflicts characters as much as actors. The crofter's wife is locked into a loveless marriage; it is hard to imagine her life improving. Jordan has to play the role of an English gentleman if he is not to risk losing his cover, and the sheriff's position allies him to the police so securely that he cannot believe Hannay, while the gang members who kidnap Hannay and Pamela are uncertain when to give up the pretence of being policemen. The dilemmas are there, even if Hitchcock ignores them in favour of the chase.

Durgnat's third criticism stems from this: 'The price of such rapidity is superficiality. The corners Donat's in are tight enough, but his manner's distinctly "Anyone-for-tennis?" with just a touch of dapper grit.'[16] The accusation of superficiality has been made elsewhere. After citing Hitchcock's comment to Truffaut: 'What is drama, after all, but life with the dull bits cut out,' Gary Johnson considers that Hitchcock 'readily sacrifices credibility in favor of a headstrong rush of exciting sequences (with magnificent results)'.[17] The fault lies with Buchan, whose novel comprises a series of short, interlinked scenes in which action is all. Hitchcock and his writers change the plot but adhere to Buchan's emphasis on action. The cost in both cases is a lack of opportunity for characters to develop. Hannay's patriotic values could give an insight into his character, but they are played down in the film, only emerging explicitly during his speech in support of the Conservative candidate. Here they can be dismissed as rhetoric, with the political implications being abandoned in favour of Hitchcock's trademark teasing of the audience with suspense and disguised identities.

George Kaplan offers another perspective on the film's superficiality, detecting in Hitchcock's lack of involvement with his actors a wish to put across his own viewpoint to the exclusion of others. Only a limited range of behavioural patterns lend themselves to this technique, which elicits a crude, simplistic and generalized reaction from audiences, while the characters dwindle into ciphers.[18] Nicholas Haeffner takes a revisionist line, contending that Hitchcock worked like any other director of the period and has an unjustified reputation for treating his actors as chess pieces.[19]

'The shift from everyday life to life's hideous potential is made without recourse to melodramatic clichés which are at best abstractions—artistic McGuffins—and therefore distractions, and at worst banalities.'[20] Here, Durgnat strikes at the heart of Hitchcock's technique. The opening of *The 39 Steps* conveys an air of menace presaging film noir, with Hannay being introduced by his shadow and everybody being seen from the waist down until he is inside the music hall. This early promise of stylish cinematography is dissipated by a contrived fight in the auditorium and the appearance of the mysterious Annabella Smith, who invites herself to Hannay's flat in a perfunctory and stagy exchange. The scenes in the flat mark a further descent into routine thriller territory, interrupted by a quirky moment when Hannay fries haddock for his guest. There can be an inventive use of sound effects, such as when Hannay's cleaning lady finds Annabella's body the next morning and her scream is replaced by a train whistle, with a cut to an express emerging from a tunnel. This is an exception. Changes of scene often seem perfunctory, with no background music to ease the transition. Dialogue can be superfluous, which accords with Hitchcock's regret at the introduction of sound.[21] Impoverished cinemas continued showing silent films into the early 1930s, so audiences were used to the conventions of the older medium. The music-hall scene which opens the film is almost entirely visual. A close-up of the telephone as it rings in Hannay's flat prompts his comment, 'Hello, there's the telephone.' The effect is ponderous. The techniques of silent film are used more effectively as Hannay waits to give his election address. The chairman's introduction is intentionally inaudible, while the camera tilts upwards from Hannay's seat to reveal a row of expectant faces turned in its direction.

Hitchcock was happy to talk about his approach to film, as his conversations with Truffaut illustrate, though how seriously he should be taken is another matter. In 1936 he gave an insight into his thinking: 'I use melodrama because I have a tremendous desire for understatement in film-making. Understatement in a dramatic situation powerful enough to be called melodramatic is, I think, the way to achieve naturalism and realism, while keeping in mind the entertainment demands of the screen, the first of these being colourful action.'[22] At first sight melodrama and understatement seem contradictory, as do melodrama and realism. Hitchcock sought genuine reactions to heightened situations. Taking this to the extreme, he reputedly exposed himself to Madeleine Carroll to achieve the dismayed expression he wanted.[23] Realism was of little consequence in Hitchcock's world, judging by his predilection for back projection and crude studio sets for outdoor scenes even in his Hollywood years, while his reliance on formulaic plots was still evident in *Dial M for Murder* (US, 1954). The ending of *The 39 Steps* was lifted from his previous work, *The Man Who Knew Too Much* (GB, 1934). Ken Mogg points to other borrowings.[24] The 'entertainment demands of the screen' were dominant: if something worked, Hitchcock was willing to use it again, while those obvious studio sets emphasize the melodramatic elements. Using the term *entertainment* in Graham Greene's sense puts Hitchcock's work in opposition to the dramas of Carl Dreyer or Ingmar Bergman. This does not mean that serious themes cannot be embedded within crime or adventure stories, as Greene's own work demonstrates, but Hitchcock does not attempt this. As Charles Higham puts it in an early and swingeing attack on Hitchcock, 'When the script is saying something quasi-serious, the director withdraws with a yawn.'[25]

David Thomson sides with Durgnat, acknowledging the power of some of Hitchcock's films, but questioning not only the contrived plots, but the director's technical expertise. His conclusion is damning:

> To plan so much that the shooting becomes a chore is an abuse not just of actors and crew, but of cinema's predilection for the momentary. It is, in fact, the style of an immense, premeditative artist—a Bach, a Proust, or a Rembrandt. And beside those masters, Hitchcock seems an impoverished inventor of thumbscrews who shows us the human capacity for inflicting pain, but no more.[26]

Hitchcock offers a cynical view of humanity. The final frames of *The 39 Steps* presage something more tender, but that might be a nod to the conventional happy ending which also rounds off *The Lady Vanishes*. We are left with the chase, but its moral and political implications are glossed over. It is not even clear what Hannay hopes to gain by going to Scotland, beyond providing Hitchcock with an opportunity to parade some colourful characters and stage such set-piece scenes as the escape on the Forth Bridge, which never add up to a satisfying whole.

Charles Thomas Samuels echoes Higham in concluding that 'Throughout his career, Hitchcock has posed moral problems only to evade them.'[27] He also concurs with Thomson in judging Hitchcock to be an indifferent technician with little interest in locations. Samuels's judgement on *Psycho* applies equally well to the earlier film:

> The key to *Psycho* is less Sigmund Freud than Richard Strauss. That is why most of Hitchcock's best films are devoid of meaning, peopled by mere containers of stress and set against backgrounds chosen because their innocuousness counterpoints terror. Primitive in insight, Hitchcock is a sophisticated man revelling in pure form whose films are ends in themselves and so can please both the plebs who want thrills and the cognoscenti thrilled by such an arrogant display of craftsmanship.[28]

The comparison with Richard Strauss is apt. There is a similar stress on bravura effect over structure and real feeling. Two marked differences are the absence in Hitchcock's work of anything comparable to Strauss's surface sheen (those studio

sets give the feeling of high-class amateur dramatics, even in *Vertigo*) and the paro-
dies which marked Hitchcock's final decade at an age when Strauss achieved a new
maturity. The observation by Samuels later in the same article that the beginning and
end of Hitchcock's films are the best parts certainly applies to *The 39 Steps*. Hitchcock was nothing if not a master of pacing, and the tempo here could be described
as allegro, with moments of rubato when romance seems about to blossom. At least
Strauss spun heartfelt melodies.

A literary parallel with Edgar Allan Poe suggested by Dennis R. Perry reinforces
Samuels's point: 'Hitchcock discovers Poe's significance for his own art in his focus
on an audience, satisfying its desire for a fearful yet safe cinematic experience.'[29]
Hitchcock was an entertainer: in the trailer for *Psycho* and in the television series
Alfred Hitchcock Presents (CBS, 1955–62), he revelled in playing the ringmaster,
manipulating audiences in a way which they enjoyed and in which he excelled. In
Higham's words, he was 'a cunning sophisticated cynic ... contemptuous of the audience which he treats as the collective victim of a Pavlovian experiment'.[30] At the
same time, Hitchcock's reflexivity—his perceived ability to comment on the cinema by using its techniques—made him a seminal figure for the French *Nouvelle
Vague*. In Perry's terms, 'For both Poe and Hitchcock process and story meet—their
art is self-expression.'[31] Hitchcock's influence on his successors, together with his
divergent aims of being a director seeking to tailor his work to his audiences' demands while at the same time probing his own insecurities, make him an interesting
rather than a great film-maker. Kaplan detects a similar dichotomy, concluding that
Hitchcock's work is too removed from a healthy concept of norms or morality to
have a Shakespearean centrality in film culture, as Robin Wood proposes.[32] This
position as a marginal figure is an ironic judgement on a film-maker who sought a
mass audience. The twist in the tail is that George Kaplan was the alter ego of Robin
Wood, who appropriated the name of a character in Hitchcock's *North by Northwest*
(US, 1959) for this exercise in self-criticism.[33] The great man would have enjoyed
the joke.

5

Modern Times (US, 1936):
A Tramp for All Seasons

Production companies: Charles Chaplin Corporation/United Artists
Producer/Director/Screenplay/Music: Charles Chaplin
Photography: Roland Totheroh, Ira Morgan
Production Designer: Russell Spencer
Art Director: Charles D. Hall
Editor: Willard Nico
Cast: Charles Chaplin (factory worker), Paulette Goddard (gamin), Stanley Sand-
    ford (Big Bill), Chester Conklin (mechanic), Allan Garcia (company president)

Synopsis

While factory workers toil on the assembly line, the company president plays with a
jigsaw puzzle in his office and reads a comic. He breaks off to watch the workers on a
television screen and orders the conveyor belt to the speeded up. The workers can hear
his voice over the speakers and see him on a screen. Charlie works on the assembly
line. He clocks out to go for a smoke, but the president is monitoring the washroom
and orders him back to work.

A mechanical feeding machine is shown to the president as a way of increasing
the workers' efficiency. It is demonstrated on Charlie, but the machine malfunctions,
pouring food over him. Later that afternoon, he causes havoc on the assembly line by
getting caught in a chute. He is chased out of the factory, only to be pursued inside
again by a policeman. The chase leads him to the control room, where he disrupts
the machinery. He squirts oil at his fellow workers until he is restrained and taken to
hospital. After his discharge, he becomes caught up in a political demonstration and
is arrested. In prison, he overcomes armed villains and is rewarded with a luxurious
cell. When he is pardoned, he is reluctant to leave. Forced into the outside world
again, he has trouble keeping a job.

The gamin is first seen stealing bananas to feed her family. When her father is
killed and her siblings are taken to an orphanage, she is alone. She is caught stealing
bread, but Charlie is on hand and takes the blame. The couple are taken to a police
station, but they escape from the police van. Charlie gets a job as a night watchman

in a department store and invites the gamin to stay there. Burglars break in on his first night. One of them is Big Bill, who worked alongside Charlie on the assembly line. Charlie and the gang get drunk on spirits taken from the store. He is found next morning in the women's clothing department, sleeping off his drinking bout. This leads to his rearrest.

The gamin is waiting for Charlie when he is freed from prison ten days later. She has found a shack where they can live. The factory reopens and Charlie is hired as mechanic's assistant, but a strike throws him out of work again. He is arrested for hitting a policeman; once more the gamin is waiting for him on his release. She works as a dancer in a cafe and has found him a job as a singing waiter. Charlie proves hopeless as a waiter, but successful as a singer. The police have tracked down the gamin and choose that moment to arrest her for vagrancy. She escapes with Charlie. The next morning, the couple are seen on a country road, with Charlie trying to cheer up the despairing gamin. They are last seen heading towards the distant mountains.

Cultural Context

Chaplin undertook a world tour in 1931 and saw the effects of the Depression at first hand. This prompted an interest in social issues which found expression in *Modern Times.* The film was begun in 1933, but by the time of its release in 1936, an economic upturn and Roosevelt's New Deal were ameliorating the worst of America's social problems. Audiences heard Chaplin's voice on film for the first time, though they had to wait until the nonsense song in the final minutes. They were unimpressed: *Modern Times* grossed at least half a million dollars less than each of Chaplin's three previous films on its American release, only covering its costs when it was distributed abroad.[1]

Reviewers praised Chaplin's performing skills, but with reservations. At the enthusiastic end of the spectrum came Frank S. Nugent of the *New York Times,* who was initially apprehensive about the long wait since *City Lights* in 1931: 'But there is no cause for alarm and no reason to delay the verdict further: *Modern Times* has still the same old Charlie, the lovable little fellow whose hands and feet and prankish eyebrows can beat an irresistible tattoo upon an audience's funnybone or hold it still, taut beneath the spell of human tragedy.'[2] Graham Greene was no paid-up Chaplin supporter judging by his *Spectator* review: 'But Miss Paulette Goddard, dark, grimy, with her amusing urban and plebeian face, is a promise that the little man will no longer linger at the edge of mawkish situation, the unfair pathos of the blind girl and the orphan child.'[3] Greene loved the humour of the mechanical feeding device but concluded that Chaplin's change of approach was not a total success: 'He presents, he doesn't offer political solutions.'[4] For the reviewer in *The Times,* 'If, for a moment, Mr Chaplin's invention slackens, the whole film instantly sags, for it has no shape, no narrative expectancy to sustain it.'[5]

The same concerns are apparent in the *Monthly Film Bulletin,* where the film was summed up as 'a succession of humorous incidents—most of them very well

engineered'.[6] Otis Ferguson writing in *New Republic* was prescient and more critical, considering that Chaplin 'may personally surmount his period, but as director-
producer he can't carry his whole show with him and I'll take bets that if he keeps
on refusing to learn any more than he learned when the movies themselves were
just learning, each successive picture he makes will seem, on release, to fall short of
what went before.'[7] Similar reservations surface in recent reviews, but now they are
relegated to the background. Mick LaSalle of the *San Francisco Chronicle* is typical:
'*Modern Times* is an ungainly masterpiece, but Chaplin's ungainliness is something
one can grow fond of. He was a thinker, but he was too emotional to think straight,
and, at this stage, too much of a performer to let ideas get in the way of a great
gag.'[8] Chris Dashiell of *CineScene* echoes these sentiments: '*Modern Times* is more
episodic than Chaplin's previous film *City Lights,* and is therefore ranked slightly
lower than that film (and rightly so, I think). But it's very funny indeed, and show-
cases Chaplin's comic timing and athleticism to great effect.'[9] *Modern Times* ranks
seventy-second among the top 250 films on the IMDb website.[10] A 2007 newspaper
poll for the top fifty comedy films failed to include anything by Chaplin.[11]

   Modern Times was similar enough to René Clair's *À nous la liberté* (France,
1931) for Tobis, the distributors of Clair's film, to accuse Chaplin of plagiarism. As
Tobis was German-controlled, Chaplin's anti-Nazi sentiments may have triggered
what became a protracted dispute. *Modern Times* was banned by Hitler.[12]

Subjective Impression

My first encounter with Chaplin was as a child in the 1950s, when a local cinema
included a silent one-reeler in a cartoon programme. It was older than anything else
on the programme, the dated sets and jerky figures causing more bemusement than
laughter. The film broke and everybody booed. Some six years later, *The Great Dicta-
tor* (US, 1940) was screened at an almost empty cinema in the town centre. It bored me.

   These experiences are relevant for two reasons. First, they colour my response
to Chaplin's work. Secondly, his style of humour with its balletic movements was
little changed in the two films from different stages of his career. Seeing the routines
again in *Modern Times,* I find them ingenious rather than funny. Chaplin draws on
his music-hall roots in playing to the audience, trying to elicit their sympathy, where
Buster Keaton and Harry Langdon give the impression of stumbling into surreal
situations and being surprised by what is happening to them. Laurel and Hardy dif-
fered from Keaton and Langdon in making a successful transition to sound. They
are aware of their audience—Stan's bafflement and Ollie's despair are presented to
the camera—but Stan's innocence and Ollie's punctured dignity enhance our glee
in watching their schemes unravelling. Charlie is more knowing. The situations in
which he finds himself provide opportunities for virtuoso displays of physical comedy, such as when he is carried along the conveyor belt and into the machine, repris-
ing Oliver Hardy's journey through a sawmill chute in *Busy Bodies* (Lloyd French,

US, 1933). We know that nothing terrible will happen: somebody who assumes the roles of writer, producer, director, performer and composer cannot afford to lose his dignity, let alone his control. The point is made in the sequence where Charlie returns to the factory as mechanic's assistant. The mechanic is played by veteran silent comedian Chester Conklin. It is Conklin who narrowly avoids being squashed in the press, whose pocket watch gets flattened and who finally gets caught in the machinery so that only his head is visible. Then Charlie takes centre stage, exploiting his freedom of movement and showing his generosity by feeding Conklin. The contrast is with the earlier scene in which Charlie grapples with the mechanized feeding machine. This is a solo sketch, for Chaplin was never a team player like Stan and Ollie. The machine constrains him, but he allows himself more movement than he gives to the hapless Conklin, while ensuring that he gets the laughs and the sympathy.

Aside from the use of sound, what makes *Modern Times* different from earlier Chaplin films is the presence of Paulette Goddard. Previous leading ladies were foils and the object of Charlie's pathos. Goddard's vivacity redeems a self-indulgent work. It is hard to believe that such a modern and sexy woman should appear in this throwback to a previous era. Chaplin looks studied beside her, unable to slough off his old persona. For all his clever business, it is Goddard who holds the attention, displaying an energy which eludes Chaplin. Both characters are outcasts and alone, yet the gains appear to be almost all on Charlie's side. Why does the gamin wait for him whenever he is released from prison? Why does she provide a home for him, except to set up one of the film's better sequences? We see Charlie's delight when he comes out of prison after the department store incident and finds her waiting for him. In the shack she has found for them, he discovers the pleasures of domestic life, while being careful not to dampen her enthusiasm by pointing out that their new home is falling down. We have to wait until the final scene before he offers her any emotional support. Even in his swansong, the little tramp has not grown up.

What do I learn as the viewer? The obvious moral of the dehumanizing effect of factory work is hardly revelatory: writers from Mrs Gaskell onwards have made the same point. I feel sympathy, but no emotional involvement when Charlie suffers one misfortune after another. His problems seem largely self-inflicted: when asked for a wedge in a boatyard, of course he takes the one holding the boat on the slipway. Innocence allows Stan Laurel to get away with such a gag; Chaplin strives for significance as much as laughter and misses on both counts. If I gain anything, it is an appreciation of the risks of being a celebrity and of trying to do too much.

Analysis

Chaplin's critical fortunes have been mixed. Among nine reviews brought together by Alistair Cooke in 1937, the consensus was that Chaplin never really outlived the silent cinema, he was prone to sentimentality and his ambition extended beyond his talent for comedy sketches.[13] Despite such doubts, two of Chaplin's works featured among the ten best films listed by *Sight and Sound* in 1952.[14] His final two films were neither critical nor commercial successes, and, by the late 1960s, his work was unavailable at a time when Buster Keaton's stock was rising. Chaplin's supporters included Andrew Sarris, who in 1968 ranked him alongside Welles among the great directors.[15] David Robinson also remained faithful, belatedly defending *Modern Times* against criticisms made in the Cooke volume: 'After thirty-six years all this seems far-off whimpering, while the film begins to look, with all its faults, something like a masterpiece.... With the years the archaic techniques which seemed so affronting in 1936 have melted into a kind of timelessness.'[16] Thirty-six years on, this judgement deserves revisiting.

The charge of being outdated is hard to deny. Though Chaplin toyed with a dialogue version of *Modern Times,* he abandoned the idea, reverting to what amounts to a silent comedy with sound effects. This could be interpreted as excessive caution or hubris. As a harbinger of things to come, *Modern Times* shared its opening programme with a Technicolor interest film and a Disney cartoon.[17] Chaplin's disdain for the talkies was expressed in a 1931 article, his contention being that fewer children were attending the cinema because they were unable to follow the dialogue: 'Silent comedy is more satisfactory entertainment for the masses than talking comedy, because most comedy depends on swiftness of action, and an event can happen and be laughed at before it can be told in words.'[18] The proliferation of children's cinema clubs gives the lie to the notion that children were abandoning films, though they may have abandoned silent comedy in favour of newer novelties like cartoons. Given that Chaplin only made two films in the 1930s, he was no longer the best judge of what audiences wanted. Whether the problem was a sentimentality at odds with the times, the intrusion of politics into entertainment, or the anachronism of a silent film is not clear. Andrew Sarris's suggestion that Chaplin kept up demand for his work by restricting supply is hard to justify.[19] If true, the ploy failed, judging by the poor box-office returns. It would be interesting to know whether audiences were made up predominantly of fans who remembered him from the silent era, or viewers who had grown up since the coming of sound. Nor is it clear that silent comedy is swifter, given the need to set up scenes. When slapstick is abandoned in *Modern Times* in favour of narrative development, the film becomes laboured.

Julian Smith defends the use of sound effects as integral to the film but evades the question of why Chaplin eschewed dialogue.[20] While Garrett Stewart concurs with Smith on many points, his conclusion catches the ambiguity of the star's situation: 'Deaf to the drawbacks of the silent film, Chaplin has given us in *Modern Times* his last scrambled word on the talkie. In the process, however, he has profoundly imagined his own immolation as a screen artist on the wheels of progress.'[21] This is a film out of its time: a silent feature released when musicals and screwball comedies were becoming popular. Whether timelessness has overtaken it as Robinson contends is debatable. Films cannot be wrenched from their social context, or from the technology which made them. To reject dialogue, relegate sound to the background and revert to inter-titles once Charlie has sung seems an indulgence or a miscalculation on Chaplin's part. As in the case of *The Battleship Potemkin,* the qualification is that we are viewing the film out of context. In Chris Dashiell's words: 'Seeing [*Modern Times*] on a big screen with an audience—an appreciative audience roaring with laughter—is a vastly different experience than seeing it on TV and chuckling to oneself.'[22] Humour is an emotion which is expressed socially as laughter. Chaplin's physical comedy is predicated on the response of audiences, not to provide feedback to the actors as in live theatre, but because laughter is infectious and audience members can share the feelings of those around them. This is an emotional response to film at its most basic.

Sentimentality can be defined as eliciting a superficial emotional response leading to a predetermined resolution. It becomes evident when Chaplin's silent comedies are compared with those of his rivals. Jonathan Rosenbaum will have none of this because it entails 'a reductionist reading that excludes too many things that matter at least as much'.[23] For Rosenbaum, mismatched shots at the end of *City Lights* can be forgiven because emotion and ambiguity are all that finally register and matter.[24] This makes clear his emotional credentials and justifies the inclusion of *City Lights* in his list of favourites, but if he wishes to argue for the essentiality of the canon and the inclusion of Chaplin's films, the charge of sentimentality cannot be dismissed so lightly. The same accusation has been levelled against Dickens, with whom Chaplin can be compared not only in his approach to storytelling, but in his history of childhood deprivation. The latter may have been exaggerated in Chaplin's case, which is indicative of his tendency to reflect the world through the prism of his own life.[25] In the words of David Thomson, who accepts Chaplin's autobiography uncritically, 'He spoke to disappointment, brutalized feelings, and failure and saw that through movies he could concoct a daydream world in which the tramp thrives and in which his whole ethos of self-pity is vindicated.'[26]

The nadir of this process is *City Lights:* Harold Lloyd never made so much fuss about getting his girl. *Modern Times* is an improvement. The social issues of unemployment and mechanization help to displace self-pity, while Paulette Goddard changes the dynamics of the film by radiating optimism rather than wistfulness. The couple married in 1933: would Chaplin have allowed his heroine such leeway if it had not been for their off-screen relationship? The 'Buckingham Palace' scene in which the couple live together in a shack is touching and amusing. Only in the final sequence does whimsy threaten to become mawkish, but Goddard looks awkward doing sentimentality, and the episode is brief enough for the danger to be averted. Mercifully, Chaplin abandoned his original ending, which involved the gamin becoming a nun, never again to see Charlie, who was in hospital recovering from a nervous breakdown (stills of Goddard in nun's costume appear on the mk2 DVD). This would have toppled the film into bathos and drawn greater opprobrium. As it is, a more likely response is cringing at the nonsense song in the Red Moon Cafe scene.

The contrivance is clumsy and Chaplin was not a good singer, which makes the enthusiasm of the cafe customers unconvincing. If you laugh, you laugh at Charlie, not with him.

Accusations of sentimentality have become muted, with attention focusing instead on Chaplin's links with Surrealism, an early exemplar in English being J. H. Matthews in 1971.[27] Although the Surrealists appreciated Chaplin and he returned the compliment, their most notorious exemplar, the film-maker Luis Buñuel, eventually lost patience with him.[28] Chaplin might be called an accidental Surrealist. His desire was to please the mass audience, not to shock.

Success gave Chaplin the power to exert increasing control over his work, a harbinger in 1919 being the formation of United Artists with Mary Pickford, Douglas Fairbanks and D. W. Griffith. Technical, artistic and business decisions became dependent on Chaplin's judgement. This might have created one of the screen's first auteurs, but the cost of avoiding collaborative friction was self-indulgence, notably in Chaplin's refusal to embrace sound and the perpetuation of his tramp image. The opening scene of *Modern Times* demonstrates how problems go unaddressed. A shot of sheep is followed by a shot of workers streaming out of a subway. This leads the viewer to equate workers with sheep in accord with Eisenstein's principles of montage, but as Charles J. Maland points out, there is no context. It is not clear whether criticism is being directed at the workers who submit to the discipline of the factory, the capitalists who own factories, the weak democracy which allows capitalists to flourish and exploit the workers, or the economic system within which business operates.[29]

Another structural problem is the way the film breaks down into a series of sketches, but the same could be said of the Marx Brothers' offerings, or Laurel and Hardy vehicles such as *Swiss Miss* (John G. Blystone, US, 1938). This was another legacy of music hall, which Chaplin did not perceive as a problem. Reputedly he told Cocteau about the gags: 'I could show them separately, one by one, like my early one-reelers.'[30] Chaplin's work in the 1930s reveals him striving to master the full-length feature. His later films show a surer sense of structure, whatever their faults.

Politics intrudes into *Modern Times*. The inclusion of placards in Spanish during the demonstration headed by an unwitting Charlie gives the film an international dimension. And while in Berlin, did Chaplin visit the AEG turbine factory (designed by Peter Behrens in 1909), using it as a model for the factory in *Modern Times?* Chaplin came from an impoverished background, but fame and wealth changed his outlook and gave him the opportunity to pronounce on political and social issues. His contradictory economic views were spelt out when *Woman's Home Companion* serialized his memoirs: to reduce government, amalgamate the English colonies into an economic unit, encourage world trade, abolish the gold standard, support private enterprise so far as it would not affect the well-being of the majority and create a government bureau of economics for controlling prices, interest and profits.[31] As Jorn K. Bramann points out, Chaplin's response to the ills of capitalism is individualistic, which becomes a troubling aspect of *Modern Times*. In both the factory and the prison, Charlie is the isolated and victimized outsider. No collective solution is offered, with unions being castigated as much as management.[32] The distress of the gamin's younger siblings when they are taken into care might reveal Chaplin's ambivalent attitude towards authority, but what would he prefer should happen to them?

Maland provides three examples of how Chaplin's viewpoint embodies middle-class American values. The first occurs in the prison scene, when Charlie reads the newspaper headline 'Strikes and Riots! Breadlines Broken by Unruly Mass.' He turns to the camera and shakes his head in despair at this attack on the status quo. Secondly, as Charlie lies on a grass verge and fantasizes about domesticity, his aspirations resemble those of the middle-class couple in the house behind him. The third example occurs in the department store scene, when the gamin luxuriates in a white fur coat.[33] Even the film's ending is tailored to please middle-class optimism: love will solve all economic ills. This from a figure who was to be investigated by the FBI for his communist leanings.

A character who hogs the limelight, wrecks every workplace where he is employed and announces in the final scene: 'Buck up—never say die! We'll get along,' before shrugging his shoulders and walking away from his problems is making no significant contribution to solving the world's economic woes. Nor was the tramp an apt symbol in an era when too many people were reduced to poverty. Charlie's privations no longer seemed funny. Fred and Ginger provided more escapist fare for anybody who could afford a cinema ticket.

Ageing, the coming of sound and changing acting fashions put an end to many acting careers. Whether from luck, talent, or adaptability, the fortunate few transcend the changes. Chaplin was in his forties when *Modern Times* was made, so he had to confront the problem of how to portray a relationship between a young, attractive heroine and an ageing star. The strategy adopted by Clint Eastwood and Woody Allen when faced with increasing age was to go behind the camera. Chaplin's solution, as when faced with the coming of sound, was to ignore the problem. The result is a fairytale romance in which two people play at being a couple, most obviously in the department store, where the gamin sleeps on a bed in the furniture department. It is not an approach which sits well with the film's political message.

Stewart defends *Modern Times,* seeing in 'one of the film's most undiluted instances of the myth of descent, the archetype of the dying and rising god, when Charlie is engulfed and dragged down into the intestinal frenzy of the huge engines. It becomes a moment of incontestable meditation of the cinema upon its own means.'[34] Stewart goes on to equate this episode with Charlie being drawn through a projector, 'an image of perhaps the screen's best-known human image undergoing the very process by which that image is made over to us in the theatre'.[35] The metaphor is impressive, if elaborate, and certainly not incontestable. The tramp never grew up. The interesting question is whether Chaplin appreciated the irony of criticizing the system which had brought him fame and riches.

6

Citizen Kane (US, 1941):
The Tragedy of Ambition

Production companies: Mercury Productions/RKO Radio Pictures
Producer/Director: Orson Welles
Screenplay: Herman J. Mankiewicz, Orson Welles, John Houseman
Photography: Gregg Toland
Art Director: Perry Ferguson[1]
Music: Bernard Herrmann
Editor: Robert Wise
Cast: Orson Welles (Charles Foster Kane), George Coulouris (Walter P. Thatcher), William Alland (Jerry Thompson), Agnes Moorehead (Kane's mother), Everett Sloane (Mr Bernstein), Joseph Cotten (Jed Leland), Ruth Warrick (Emily Norton Kane), Dorothy Comingore (Susan Alexander), Ray Collins (James W. Gettys), Paul Stewart (Raymond)

Synopsis

The film opens as Charles Foster Kane is dying in his unfinished mansion of Xanadu. A paperweight falls from his hand as he utters his final word, 'Rosebud'. There follows a newsreel of Kane's life. He came from humble origins, gaining his fortune when he was left the deeds of a supposedly worthless mine which proved to be valuable. His empire expanded from the media into shops, property and mining. He was branded a communist by his trustee and banker, Walter P. Thatcher, and a fascist by a union organizer. His pivotal role in recent American history is revealed, including an attempt to gain political office in 1916.

The newsreel is being shown to reporters, who speculate on what Rosebud means. Jerry Thompson is ordered by his editor to discover the secret; the remainder of the film follows his quest. He visits Kane's second wife, Susan Alexander, who is drunk and unwilling to talk. Thompson moves on to the palatial library endowed by Thatcher, where he reads the banker's reminiscences. A flashback shows Kane's mother signing the deed which allowed Thatcher to become the boy's guardian and control his trust fund. The document recounts how Kane became a crusading newspaper owner and ran a campaign against Thatcher. The 1929 stock market crash meant that Kane had to cede control of his empire to Thatcher's bank.

Thompson's quest takes him to Bernstein, who managed Kane's first newspaper office. Bernstein recalls Kane's declaration to tell people the truth. At a party held to celebrate the paper's rising circulation, the dramatic critic, Jed Leland, predicted that success would change their employer.

Jed is in a geriatric ward. He remembers his former employer and old college friend as a self-centred man, devoid of principles. Kane sought to extend his power by entering politics. Both his marriage to Emily and his political ambitions ended when the rival candidate, Jim Gettys, exposed Kane's affair with Susan Alexander. Kane subsequently married Susan and promoted her operatic career, building an opera house for her. When Jed gave her a bad review, the friendship between the two men was severed.

Thompson revisits Susan, who reveals that when she tried to abandon her singing career, Kane forced her to continue, precipitating her suicide attempt. She passed her time in Xanadu doing jigsaw puzzles. The couple quarrelled as friends partied outside. Susan left, not listening to Kane's pleas to stay.

When Thompson visits Xanadu, Kane's possessions are already being sold. The final interviewee is Raymond the butler, who recalls watching with the other staff as Kane wrecked Susan's room after her departure. Thompson confesses to his colleagues that he has failed to discover what Rosebud means. He is unaware that among the furniture being thrown into the furnace is a sledge which Kane was given by his mother. As flames consume it, the name *Rosebud* is glimpsed on the backrest.

Cultural Context

Citizen Kane was Orson Welles's first film. Herman J. Mankiewicz wrote the script, but how much Welles and John Houseman contributed remains a matter for conjecture.[2] Most of the cast were known to Welles from his stage and radio work, but with the exception of George Coulouris, they were not familiar faces on film.[3] The 1941 premiere took place to general critical acclaim. Bosley Crowther of the *New York Times* shared this enthusiasm: 'For, in spite of some disconcerting lapses and strange ambiguities in the creation of the principal character, *Citizen Kane* is far and away the most surprising and cinematically exciting motion picture to be seen here in many a moon. As a matter of fact, it comes close to being the most sensational film ever made in Hollywood.'[4] Doubts soon emerged, typified by Crowther's response two days after his first review. He still felt that the film was surpassingly magnificent technically, 'But this corner is inclined to suspect that the enthusiasm with which Mr Welles made the film—the natural bent of a first-class showman toward eloquent and dramatic effects—rather worked against the logic of his story.'[5] Richard Griffith of the *Los Angeles Times* was less restrained: 'Though the attempt is praiseworthy, the results are shockingly unsatisfying.'[6] The critical response in Britain was favourable. For the correspondent of *The Times,* 'The rare distinction of having made a film entitled to rank as a work of art belongs almost exclusively to the director, Mr Orson Welles.'[7] Dilys Powell concurred: 'This is an adult film, technically and psychologically adult, recognising the ultimate obscurity in which every human life moves; one of the few, the very few, films to present not an abstraction, but a man.'[8]

The film was by hit by scandal long before it opened because of alleged similarities between Kane's story and that of the newspaper magnate William Randolph Hearst. The controversy gave the film a whiff of notoriety for audiences, though it may have coloured some reviews as well as limiting exhibition: Hearst's power was such that some cinemas in America booked the film but never screened it. If this had an adverse effect on box-office receipts, it does not fully explain the public's disinterest in *Citizen Kane* beyond metropolitan centres. The film had lost US$150,000 by the time RKO withdrew it from domestic circulation in 1942.[9] British audiences were also indifferent, though the film had a better public reception in France after the Occupation.[10]

The revival of interest in *Citizen Kane* began in 1955, when RKO sold the television rights to its film library and Welles's film was widely seen.[11] It headed *Sight and Sound*'s list of best films in 1962 and has maintained that position.[12] Roger Ebert is representative of recent critical opinion: 'Its surface is as much fun as any movie ever made. Its depths surpass understanding.... The more clearly I can see its physical manifestation, the more I am stirred by its mystery.'[13] This view is not limited to critics, given that *Citizen Kane* ranks twenty-fourth among the top 250 films in the IMDb ratings.[14] Something about a film made more than sixty years ago still fascinates critics and public alike.

Subjective Impression

The film's beginning portends a Gothic horror story, with a fantasy castle atop a hill surrounded by an enchanted garden. This stylized opening to the saga of a self-made man gives the piece the air of a nineteenth-century tale, an impression strengthened by the dated clothes. Notwithstanding the mock newsreel, the film stands as a period piece in my mind, distancing me from events as effectively as if I were watching a fairy story. I find the disjunction between the topicality of the newsreel and a distant past unsettling, confounding my initial expectations.

The opening scenes set at Xanadu reveal the extent of Kane's wealth and status. The newsreel recounts the facts of his life and the sort of people he mixed with, but necessarily it dwells on public moments. The rest of the film presents the viewpoints of people who knew him. His relationships with Jed and Susan turned sour, while Thatcher's memoir is unremittingly hostile. Bernstein presents the most balanced account, born of a long working relationship. I want to know more about Kane the private man. Raymond the butler could give an intimate portrait of life at Xanadu in Kane's final years, but he is reticent in his short interview. Kane's first wife could tell us, but her perspective is missing. Kane's early years with Thatcher are also glossed over, while his college friend Jed never illuminates what drove the youthful Kane's ambition. Even as he wrecks Susan's room after she leaves him, Kane is giving a performance for the assembled domestic staff. A moment of genuine feeling occurs when he visits her apartment for the first time. He explains that he was on his way to see his mother's furniture, which is in store. The bond remains between Kane and his mother. We feel the trauma of being sold to Thatcher like a chattel. When Thatcher gives the boy a sledge, Kane's lack of gratitude tells of his resentment. This is all we see of the growing Kane. The desire to prove himself helps him to prosper in business. The cost becomes clear in the breakfast scene between Kane and Emily, when glimpses of subsequent stages of their deteriorating relationship reveal the price of ambition. We come to understand his ruthless approach to business. When he assumes personal control of the newspaper, he parades his social concern. As the paper prospers, power becomes an end in itself. The overlong song and dance routine at the office party is crass and alienates me further from events on screen, but that may be my British sensibility showing.

Kane fails to learn from experience, which becomes evident in his relationship with Susan. She shows no enthusiasm for becoming a singer as her mother hoped, but Kane propels her into a solo career in defiance of her lack of talent. When she attempts suicide, his primary concern is the adverse publicity. Afterwards, he treats her with disdain. When she leaves him, his response is anger at being thwarted. There is no sign of remorse. As Jed tells him, 'You want love on your own terms—something to be played your way, according to your rules.' Two marriages teach Kane nothing. His other relationships are no better. The antipathy with Thatcher is never resolved. Jed is old and sick. He calls his erstwhile employer a swine, but there is no longer any passion behind his words. He long ago realized that Kane was an egoist rather than a crusading publisher. Bernstein has pursued a successful business career, becoming a company chairman. He recalls Kane's early days as a newspaper publisher without offering any insights. The years with Kane have left him unaffected, perhaps because he kept his distance: he was always 'Mr Bernstein', unlike Jed with whom Kane was on first name terms. Thompson should bring the scraps of information together, but he learns little beyond the bare facts. He even fails to discover what Rosebud means.

Kane's first wife, Emily, has most to learn. The breakfast scene offers an insight into her marriage. The note from Gettys revealing her husband's infidelity causes no surprise. She forces Kane to go with her to Susan's apartment. When he has to choose between the two women, Emily proves dispensable. From that moment, we are fearful for Susan. Initially Kane indulges her; later she comes to understand his true nature.

The film offers a familiar message about the dangers of capitalism which accords with Welles's left-wing sympathies. The story is personalized, showing how ambition can pervert aspirations and destroy relationships. Yet I can arouse no concern for Kane. He is a monster, but I never understand him enough to sympathize with him, or pity him. Like Frankenstein's creation, he is no more than an automaton who blunders through people's lives. There are moments when characters come alive. Bernstein's tone is wistful as he recalls a youthful vision of a girl in a white dress whom he glimpsed on a ferry. She remained a stranger and he never saw her again, but her image stayed with him. Emily retains her dignity when Kane spurns her for another woman. Susan shows her girlish side when she first entertains Kane in her apartment. Jed displays real passion when he denounces Kane's lack of principle at the election. The trouble is that these moments are fleeting and interspersed between the bludgeoning activities of Kane himself. I am left feeling that he got what he deserved, which might have been Welles's intention.

Analysis

Most commentators are willing to acknowledge that *Citizen Kane* has flaws, but these are dismissed as insignificant by comparison with Welles's achievement. Pauline Kael concedes that there is no one to hear Kane's deathbed utterance, the newspaper office scenes and the first meeting of Kane and Susan are clumsily staged, there is no sexual interest, Cotten's 'sentimental old codger' in the hospital is a disgrace, Emily is a stereotype of refinement and Susan too thin a conception. Despite these criticisms, Kael is still won over by Welles's 'mysteriously beautiful' performance.[15] Peter Wollen is less partisan, acknowledging the film's impact on film-makers, but accepting that its content cannot be taken seriously.[16] This prompts the question why a film with so little substance should achieve such prominence. The four aspects to be considered are characterization, technical innovations, structural problems and intellectual content.

As Simon Callow is an actor as well as a writer, his views on Welles are illuminating:

> He was not interested in psychology. His notes to actors, as to Paul Stewart as Raymond, were based on a notion of character which expressed itself in paradoxical types (the butler who steals). This approach can best be described as anecdotal; its impact is cerebral, not visceral. The audience feels that they've got the point of the character, not that they've experienced him in all his richness. Welles's real concern was not with the essence of the character but his tempo, pitch and rhythm: his texture.[17]

Welles's approach to acting is in contradistinction to Lee Strasberg's method school, which came to dominate American cinema. By 1941, Welles's declamatory style was already dated. Whether its use in *Citizen Kane* was the result of a firm directorial hand, the cast's earlier work with Welles, or their common theatrical background is a matter for conjecture. James Naremore contends that Welles's own scenes were designed to accommodate his physical limitations, which included a sprained ankle and a corset. Because Welles was graceless in movement and more convincing when playing an old man or when seated, his immobility locked his fellow actors into rigid structural patterns around him.[18] This may explain why the film dwindles into a series of tableaux, each with Welles at its centre. His fellow actors have little opportunity to develop their characters: on occasions when Kane is not present, all they do is talk about him. They rarely move. The actor who escapes from Welles's prescriptive style is Agnes Moorehead. She conveys a sense of holding back genuine emotions, as commentators as diverse as Callow and David Thomson have noted.[19]

Is Kane a maligned character? Bosley Crowther came to this conclusion in his second review: 'Yet at no point in the picture is a black mark actually checked against Kane. Not a shred of evidence is presented to indicate that he is anything but an honest publisher with a consistently conscientious attitude towards society.'[20] This may be correct in terms of business practice, even if it ignores Kane's egomaniacal character and his treatment of the people around him. Crowther's view was unusual even among the flux of critical opinion which surrounded the film in its early days. It provides an instance of a critic's political values colouring a review. Whether it coincided with Welles's view of capitalism is another matter.[21] A clue to Kane's attitude is revealed during the newsreel, when his words appear on screen: 'I am, have been, and always will be only one thing—an American.' This is presented as justification for his actions. Later in the newsreel, he tells the interviewer after his travels abroad: 'I'm always glad to be back, young man. I'm American. I've always been American.' This emphasis on nationality is used to imply a set of values which are its concomitant and which audiences were expected to know and support. These include a dislike of vested interests (Thatcher the banker is held in contempt by Kane and Bernstein) and the endorsement of capitalism as a way of achieving power, with its ever-present risk of losing what has been achieved. Liberals might feel uneasy that Kane gains his fortune by luck rather than hard work and shows more interest in consolidating his power than upholding the free market, but these possibilities never troubled Crowther.

In establishing the look of the film, Welles found a willing partner in his cinematographer, Gregg Toland. Deep-focus photography is exploited in the party scene at the newspaper office, where the camera is placed at the end of a long table and takes in all the diners. Renoir toyed with the technique in *La Règle du jeu*, as did D. W. Griffith before him, but Welles and Toland used it more consistently.[22] Nor was optical printing new—projecting a film onto a camera lens, so that images could be superimposed. Welles used the process to achieve such effects as the pan through a skylight into Susan Alexander's night club.[23] Having ceilings to the sets (even if they were of muslin to facilitate microphone placing) allowed the camera to be placed at a low level. The effect recalls German Expressionism, the deep shadows helping to disguise the partial sets used for the interior of Xanadu.[24] But Expressionism was twenty years old and its tropes had been incorporated into the horror film. This is appropriation rather than innovation.

There were comparable technical advances in the use of sound. In his radio work, Welles abandoned the stage convention of waiting until the other character finishes speaking. This is notable in the boarding-house scene from Kane's childhood. The voices overlap, the depth of focus allowing the speakers to be kept in view. One virtue of this technique is that it delineates power relationships, with the dominant character cutting off the subordinate, but such innovations cannot prevent the film from evoking a previous age.[25] That Gothic opening and the clothes locate events in the past, while the overemphatic acting harks back to the cinema of Welles's childhood. There is little which is contemporary other than the newsreel and the projector which screens it, the illuminated sign over the club where Susan sings, the telephone booth in the club entrance and the procession of cars setting off for a picnic at Xanadu. It is as though Welles feels at more ease in the past, despite his fascination with technology. His enthusiastic use of technical developments led to the accusations of showmanship evident in Bosley Crowther's second thoughts. And the doubts lingered. Richard Rowland wrote in 1947: 'The brilliant camera work which Orson Welles gave us in *Citizen Kane,* we realize sadly, was largely trickery and mechanical cleverness used to conceal the emptiness of the film.'[26] This kind of criticism was largely forgotten after *Citizen Kane's* rediscovery in the 1950s. If anything, the cleverness which Rowland perceived as a weakness was reinterpreted as a virtue, not least by Kael, while Andrew Sarris saw in Welles's defiant rejection of current filmmaking techniques a redefining of the cinema.[27] Welles only intermittently lived up to the promise of *Citizen Kane,* suggesting that the film's technical innovations were not a sufficient basis for a career.

The device of a man being remembered by several people had been used in *The Power and the Glory* (William K. Howard, US, 1933), another story of the corrupting effects of power. Though Welles claimed not to have seen the earlier film, he was likely to have been aware of it.[28] Charles Higham exposes a problem with Welles's use of this flashback structure:

> Yet if much of the film reflects a sentimental romanticism, its structure is cynical. The cynicism lies in the technique of having people comment on Kane who are themselves comically overdrawn witnesses to a serious career. If we cannot take them seriously, we cannot take their views seriously; and if Kane emerges from their accounts making any sense at all, it is in spite of them.[29]

Overlapping accounts of a character's life can become repetitious. Welles and Mankiewicz attempted to minimize this danger by organizing the memories into a roughly chronological sequence, with each speaker recalling different events. The audience is given a context by the device of the opening newsreel, which presents Kane's public persona. This obviates the need for a narrator, but then the scriptwriters compromise by introducing the reporter, whose questions prompt the flashbacks. If he discovers little about Kane, we find out nothing about Thompson. He is arbitrarily introduced to move the action forward. As Welles put it, 'He's not a person. He's a piece of machinery.'[30] Does any other great film have a central character who remains so anonymous and can be dismissed so casually?

The newsreel device introduces another problem. A newsreel was an integral part of every cinema programme and was screened immediately after the trailers for forthcoming attractions. Inserting an ersatz newsreel near the beginning of the film risks making the brief preceding scenes resemble a trailer, which is unworthy of full attention. The more authentic the newsreel, the more likely it was to be perceived as genuine, provoking audiences into restlessness as they waited for the main feature to begin. Film diaries, exhibitors' returns, or interviews with audience members might clarify this point. RKO was an early user of Gallup Polls. These give glimpses of American audiences' tastes, including their opinions on Welles, but Susan Ohmer makes no mention of any feedback on *Citizen Kane* in this cache.[31]

Two further structural flaws become apparent in Thatcher's memoir. First, why does a loving mother sell her son? The explanation given—to get him away from his feckless father—never seems convincing given the mother's dominating position in the household. The trouble is that the contrivance of Rosebud depends upon it. David Thomson attributes the incident to the cinematic adoration of a mother who severs bonds with her son, which raises the spectre of a Hollywood cliché at the heart of the film.[32] The second blemish is the scene in which Kane cedes control of his empire to his bankers after his power is weakened by the 1929 Wall Street Crash. It disrupts the story's linear progression, while serving no dramatic purpose: nothing leads up to it and it is never referred to again. Kael notes that Welles was unhappy with the scene and meant to come back to it, but the sequence it coordinated was never restored during editing.[33] Such a glaring loose end diminishes Welles's achievement.

Sarris concedes that the film's intellectual content is superficial.[34] Certainly *Citizen Kane* displays no intellectual pretensions. There is no critique of the American political system, Kane's attempt to garner power by running for political office being presented as a personal battle with Gettys.[35] No guide to how Kane built up his empire is offered. Nor are the problems and responsibilities of power addressed. Welles made no pretence that *Citizen Kane* was an intellectual film, but neither does he explore the emotions of his characters, or touch the emotions of audiences. So where lies the film's greatness? Rosebud encapsulates the problem. Welles reputedly admitted that the device was 'dollar-book Freud', but this proved no deterrent.[36] Perhaps Edgar Allan Poe's apocryphal deathbed cry of 'Reynolds' inspired the idea. The sledge named *Rosebud* was given to Kane by his mother and signifies his love for her and the trauma of separation. This is hard to discern from watching the film, unless the viewer is attentive to the names on sledges. Such detail is more likely to be gleaned from commentaries on the film, which is no compliment to Welles. Tangye Lean, writing in 1941, detected an importance beyond anything Welles admitted in the revelation of the name: 'If you accept the discovery of *Rosebud* as something more significant than an O. Henry ending, a vast pattern of interrelated human themes becomes clear—as a different one does in the last volume of *A la recherche du temps perdu.*'[37]

A student in the audience felt the same way: 'It was the flaming consummation of sex and politics we had been waiting for in movie theaters all our lives.'[38] But the film never builds on the discovery of what Rosebud means. The immolation scene as flames consume the sledge has a Wagnerian splendour, but it is a hollow gesture which provides no emotional catharsis because we have not become involved with the characters. Rosebud is a 'piece of machinery', like Thompson, and the conundrum is neatly resolved in the final reel. *Millions Like Us* (Frank Launder and Sidney Gilliat, GB, 1943) is an example of a film which is more successful in this respect. When the husband of newly married Celia (Patricia Roc) is lost on a bombing raid over Germany, she gradually joins in the singing at a variety concert in the factory canteen, drawing strength from the community around her. *Citizen Kane* never tugs at the heart like this scene. Nor can Welles provide an intellectual resolution comparable to the final conflagration in an equally brittle film, *The Draughtsman's Contract* (Peter Greenaway, GB, 1982), for no philosophical conundrum has been resolved.

Those early reservations about *Citizen Kane* deserve reappraising. The film is the work of a director in love with the cinema's potential, but it has an emotional and intellectual vacuum at its core which all Welles's bravura fails to hide.

–7–

It's a Wonderful Life (US, 1946): Seeking the American Hero

Production company: Liberty Films
Producer/Director: Frank Capra
Source: Philip Van Doren Stern (story: 'The Greatest Gift')
Screenplay: Frank Capra, Frances Goodrich, Albert Hackett, Dorothy Parker, Jo Swerling, Michael Wilson
Photography: Joseph Walker, Joseph Biroc
Art Director: Jack Okey
Music: Dimitri Tiomkin
Editor: William Hornbeck
Cast: James Stewart (George Bailey), Donna Reed (Mary), Lionel Barrymore (Mr Potter), Thomas Mitchell (Uncle Billy), Henry Travers (Clarence), Gloria Grahame (Vi)

Synopsis

One snowy night, the inhabitants of Bedford Falls pray for their fellow citizen, George Bailey. The film looks back over his life. As a young man, he turns down his father's suggestion that he should take over the family savings and loan business, preferring to travel before training as an engineer. Potter is a banker and the town's most prominent businessman, whose opposition to the Bailey family is placated with a seat on the board. The death of George's father changes everything. To prevent Potter from closing the business, George takes charge while his brother goes to college. After marrying his teenage sweetheart, Mary, George discovers that the bank has precipitated a run on the company by calling in the loans. He reassures worried investors that their money is secured in property. Those who are still nervous are repaid using cash intended for the honeymoon. His strategy works and the business is saved.

Potter's income from rents declines because people are buying homes with the help of Bailey's company. As George is the company's lynchpin, Potter tries to buy him off by offering him a job as manager in the bank. George refuses. When he returns home to tell Mary of the offer, she reveals that she is pregnant.

George's brother, Harry, becomes a decorated naval flyer during the Second World War and the hero of Bedford Falls, while George continues to run the business. Christmas approaches and Uncle Billy goes to the bank with the company's takings. There he is distracted by reading of Harry's exploits. The copy of the newspaper belongs to Potter, who subsequently finds the money among the pages. He says nothing. A distraught Billy confesses to George that the money is lost, while a bank examiner chooses that day to examine the books. George is forced to appeal to Potter for help. The banker refuses. As George prepares to kill himself, an angel named Clarence intervenes. In response to George's wish that he had never been born, Clarence shows him what the town would have become without him. It is filled with bars and gambling clubs. The Bailey family business has long since disappeared. Harry is dead because George was not there as a child to rescue him from a frozen lake. Mary is unmarried. When George tries to talk to her, she becomes alarmed. The men of the town turn on him and he is forced to flee. The experience makes George decide to live. He returns home to find that the townspeople have clubbed together to make good the company's loss. They all celebrate Christmas.

Cultural Context

Philip Van Doren Stern published his story 'The Greatest Gift' at his own expense. RKO bought the film rights for $10,000 in 1943 and Dalton Trumbo wrote a script which was rewritten by Clifford Odets and Marc Connolly. When RKO dropped the project, Frank Capra purchased the rights in 1945 for $50,000. To gain independence from the studios, he formed the production company Liberty Films with William Wyler, George Stevens and producer Samuel Briskin. Capra, Frances Goodrich, Albert Hackett, Jo Swerling, Michael Wilson and Dorothy Parker all had a hand in the script of *It's a Wonderful Life,* though witch-hunts against communists meant that some of these names went uncredited, with Capra himself coming under suspicion at one stage.[1] Capra had Stewart in mind for the part of George Bailey from the outset. Jean Arthur was first in line for the role of Mary, but she was unavailable. Ginger Rogers was columnist Hedda Hopper's choice, Capra's rejection of her precipitating a break between the two men. Rogers thought the role too bland.[2]

Charles K. Wolfe has collated reviews in his bibliography of Capra.[3] American critics were generally positive, except for those in New York. For Bosley Crowther of the *New York Times,* 'the weakness of this picture ... is the sentimentality of it—its illusory concept of life.' The charming characters, the beguiling small town and the optimistic resolution 'all resemble theatrical attitudes rather than average realities'.[4] Virginia Wright's review in the *New York Daily News* was equally dismissive, calling the film 'an uneven collection of fantasy, homely philosophy, slapstick, sentimentality and humor'.[5] For Pauline Kael, 'In its own slurpy, bittersweet way, the picture's well done.... Capra takes a serious tone here though there is no basis for the seriousness; this is doggerel trying to pass as art.'[6] British critics took a similar tone, the review in *The Times* being representative:

> Mr Frank Capra has exploited the sentimental possibilities of his themes to the full and has reserved subtlety for the incidental touches and humours. It is not a good film, but it is a generous one … at the end the audience feels as though it had been listening to a large man of boisterous good nature talking at the top of his voice for over two hours.[7]

Dilys Powell provided a more penetrating analysis:

> Since Capra came of age as a director, the celestial messenger has caught on as well as the celestial choir; and so the problems of mortality must be solved not by mortal means, but by Henry Travers as a guardian angel winning his wings. Capra, in fact, shrinks … from pursuing the inquiry into human nature; so far as the easy superficial goodness, but no farther.[8]

The film was a failure at the box office, losing US$480,000 on its domestic release.[9] It was forgotten after 1947, not coming to public or critical attention again until 1974, when the bankrupt owners failed to renew the copyright and the film entered the public domain. This led to frequent screenings as a Christmas film by television companies. The complications of derivative rights on such items as the music and the story meant that the legal situation was not resolved until NBC acquired the rights to the film in 1994.[10] The rise of the auteur coincided with the film's reappearance in the 1970s, heralding a re-evaluation of Capra. John Mariani could write in 1979: '*It's a Wonderful Life* now seems to be Capra's most complex movie—and, I think, one of the cinema's great works—because its characters, themes, textures, and imagery are so smooth, so compelling and so arresting, so wise about the basic facts and fantasies of human life.'[11] *It's a Wonderful Life* was voted the most inspirational film of all time by 1,500 film professionals in a 2006 AFI poll and ranks thirty-first among the top 250 films chosen by IMDb users.[12]

Subjective Impression

The film's opening with snow falling on small-town America makes my heart sink. As the citizens pray for George Bailey to the accompaniment of a Christmas carol, I prepare for two hours of schmaltz. Things get no better when an angel discusses with his superior how to help George. Such blatant sentimentality may prove infuriating, but at least we discover that heaven is hierarchical.

Even during childhood, George dreams of foreign travel. As a young man, he sets out to buy a suitcase, insisting that it must be large enough to take labels from all the places he will visit. Only then does he discover that the chemist in whose shop he worked as a child has ordered a case for him as a present. George's dreams are public property. He swings the case proudly as he leaves the shop, yet his preparations prove unnecessary. At first it seems that his burgeoning relationship with Mary will prevent him from leaving, but the couple grow apart. The defining event proves to be his father's stroke. George is drawn into the family business at the cost of abandoning his dreams of travel. He throws away the travel brochures which have sustained him and attempts to renew his relationship with Mary, newly returned from New York. At least one of his dreams comes true when he marries her. The couple sets up home in a ramshackle house which he scorned as a teenager. Mary decorates it with travel posters, which seems a cruel reminder of George's dreams. Anybody whose youthful ambitions are subverted by circumstances will empathize. His world collapses on the day when Uncle Billy loses the company's money and the bank examiner calls. George snaps at his family, which is uncharacteristic enough to show the strain he is under. With certainties gone, suicide seems the only solution.

It's a Wonderful Life is about learning, as the intervention of the angel makes clear. George wishes that he had never been born and he is shown the consequences if his wish were granted. He wanders through Bedford Falls as a stranger, discovering the extent of Potter's power had he not been there to limit it. Even the name of the town has been changed to Pottersville. Family businesses have gone. The people show none of the goodwill which George remembers. The culminating incident which makes him realize the importance of his marriage is not being recognized by Mary, though surely the men who rally to her defence against this aggressive stranger are showing community spirit. George seems reconciled with his lot when he returns to the real world. Family and townsfolk rally round, but does he still harbour dreams? Can his future life be wonderful, or is he only conscious of its emptiness? And does it take an angel, that most threadbare of dramatic devices, to convince George and the audience that everything is all right?

Mary's dreams have to be inferred. New York proved disappointing enough for her to return home. George visits her as she awaits a telephone call from his rival. When the call comes, her preference becomes obvious. She soon learns that George's commitment to the community extends to giving creditors the money intended for the honeymoon. This does not deter her from creating a home and bringing up a family with him. Her ambitions might be traditional, but they are real enough and they are achieved. She is tested when things go wrong for George. It is Mary who holds the family together and organizes the townspeople to support him. She proves stronger than George, though Capra does not emphasize this. The couple approach life from opposing directions. George looks outwards with his longing for travel, yet he discovers a world in microcosm in the community where he was raised. Mary is the one who travels further. Rather than turning inwards to the family, she looks to the community for support when George is in trouble. Her faith in the townspeople is vindicated.

This is a moralistic film, but is the moral that people should abandon youthful ambitions and be content with their lot, or that relationships matter more than commerce? One clue comes from the copy of *The Adventures of Tom Sawyer* which the angel leaves for George. It is inscribed 'Remember *no* man is a failure who has friends.' The official who comes to arrest George for financial irregularities tears up the warrant and joins in the Christmas celebrations. The bank examiner makes his own contribution to the fund covering the shortfall. Everybody sings 'Hark the Herald Angels Sing,' which George's daughter was practising on the piano when her father turned his anger on the family. Everybody has been transformed, or so we have to believe. The exception is Potter, who remains as irascible as ever. George is part of the same financial system, and, as he points out to Mary in their courting days, all is fair in love and war. By the end of the film, George might have won the battle against Potter, but the war continues.

The values the film espouses seem confused. Like *Citizen Kane,* it is torn between a mythical past and the contemporary world, which might be a comment on America in the 1940s, or the values of those film-makers who were the grit in the Hollywood system.

Analysis

James Martin, writing in 1997, ascribed the popularity of *It's a Wonderful Life,* among other reasons, to how easy it was for the baby-boom generation to empathize with George in his desire to cast off all responsibilities and travel. Martin also noted the film's value as a source of cultural references.[13] Enter the title into an internet search engine and the surprise is how many articles on law, banking and business refer to the film. The sticking point for many people is the heart-on-sleeve emotion. For Aljean Harmetz writing in 2005, Capra confuses sentiment with sentimentality, which is a consequence of writing the script himself rather than turning to his regular collaborator, Robert Riskin.[14] This ignores the other hands involved, though Capra had the final say as producer-director. Nor can Harmetz's view that *It's a Wonderful Life* is relentlessly cheerful be accepted unequivocally. Despite these reservations, it is hard to disagree that the film 'drowns in the treacle of Stewart's adorable daughter praying, "Dear God, help Daddy"'.[15] Elliott Stein, writing in 1972, also bemoaned the film's greeting-card sentiments.[16] Given that similar accusations were made by the first reviewers, this is not a case of sensibilities changing over time. 'Capra corn' is a fusion of idealized settings, cute children, simplistic adult characters in predictable relationships and superficial emotionalism, often emphasized by trite music. Those who do not find Capra corn an insurmountable obstacle have to glory in it, ignore it, or rationalize it; but it is there, even if Capra-esque has become the accepted and less pejorative term.

Those appeals to God at the start of the film may prove a sticking point for some. J. B. Priestley's plays used a similar device of rerunning characters' lives without resorting to angels. Those who feel comfortable with the film's religious aspects can enjoy finding theological parallels. As Martin points out, it abounds in popular theology: the story starts in heaven (Genesis) and George devotes himself to helping the poor and disadvantaged (St Francis of Assisi) with the help of his wife (Mary). Evil as represented by Potter reduces George from prosperity to poverty (Job), but a vision helps him to understand life (St Paul). He returns home to his disgrace (the prodigal son), but the people recognize his goodness after his resurrection.[17] There is even the temptress Vi to lure the pilgrim from his chosen path, but needless to say he resists her charms. Against such a reading, George never turns to the Church. Leland Poague argues that because Clarence's intervention has little bearing on the lesson George learns, the message is not specifically Christian.[18] If the film is seen as conforming to the mythic mode, the specifically Christian references appear incidental. The hero is tested and approaches his innermost core (suicidal thoughts). He undergoes an ordeal (the glimpse of Pottersville) and with the help of his mentor (an angel) is rewarded by being shown the right path. His return to the everyday world is a cause for celebration.[19] By either religious or mythical interpretations, his life will never be the same again.

Characterization constitutes an equally contentious problem. It is easy to see why Ginger Rogers turned down the role of Mary. George is the only character with any substance. He is driven by a sense of duty, which is difficult to convey on screen by comparison with the inherent drama of risk-taking. The film is George's story and he is rarely off screen, which is unfortunate given that he is presented as a decent, ordinary man rather than a villain or egoist, who might have made a more interesting character. Mary functions as his consort; Glenn Erickson finds it insulting to believe she would become a frigid old maid without George.[20] Uncle Billy provides comic relief as the stock bumbling minor official with a weakness for drink. Barrymore plays Potter as the villain everybody loves to hate, leaving no room for subtlety. The trouble is that in a morality tale, it seems remiss to ignore the villain once he has set the story in motion. Revenge might fly in the face of the Christian ethos, but at least the issue of forgiveness could be addressed if Potter's hubris got the better of him.[21] *It's a Wonderful Life* is often presented as a quintessentially American film.[22] Perhaps it takes an outsider to catch the character of a nation, as it took the Hungarians Emeric Pressburger and Alexander Korda to stand up for Britishness. The Sicilian Capra portrays the self-help values of small-town America coming into conflict with the soulless profiteering of big business, this being expressed as a struggle between Potter and George. Crucially it remains at this level rather than being universalized. As Stein puts it, '[The film's] spiritual meat is that the only thing wrong with capitalism is Lionel Barrymore.'[23] If big business is suspect in Capra's America, so is government as represented by the bank inspector. His inflexibility mirrors government bureaucracy, but even he turns out to be human when regulations are forgotten and the community wins out. Jonathan Munby detects in the film the contradictions of postwar life: the balance between individual aspiration and social responsibility, big city and small town values, and good and bad versions of capitalism.[24] Such contradictions are certainly present, though whether they are distinctively postwar phenomena is less certain.

Running counter to Munby is a thought-provoking commentary from Ray Carney. His contention is that much American film criticism employs a 'surface-depth' model, looking beyond events and characters to the deeper meanings they represent, such as the condition of postwar America. 'Tendentious sociological interpretations drain life of its idiosyncrasy and uniqueness,' devaluing the life of the body and the senses.[25] For Carney, Capra's characters function as critics of society. George Bailey 'honors the uniqueness of personal consciousness and affirms the power of the individual to escape repressive systems of understanding', while Potter is 'devoted to forcing various kinds of metaphoric, symbolic or allegorical interpretations onto experience, robbing life of its mystery and denying individuality and imaginative freedom to others'.[26] The film becomes a journey from George's everyday world into a rich inner life: 'One can stay at home and still be a cosmic traveller in space and time, as George and an imaginative viewer of the film both learn.'[27]

As Carney points out, the temptation to weigh down a film with sociological significance is hard to resist. Against such an argument, film is valuable primary source material for historians precisely because its makers can catch the mood of the times. Carney comes close to transgressing his own principles when he complains that Stein personalizes a predicament whose essential interest is beyond personalities. But rather than succumbing to contradictions, Carney sets himself apart from other commentators by his concern with how institutions can inhibit the inner lives of characters: 'What is wrong with capitalism, according to Capra, is, of course, nothing traceable to or localizable in any individual but rather its fundamental repression of our free imaginative energies, its demands that we relentlessly channel them into socially and ethically responsible careers of action.'[28] It is possible to applaud Carney's methods while having reservations about his willingness to ignore Capra's sentimentality and questionable decisions about structure. George's life is sketched in flashback for Clarence and the audience in preparation for his redemption, but three-quarters of the film has to pass before Clarence intervenes and events begin to unfold in real time. The vision of George's journey through the town as if he had never lived has dramatic power, but it comes when the film's mood is already established. It is only at this stage that the significance becomes apparent of seemingly incidental events such as saving his brother from drowning as a child. On the basis of internal evidence, Erickson suggests that the film was recut as a series of flashbacks because a linear approach proved unsatisfactory.[29] Capra had other options. If George had committed suicide, the emphasis would shift to Mary's response, making this a woman-centred film with no need for angels—or flashbacks.

In a reversal of the usual viewpoint, Patrick J. Deneen sees George as vying with Potter to change the environment with airports, skyscrapers and bridges.[30] This is the America of mobility and impermanence. George's grandiose dreams dwindle to transforming his home town by building Bailey Park, where pavements and porches, the traditional places for social interaction, are banished in favour of garages and patios. The result is that families are thrown onto their own resources rather than looking outwards to the community. George was friends with the Martini family, who ran a local bar. When he goes with Clarence to their home in Bailey Park, he cannot find it, stumbling instead through a cemetery. Then we realize that he swept away the cemetery to build his suburb, obliterating the town's links with its past. As Deneen puts it, 'A deep irony pervades the film at the moment of its joyous conclusion. As the developer of an antiseptic suburban subdivision, George Bailey is saved through the kinds of relationships nourished in his town, which will be undermined and even precluded in the anomic community he builds.'[31] Potter's vision does not seem so bad after this.

Erickson sees *film blanc* with its presentation of a world after death as a genre threading through cinema history in such disparate works as *Destiny* (Fritz Lang, Germany, 1921), *Liliom* (Fritz Lang, France, 1934) and *The Blue Bird* (Walter Lang, US, 1940). A heavenly waiting room is a distinguishing feature of a genre which has a utopian aspect but carries the risks of smugness and righteousness. *It's a Wonderful Life* fits Erickson's definition of *film blanc,* though he concedes that the *noir* elements have attracted more attention.[32] Bosley Crowther compared the film unfavourably with *Stairway to Heaven,* aka *A Matter of Life and Death* (Michael Powell and Emeric Pressburger, GB, 1946), the most distinguished British contribution to film blanc.[33] A detailed comparison of postwar attitudes in the two works would be revealing.

The title *It's a Wonderful Life* sums up the problem of how to approach the film. Should it be taken at face value, or as something more equivocal? The temptation is to see it as an ironic comment on George's life, or is this to impose a postmodern gloss on the work? Stephen J. Brown points out that the title in the film's opening credit sequence is in quotation marks, implying ambiguity on Capra's part, but did audiences take it this way?[34] Munby argues that *It's a Wonderful Life* was not intended as a holiday film, but as something more cynical and desperate.[35] For Vito Zagarrio, Capra probed moral dilemmas within the conventions of Hollywood. Like social conflict, suicide is a recurring and disturbing motif in his films, jolting them out of their cosiness.[36] A Catholic upbringing and an interest in Christian Science make it likely that Capra's concern was redemption rather than nihilism and that beneath the whimsy is a darker undertow. This is enough to make the film interesting, but quality has to be argued for.

It's a Wonderful Life is taken more seriously than on its first release. If it can no longer be dismissed as a Christmas confection, its flaws cannot be ignored. Capra offers a glimpse of a world without George, but this is also a world seemingly untouched by the New Deal, where real men sort out their own problems.[37] The nostalgia for traditional American values is undercut by George's own brand of capitalism, which is less blatant than Potter's, but just as pernicious. As Dilys Powell perceived in her 1947 review, Capra settles for easy, superficial goodness. The people around George function as satellites. In Erickson's words, 'In the Capra universe, all souls are equal, but some more equal than others. You're either the star, or destined to be some quaint but irrelevant bit player.'[38] The star is obviously James Stewart. George Bailey's journey of the soul is diminished by Capra's lack of balance and his play for easy emotions. Capra corn has to be confronted, from the opening prayers to the final carol singing. It may be attributed to Capra's Italian background, or conformity to the Hollywood conventions which he helped to define. For Munby, the irony is that the film has become a myth, while Capra sought to move away from the Hollywood version of how life was lived towards something more realistic.[39] If the time model of greatness is accepted, the film should transcend its era, even if some of its meaning is lost or changed. It has yet to be demonstrated that *It's a Wonderful Life* achieves this, despite Carney's advocacy.

Black Narcissus (GB, 1947):
Nuns in Exotic Places

Production company: The Archers
Producers/Directors/Screenplay: Michael Powell, Emeric Pressburger
Source: Rumer Godden (novel: *Black Narcissus*)
Photography: Jack Cardiff
Production Designer: Alfred Junge
Music: Brian Easdale
Editor: Reginald Mills
Cast: Deborah Kerr (Sister Clodagh), David Farrar (Dean), Flora Robson (Sister Philippa), Kathleen Byron (Sister Ruth), Jean Simmons (Kanchi), Sabu (Young General), May Hallatt (Angu), Judith Furse (Sister Briony), Jenny Laird (Sister Honey)

Synopsis

When an Indian ruler, the Old General, presents nuns with the hilltop palace of Mopu in the Himalayan foothills, his English agent, Dean, predicts that they will leave by the time the rains arrive. At first it seems that the prediction will be proved wrong, for the school and dispensary which the nuns open are well attended. It transpires that the Old General has paid the villagers to attend. Dean explains to Sister Clodagh, who runs the mission, that the payments will be tapered off once the habit of attending is established.

The nuns have their own problems. Sister Philippa, who tends the garden, is disoriented by the strange surroundings; she plants flowers instead of vegetables. Sister Ruth is attracted to Dean, contriving every opportunity to glimpse him. She has a rival in Sister Clodagh, whose thoughts turn to the man she left behind in Ireland whenever she encounters Dean. He brings Kanchi, a disruptive orphan of seventeen, to be looked after by the sisters. She is attracted to the Young General, who attends the mission for lessons. His black narcissus cologne bought from a London department store gives the film its title.

Sister Briony heeds Dean's advice, refusing to treat a baby with a life-threatening illness. Sister Honey is swayed by the mother's appeals and dispenses castor oil without telling her more experienced colleague. When the baby dies, the sisters are blamed and the villagers desert the mission. The Young General abandons his lessons and leaves with Kanchi. In her rounds of the palace, Sister Clodagh finds Sister Ruth wearing a red velvet dress, having decided to give up the sisterhood. The rebellious sister taunts her superior. Sister Clodagh intends them to pray together through the night but falls asleep, giving Sister Ruth the opportunity to slip out and confront Dean. When she confesses her love, he urges her to return to the palace. She agrees reluctantly. As Sister Clodagh calls the nuns to prayer by ringing the bell on the cliff edge, Sister Ruth is overcome by jealousy and attacks her, but it is Sister Ruth who loses her footing in the struggle and falls to her death. The nuns abandon the palace as the rains come, fulfilling Dean's prediction.

Cultural Context

Black Narcissus was Powell and Pressburger's first foray into adapting a popular novel for the screen. The fan magazine *Picture Show* called the film 'sincere and unusual entertainment'.[1] The *Monthly Film Bulletin* showed blanket enthusiasm, praising the acting, the brilliant cutting, the exotic settings and the beautiful, natural colour.[2] This favourable critical response was confirmed when *Black Narcissus* was voted among the runners-up for the Empire Award in Canada, the winner being *Great Expectations* (David Lean, GB, 1946).[3] Among dissenting voices, the reviewer for *The Times* noted 'the tendency of the dialogue to drop unexpectedly into artificiality and bathos', while 'all the careful planning of the fact that the wind, the air, the mountains, and the far horizons work subtly on the imagination leads only to a conventional gesture of melodrama.'[4] Dilys Powell praised the use of colour, 'But [the film] is weakened by the conflict of themes; there is not concentration enough on the feeling of the place; and the flash-backs by which the history and state of mind of the young Sister Superior are indicated have an obviousness alien from the rest of the piece.'[5] James Agee also praised the photography but found the overall effect tedious and vulgar, the faults lying with the novel.[6] The trade press gave the film a cautious reception: while *Variety* praised the cinematography and Kathleen Byron's performance, *Kinematograph Weekly* doubted whether the film would be successful in 'tough industrial areas'.[7] The absence of box-office figures makes it difficult to gauge whether this judgement was correct.

A renewed interest in British cinema rescued Powell and Pressburger from obscurity. Their rehabilitation was aided by Powell's autobiography and the proselytizing of supporters like Ian Christie.[8] The reputation of Powell in particular rose to auteur status, even if this glosses over the duo's later misfires.

Today, *Black Narcissus* is rated highly. In the *Time Out Film Guide*, Geoff Andrew proclaims: 'Powell's use of colour, design and music was never as perfectly in tune with the emotional complexity of Pressburger's script, their talents combining to create one of Britain's great cinematic masterpieces, a marvellous evocation of hysteria and repression, and incidentally one of the few genuinely erotic films ever to emerge from these sexually staid isles.'[9] The *Radio Times Guide to Films* is no less effusive, describing *Black Narcissus* as 'one of the most striking examples of studio-controlled artifice in film history'.[10] Internet guides are equally enthusiastic, with Mark Duguid describing *Black Narcissus* as 'one of the most erotic films ever to emerge from the British cinema'.[11] Martin Scorsese in his commentary included with DVD version compares the experience of watching the film for the first time to 'being bathed in color'.[12] The public is less keen, judging by the film's absence from audience polls.

Subjective Impression

Powell and Pressburger conjure a strange, exotic world by their use of music, costumes and scenery. Into this world come the nuns, whose lifestyle would also be considered unusual by many people. They are isolated from the world they know and have to grapple with the alien environment.

Sister Clodagh is young to be heading a mission. She thinks too highly of herself, as the Mother Superior is not reticent about telling her. Dean detects the same character trait. As he remarks, 'You'll like the General, Sister. He, also, is a superior being.' Her leadership qualities and her faith are tested by the clash with the villagers, though the palace is already a troubled place, with the nuns becoming increasingly wayward. Dean stirs memories of the upper-middle-class life she gave up. When she turns to Dean for help, she seems closer to the conventional passive heroine than a superior being. She tries to give strength to the erring Sister Ruth by sitting with her through the night but renders her gesture futile by falling asleep. The abandonment of the palace signals her failure to restore her authority.

Sister Ruth's vocation is in doubt from the start. Sister Clodagh has reservations about the wayward sister's suitability for the posting, but the Reverend Mother feels that she will do better in a small community. Like Sister Honey, Sister Ruth shows her emotions too readily, which is perceived as a problem. Her vocation vies not only with desire for Dean, but jealousy towards her superior. This becomes apparent when she goads Sister Clodagh by applying lipstick. Dean's rejection intensifies her jealousy, precipitating the final tragedy. Sister Ruth's emotions prove her undoing, vindicating the reservations of her superiors.

The daunting reputation of Powell and Pressburger prefigures my response. I expect a visual feast and strong emotions, yet the story seems drawn from romantic fiction, which is not meant to be taken seriously. The result is uncertainty about how to respond to the film. My instinct is not to expect profundity; background knowledge tells me that I should reserve judgement.

Dean begins the film as a detached and ironic observer, which is my position as a viewer. I share his awareness of the mysteriousness of the palace and how it disorients the newcomers. Sister Honey exasperates me with her silliness. I understand why villagers boycott the palace when the baby dies, but I root for Sister Clodagh in her attempts to keep the mission running. Becoming involved in the nuns' battle against the elements increases my sympathy towards them, distracting my attention from the clash of cultures and turning it towards tensions within the palace. When Dean is drawn into advising the nuns, I appreciate his divided loyalties, even if Powell and Pressburger make little of this. My greatest problem is with Sister Ruth, who wrenches the film into the realm of Gothic fiction. The director seems obsessed with her meaningful glances, while her visit to Dean's house seems unconvincing both in its hysterical pitch and the jungle surroundings, which are so at odds with the world of the mountains. It is hard to understand why she became a nun, and no explanation is forthcoming. She is a dramatic device rather than a real person. Psychological truth is missing, which unsettles the film and unsettles me.

It is Sister Clodagh who has most to learn as the mission fails. How the experience changes her is outside the scope of the film, though we can assume that she no longer considers herself a superior being. Dean has his prejudices confirmed. Do we learn anything? A few masculine prejudices are reinforced, but that is all.

Analysis

Adapting a tried and tested literary work brings its own problems. Lovers of the book can be alienated—no realization rivals the film in the reader's head—while the adapter has the dilemma of whether to remain faithful to the source, or use it as a springboard for a more innovative treatment. Powell and Pressburger change the novel's emphasis, but they reproduce much of Rumer Godden's dialogue verbatim, exposing the flatness of speech which was intended to be read rather than spoken. A major simplification is the omission of stern Sister Adela, who takes Sister Philippa's place when she leaves the mission. This avoids introducing a new character halfway through the film.

The book portrays two culture clashes. A conflict of interests exists between the rulers and the ruled, though the British Empire hardly impinges on this frontier region. Even the Old General leaves the locals to settle their own disputes. Dean's position as agent is ambivalent. He comes from the same colonizing power as the nuns and speaks of the population as children, yet his employer is Indian. Like a Graham Greene character, Dean finds solace in drink and local women; the difference from Greeneland is that Godden makes the sisters Anglo-Catholic and Dean an agnostic.

The complexities of Indian culture hinted at in the novel are omitted from the film. Apart from the boy translator, Joseph Anthony, the only Indian characters with significant roles are Kanchi the temptress, Angu the eccentric caretaker and the vain Young General. By presenting this adult trio as comic oddities and the boy as cute, effectively the racial theme is neutralized, throwing the focus on the sisters' response to a world which is geographically and culturally alien. When they are blamed for the death of the baby, the truce between East and West ruptures and the exotic becomes threatening. Following Dean's advice, they look to their own resources, cutting themselves off from the local community. The threat becomes an abstraction: a natural catastrophe would serve the story equally well.

The second culture clash is between discipline (the nuns) and hedonism (Dean). There are moments when hedonism seems destined to win out, which is unusual for British films of the period. Because both sides have English as their first language, this theme is easier to develop in dialogue. Powell and Pressburger accord it more attention, so the film almost becomes a parable about power: the power of religion, power within hierarchies and personal power. But power is never as absolute as its possessors like to believe: it can be subverted by events and emotions. The financial power of the Old General keeps villagers coming to the mission, but it proves useless once the sisters are blamed for the death of the baby. The sisters lose their power to proselytize on health, education and religion. Nor can they hold Kanchi, who is lured away by the wealthy and handsome Young General. As Sister Clodagh's authority ebbs away, she relies increasingly on Dean, whose own power in an alien culture is limited. Only the Holy Man remains aloof. The nuns search for Sister Ruth, not knowing she has gone to Dean. As Joseph Anthony assures Sister Clodagh, the disappearance of Sister Ruth is of little consequence to the Holy Man, and it would be inappropriate to ask whether he has seen her.

Frequent references by critics to the film's eroticism prompt the diligent viewer to search for it. Given the British Board of Film Censors' innate caution, something oblique is to be anticipated. The painting so disliked by Sister Clodagh is erotic, but it is art (meaning that ordinary people cannot be expected to understand it), it is foreign (foreigners have dubious habits), it is glimpsed from a discreet distance and Sister Clodagh does the right thing by banishing it. Kanchi's skittish behaviour in the presence of the Young General is also absolved because she is foreign; her blatant pursuit of him is more embarrassing than erotic. The sexual desire which spices relations between Dean and the sisters is expressed in lingering glances, only becoming explicit when Sister Ruth visits Dean's house. She proclaims her love, but it is not reciprocated and the couple never kiss. The censor could rest easy. Not that the film escaped unscathed: flashbacks to Sister Clodagh's life in Ireland were cut from the American version after objections from the League of Decency, who felt that such scenes cast doubt on her vocation.[13]

Eroticism has to tantalize if it is not to dwindle into pornography; it should hint that there is something more to be revealed. The object of desire may be unaware of the effect she is having, as Eric Rohmer's *Claire's Knee* (France, 1970) demonstrates to perfection. Kathleen Byron's antics in *Black Narcissus* are more likely to raise a smile. This is a matter of what Powell and Byron show rather than what they conceal. Subtlety is missing.

If *Black Narcissus* is unusual among British films of the period in its use of colour and its portrayal of unfulfilled sexual desire, wittingly or unwittingly it betrays the preoccupations of its time. Establishing a clinic and a school is an apt topic for the era of the welfare state. The film could not have been made three years earlier: the mood is wrong for wartime. Nor could it have been made three years later, after partition stopped India from being regarded as Britain's back yard. Powell and Pressburger adopt the viewpoint of the colonial power, the villagers being presented as mired in a backward culture or quaintly amusing. A perspective from the colonized comes from Dibyaduti Purkayastha, who points out that although the caretaker, Angu, and the wayward Kanchi represent the indigenous culture, both are played by British actors.[14] The irony is that the re-evaluation of the film should occur at a time when it can be criticized for perpetuating racial stereotypes. Anh Hua goes further, detecting a celebration of the imbalance of power between colonizers and colonized, with the masculine imperialist gaze feminizing what it sees and even the virginal Himalayas awaiting mastery by the conqueror.[15] There is no much left to salvage from this critique, which is a reinterpretation of the film for a post-colonial age. But applying today's values to the past is akin to cladding an historic building in plastic and provokes a comparable response from historians.

Mopu is a place of colour, poverty and primitive beliefs, where steamy jungle and snow-capped peaks are unconvincingly juxtaposed. In Purkayastha's judgement, the scenery resembles no particular place in India. This is symptomatic of a generalized vision of the East out of *Lost Horizon* (Frank Capra, US, 1938) and still persisting in *The King and I* (Walter Lang, US, 1957), where Deborah Kerr again played the visitor from the West. *Black Narcissus* is in danger of dwindling into a Rank travelogue as Dean intones over shots of smiling locals: 'The people are like mountain peasants everywhere—simple and independent. They work because they must, they smile when they feel like it and they're no respecters of persons. The men are men—no better than anywhere else. The women are women, the children, children.' Andrew Moor interprets this as parody, but its purpose is unclear given that Rank financed the film.[16]

Myth also wins over reality in the presentation of the palace. The book stresses that Mopu is designed to withstand the elements, the single storey reducing exposure to the wind, and the windows having thick glass. The palace in the film resembles a summer residence on two floors (staircases allow dramatic camera angles), with no glass in the windows to obstruct the mountain vistas. The sisters introduce the trappings of religious life, but they never manage to change the character of the place. Dean helps them, but at heart he prefers to leave things as they were. The film hints at the palace's louche past by contrasting the bright decor with the bleached robes of the sisters. But religious life need not be pallid, as the sisters demonstrate by introducing statuettes and candles.

Black Narcissus prefigures the Bollywood movie in its emphasis on colour. The significance accorded to Sister Ruth's lipstick and her red dress is only possible in colour film. Both are additions for the screen version. The trouble is that the saturated hues evoke Hollywood's worst excesses. John Huntley worked on the film and wrote of attempting to keep the dreamlike strangeness without garish colour.[17] But garishness intrudes, though transfers between media may have distorted the tonal balance.[18] There is no reason why audiences from the 1940s should have interpreted Powell and Pressburger's exuberance as anything other than escapism in the same vein as American Technicolor offerings. What Durgnat calls 'philosophy by Technicolour' has overtaken the film.[19] Even David Thomson waxes lyrical: 'They enjoyed the glory days of Technicolor, before the process opted for high fidelity, cool accuracy, and anonymity, when every color was exaggerated and it was possible to paint with light.'[20] Colour may delight an audience, but it cannot move them, however ruby red Sister Ruth's lips might be. For this we need engagement with real emotions.

An audience's sense of watching a Hollywood product is enhanced by the music, which replaces dialogue in some scenes. It is analysed in Alton Jerome McFarland's paper on the use of sound in the film.[21] The problem lies in the music's quality. Brian Easdale's score makes obvious emotional points, never rising above the mundane. One example occurs when Sister Clodagh encounters Sister Ruth wearing the red dress. A wordless female chorus rises over the orchestra in some clichéd scoring. A similar modal approach and comparable forces are apparent in *Flos Campi* (1925) by Vaughan Williams. Here the composer uses a viola to spin an astringent melodic line over spare accompaniment, creating a sense of wonderment which eludes Easdale, who studied with Vaughan Williams's friend and pupil, Gordon Jacob. Sister Ruth walks through the jungle to Dean's home to the accompaniment of rhythmic drumming. A solo string melody is introduced over the drums as she enters the building, but the oily tone conveys the same superficial emotionalism as the chorus, which is reintroduced as she faints. What should be overpowering is rendered sentimental, neutralizing genuine feeling. A comparison with Joe Losey's *The Go-Between* makes the point. Michel Legrand's score is out of period and recycled from *The Happy Ending* (Richard Brooks, US, 1969), but by employing dissonance against insistent rhythm, it catches the tension between the ordered, upper-class world and the covert relationship which crosses class barriers. The emotional impact of events on screen is enhanced rather than echoed.

The Go-Between relies on naturalistic acting; *Black Narcissus* has an equally cathartic ending but displays contrasting acting styles. Deborah Kerr's performance as Sister Clodagh is as buttoned up as her costume: her look of horror when Sister Ruth falls to her death is one of the few moments when her character's emotions break through. This is someone who takes her vows and her position as head of the mission seriously. Flora Robson and Judith Furse are equally naturalistic. The contrast is with the overwrought performances of May Hallatt, Jenny Laird, Jean Simmons and especially Kathleen Byron, whose staring eyes and flaring nostrils hark back to German Expressionism but sit uneasily with 1940s production values.

Diana Dors wrote that Powell considered her for a role.[22] It is intriguing to speculate on the result had she opted for the Grand Guignol school of acting. How her sultry presence (as Sister Honey?) would have changed the film. Whether the clash of acting styles was deliberate is unclear, but it must have been sanctioned by Powell. It makes the film unusual in a period when realism was ascendant, but this is distinct from quality.

At a time when a good story was at the heart of every successful film, Powell and Pressburger were distinguished by a relaxed attitude to narrative, which was already apparent in *A Canterbury Tale* (GB, 1944). Adapting a novel such as *Black Narcissus* means being harnessed to its narrative structure, but the duo seemed intent on pushing against their self-imposed bounds by emphasizing the story's melodramatic elements. The cost is the loss of Rumer Godden's ironic detachment, which conveys a sense of telling a morality tale rather than merely recounting a story. Her characters lose their psychological complexity in the film. Godden's Angu travelled to Europe as a maid and displays more wisdom than the nuns; in the film, she dwindles to an eccentric. Dean fails to come across as a man making moral choices, though David Farrar's monochrome performance does not help. The most serious weakness is that Sister Ruth is reduced from being a clever but highly strung teacher to the stock hysterical woman. Unsurprisingly, Rumer Godden thought the film phoney.[23]

The exotic setting, the music, the use of colour and the presentation of heightened emotions ape American popular cinema, so were Powell and Pressburger aiming at a mass audience? At a time when dollars were needed, the expensive Technicolor process was only justified for a prestige production which appealed to an overseas market. Even prestige productions have their financial limits, but expediency does not fully explain shooting at Pinewood rather than on location, or the use of hand-coloured backdrops. It is as if Powell and Pressburger were rebelling against realism. In their quest for something different from the conventional British film they may have triumphed over restrictions, but the result is distinctively British in its reliance on British actors and its ultimate denial of emotional satisfaction: Sister Ruth dies, and Sister Clodagh has to confront her failure, while Dean is left alone, loving no one. There are nods to the conventions of Hollywood such as the love interest, but the result could be seen as a tongue-in-cheek riposte to hits like *The Song of Bernadette* (Henry King, US, 1943) and *The Bells of St Mary's* (Leo McCarey, US, 1945) rather than an attempt to emulate them.

Underlying many of the conflicting opinions about *Black Narcissus* are differing attitudes to melodrama. Michael Walker is a supporter, perhaps because putting people in extreme situations offers plenty to psychoanalyse.[24] Yet this is where the film fails to cohere. Blatant overacting conflicts with the realistic approach adopted by other principals. Action is choreographed to music whose quality never rises to its intended purpose. The artifice of the palace enhances the sense of unreality but sits uncomfortably with the location shooting in the opening and closing scenes as the sisters travel to and from the palace. The tawdriness of the studio sets is exposed by Jack Cardiff's lighting, which evokes the paintings of Vermeer, that most tonally subtle of artists. Rather than being a triumph of style, *Black Narcissus* parades directorial uncertainty at every turn. It can be read as an elegy to empire, or an ironic comment on the Labour Party's attempt to change British society. We should ask how seriously Powell and Pressburger meant audiences to take their work, but this topic seems absent from the literature, which is also light on feminist perspectives.

One tactic is to present as strengths what would otherwise be considered weaknesses. To seek a satisfying narrative becomes a misunderstanding of the film-makers' intentions. Because the mood of the *Black Narcissus* can be read in its shifting colours, artifice becomes a virtue, reminding us that this is a feast for the senses rather than an attempt to capture reality. An eclectic mix of styles becomes a way of emphasizing this. A paper by Adrian Danks exemplifies this approach.[25] A snag is that it might justifiably be applied to other films which glory in artifice, such as Arthur Crabtree's *Madonna of the Seven Moons* (GB, 1944) or Peter Yates's *Summer Holiday* (GB, 1962), but these directors seem exempt from the special pleading which applies to Powell and Pressburger.

In drawing on a well-known novel and exploring colonialism, *Black Narcissus* marked a new direction for Powell and Pressburger. This makes it intriguing, if nothing more. A clue to the varied critical responses the film engenders comes from Jean George Auriol: '[*Black Narcissus*] appeared absurd and intolerably artificial in Paris, whereas in Rome people were carried away by a story of events that could not happen in the Mediterranean world and could, therefore, be appreciated only by intuition. The French, whether stupid or otherwise, make their final appeal to reason; the Italians, however highly educated, turn invariably to instinct.'[26] Reactions in Paris and Rome were reversed for *Brief Encounter.* Ignoring questionable assumptions about national sensibilities, Auriol's comment provides an explanation for why some people are attracted to melodrama (because it is instinctive), while others avoid it (because it does not appeal to reason). The surprising thing is that so many critics have taken the instinctual route; the paradox is that they should intellectualize their preference.

—9—

The Night of the Hunter (US, 1955): Return of the Big Bad Wolf

Production companies: Paul Gregory Productions/United Artists
Producer: Paul Gregory
Director: Charles Laughton
Screenplay: James Agee, Charles Laughton
Source: Davis Grubb (novel: *The Night of the Hunter*)
Photography: Stanley Cortez
Art Director: Hilyard Brown
Music: Walter Schumann
Editor: Robert Golden
Cast: Robert Mitchum (Harry Powell—the Preacher), Shelley Winters (Willa Harper), Lillian Gish (Rachel Cooper), Don Beddoe (Walt Spoon), Evelyn Varden (Icey Spoon), James Gleason (Uncle Birdie), Peter Graves (Ben Harper), Billy Chapin (John), Gloria Castilo (Ruby), Sally Jane Bruce (Pearl)

Synopsis

When Ben Harper is arrested for murder and robbery, only his children, John and Pearl, know where he has hidden the stolen money. He is found guilty and condemned to death. His cell mate is the itinerant preacher Harry Powell, who has been imprisoned for thirty days for stealing a car. Because Ben talks in his sleep, the Preacher learns of the money, but not where it is hidden. On his release, he visits Ben's home, purporting to be a former prison clergyman whose work brought him into contact with Ben. He insinuates himself into the family by courting Ben's widow, Willa. The matchmaking is encouraged by Icey, who runs the local ice cream parlour with her husband, Walt. The Preacher marries Willa. In spite of his indifference towards her, she is drawn to his evangelical brand of religion. Pearl likes her stepfather, but John is wary. The Preacher separates the children and threatens Pearl in his quest for the stolen money. When he discovers that Willa has overheard him, his wife's fate is sealed. He pretends that she has left him in the night, taking his car. Uncle Birdie is fishing when he discovers her body in the submerged car, but he is afraid of being accused of her murder and does nothing.

By threatening John, the Preacher gets Pearl to admit that the money is hidden in her doll. The children escape their tormentor and flee in a boat, taking the doll with them. Their journey lasts several days. The boat drifts into reeds, where the youngsters are found by Rachel Cooper, who takes in unwanted children. The Preacher is searching for John and Pearl in the neighbouring town when he encounters Gloria, one of the older girls who lives with Miss Cooper. He poses as a suitor until Gloria reveals where John and Pearl are staying. Miss Cooper becomes suspicious when he comes to collect them and she threatens him with a gun. When he returns that night, she shoots at him. He shelters in her barn, where the state troopers find him the next morning. At his trial, he is sentenced to hang for Willa's murder. Icey and Walt, who were so much on his side, are the first to denounce him. The children remain with Miss Cooper.

Cultural Context

Davis Grubb based his novel on the true story of Harry Power, who was hanged in 1932 for murdering two widows and three children. Laughton bought the rights to the book before publication, its subsequent commercial and critical success vindicating his judgement. The script was entrusted to James Agee, who produced an overlong version, which Laughton rewrote. It remains an open question how much Agee, Laughton and Grubb each contributed to the final script, which departs from the novel notably in the opening and closing scenes.[1] First choice for the role of the Preacher was Gary Cooper, but Laughton and Mitchum formed a close working relationship on the shoot. Mitchum helped to coach the children, but Simon Callow discounts the story that Laughton disliked them.[2]

The press were baffled by a film which belonged to no recognizable genre. Philip T. Hartung commented in *Commonweal:* 'What *The Night of the Hunter* lacks most of all, in spite of the good performances of Master Chapin and Miss Gish, is heart. It's strong on Art, but has a cool contempt for people.'[3] Bosley Crowther of the *New York Times* singled out the shaping of the story, noting that 'The toughness of the grain of the story goes soft and porous toward the end.'[4] The reviewer for *The Times* found the child actors disappointing and considered that the techniques harked back to silent cinema. These made the film funny rather than frightening, but '*The Night of the Hunter* is indeed none the less interesting for being a failure.'[5] Dilys Powell had similar reservations: 'It is a curious and unusual piece, full of literary dialogue a good deal of which doesn't come off, full of visual symbolism a good deal of which does. The weakness is in the casting.' In her view, only Gish showed the right feeling.[6] Opinions on *The Night of the Hunter* have become more positive since 1955. Roger Ebert calls it one of the greatest of all American films, an opinion endorsed by Edward Guthmann in the *San Francisco Chronicle.*[7] In the programme note for a New York State Writers Institute screening, Kevin Hagopian comments: 'Frequently, there are images so profound as to make it seem as though Laughton and Agee have set out to do nothing so much as reinvent cinema to suit themselves.'[8] In spite of this enthusiasm, the film has generated scant literature and middling public interest. It ranks 163rd among the IMDb's top 250 films.[9]

Subjective Impression

The Night of the Hunter relies heavily on suspense. The first cliffhanger is whether the Preacher will be able to prise from the children where the money is hidden. The second is what will happen when Willa discovers his true motives. Her murder provides the answer. The third is how long it will take for her murder to be discovered and the murderer revealed. When Pearl is forced into disclosing the hiding place for the money, the first cliffhanger is resolved. The issue then is whether the children will escape. The Preacher catches up with them, but will Miss Cooper believe him? The final cliffhanger is whether retribution will come to Powell. Incidental events and characters matter less than maintaining the suspense.

The story adheres to a rigid morality. The innocence of childhood is contrasted with the uselessness of men. Ben Harper and Harry Powell are thieves and murderers, Uncle Birdie is an alcoholic, while Walt is so subservient to his wife that he could be considered culpable by default. By contrast, the women subscribe to traditional religious values. Willa subordinates herself to her new husband and his brand of evangelism, putting up no resistance when he kills her. Miss Cooper devotes herself to looking after unwanted children and inculcating them with her homespun brand of religion. Icey clings to the belief that the Preacher is a holy man and accepts uncritically everything he says about Willa. Good triumphs over evil, but not without being tested. The climax is the battle of wills between Miss Cooper and Harry Powell. Judging by their interaction, each recognizes similar qualities in the other, whatever their ostensible differences.

As in any morality tale, the characters are changed by their experiences. Icey and Walt have plenty to learn, though they show no willingness to acknowledge that they were credulous. When they vent their anger on the Preacher, it is for deceiving them as much as for what he did to Willa. Under Miss Cooper's tutelage, even Ruby reverts to being a girl, albeit none too believably after emerging from her chrysalis as a young woman. She too was deceived by the Preacher. Miss Cooper has her religious values confirmed, but she cannot be said to have learned. Nor has the Preacher, who is irredeemable and pays the price.

Much of the action is seen from John's viewpoint. He has most to learn. He soon discovers the wisdom of keeping his own counsel. If he confides in his mother, she will tell the Preacher where the money is hidden. Pearl accepts the Preacher as a stepfather and will be coaxed into revealing their secret. Uncle Birdie wants to help but is unreliable. Only Miss Cooper breaks the mould, and John seems willing to trust her and become part of her extended family.

The viewer is allowed little leeway in what to take from the film. The sense of entering a fairy story is enhanced by the contrived shots and the constant visual references to nature. One notable image is of the children sheltering in a barn during their flight. A silhouette of a horseman appears on the horizon and their pursuer is heard singing. There is no sense of perspective, making it impossible to gauge distance, though the voice comes from nearby. The image could be lifted from a child's storybook. The moral is clear: Harry Powell is the big, bad wolf and evil cannot be seen to flourish, whether in fairy stories or under the Hollywood Production Code. The trouble is that the Preacher is so charismatic. Willa is colourless beside him, while Miss Cooper does not appear until late in the film. This creates a desire to root for the villain, the counterbalance being that John and Pearl are on the side of the angels and, in Eisenstein's terms, children always elicit sympathy.

The sudden switches from realism to artifice are disconcerting. I am drawn close to the characters, who suddenly slip into allegory in Brechtian fashion. This is technically interesting rather than emotionally satisfying. The overwrought poetics and Mitchum's jaunty performance irritated me on first viewing and my response has not changed: the language still seems pointlessly contrived, and Mitchum's acting still jars, while those shots of animals are incongruous. No wonder that a film which is too frightening for children and too moralistic for adults was a commercial failure.

Analysis

An early commentator to give *The Night of the Hunter* a retrospective analysis was Gordon Gow, who in 1975 included it in a series of articles on cult films.[10] He applauded the success of the slapstick interlude in the cellar as the Preacher pursues the children, while conceding that the Christmas scene at the end marked a descent into 'utterly glutinous sentimentality too sticky to be saved by the inner grace of Lillian Gish as she preaches religiously that the children "abide" '.[11] The 'slapstick interlude' strikes me as more horrifying than slapstick, though I would not dissent from his view on the Christmas scene. Neither sequence made an impression on Paul Hammond in 1979. Though he concurred with Gow that the devices used in the film were conventional, Hammond saw the mise-en-scène as radical.[12] But is he reading too much into the film by interpreting it as a fairy story for our time, a tale of social disorientation and paranoia brought on by an excess of demented authoritarianism? The Preacher is calculating rather than paranoid or demented, and his sole interest in the children is to gain information about the money rather than to exert control. More telling is Hammond's point that the film's visual style owes as much to horror films as to German Expressionism.[13] This is evident in Laughton's reliance on suspense. Expressionism requires a willingness to enter society's dark places rather than merely observing them. The image of the dead Willa seen through the water owes a debt to Vigo's *L'Atalante,* suggesting that the French Symbolist tradition provided Laughton with another source of references.

The re-evaluation of *The Night of the Hunter* has not gone smoothly, with David Thomson bucking the trend:

> After years of admiration—and a proper reading of Davis Grubb's novel—I began to see shortcomings in the Laughton film. Yes, it can knock your eyes out. Yes, there is nothing like it. But even when your eyes yield, your mind can find things to worry about, and the greatest of these may be the novel's secret bond between the figure of Powell and the boy John.[14]

Something of this bond survives in the film in John's anguish as Harry is arrested, an emotion which is unexplained and seems misplaced given all that has happened. Pearl has shown a greater rapport with her stepfather, yet she remains unmoved.

Two other points raised by Thomson deserve comment. First is the quality of the acting. This apparently simple issue elicits a spectrum of opinions from critics. As noted earlier, the *Times* reviewer found the children's acting wooden, while Hartung praised Billy Chapin, who played John. Crowther linked the children's acting to faults in the film's structure, finding them 'posey and incredible' in the final scenes.[15] I find the children stilted: it is difficult to believe that John is terrified, even when the music and photography insist that he is.

Opinions on Mitchum's performance are equally varied. It is praised in two New York reviews quoted by Callow, but the reviewer from the *Washington DC News* felt that Mitchum was wrong for the part.[16] The reviewer for *Variety* detected some depth in Mitchum's interpretation, 'but in instances where he's crazed with lust for the money, there's barely adequate conviction.'[17] For Thomson, 'Mitchum does not seem wicked or past hope,' which might stem from Laughton's reputed reluctance to destroy Mitchum's career by making the character unequivocally evil.[18] Michael Powell displayed no such inhibitions when casting Carl Boehm in *Peeping Tom* (GB, 1960). Callow's view is that both Mitchum and his character give consciously two-dimensional performances, lending the film a highly original and Brechtian dimension.[19] Such an argument is thought-provoking, but it makes distinguishing between good and bad acting difficult. Nor does Callow consider how such an approach fits into the film. It could be seen as working against the grain of the story, which needs something darker to balance the sentimentality. My view, which is closer to Thomson's, is that Mitchum slips into parody. He gives us a pantomime villain, with enough mugging to reassure us that it is all an act. It is the sort of over-the-top performance Laughton himself gave in *Hobson's Choice* (David Lean, GB, 1953). Mitchum never shows the calculating murderer, even when the Preacher is under pressure. Dilys Powell is surely correct: only Lillian Gish manages to light up the screen, making me almost believe in her contradictory character pitched between saint and warrior queen.

Willa presents particular difficulties for the performer. During the picnic, she has to transform herself from bemused widow to candidate for marriage. On marrying, she has a few short scenes in which to demonstrate a religious conversion so complete that, like a character from Bresson, she seems compliant before her fate. The difference is that for Bresson, this would be sufficient material for a film; Laughton despatches her before the real battle of wills between Harry and John begins. Shelley Winters does her best with an underwritten role, but she fails to make these sudden shifts convincing.

Thomson's second point is that despite the excellence of Cortez's photography, many shots feel like set pieces.[20] This is notable in Willa's murder. The problem is not simply the stylized quality of sets and acting, but the way they are intercut with naturalistic episodes, such as when the children listen to what is happening in their parents' bedroom. Visual poetry holds up what is in other respects an action story. In *Thieves Like Us* (Robert Altman, US, 1974), another tale of hunters and the hunted, the lyrical moments are integrated more successfully into the drama, avoiding an uneasy juxtaposition of moods.

The opening of *The Night of the Hunter* has Gish seen against an artificial starlit sky. She talks, ostensibly to the children, but in reality to the camera as she does in the final frames. The Preacher's capture mirrors that of Ben Harper at the beginning of the film, and John's reaction is the same. Both the Preacher and Rachel Cooper are sexually repressed, which makes their encounter intriguing. The film displays a symmetry which may be a hangover from Hollywood film-making, or from the well-made plays which Laughton knew as a stage actor. It may also derive from the simplicity of fairytales. Whatever the reason, it adds to the sense of artifice, of entering a world in which there is a preordained outcome, whatever happens along the way.

The film is stuffed with ideas which remain undeveloped. Does the Preacher believe his own rhetoric? This is never put to the test. His sexual repression was difficult to explore in 1955, but the love-hate sexuality symbolized by his rejection of Willa on their wedding night remains tantalizing. What drives Ben Harper to rob and murder to provide money for his children? Is Willa to blame, as she proclaims, with her incessant demands for money? What do John and Pearl think about their father's crimes? If even a few of these issues were explored, this would be a richer film. It is not a typical Hollywood product, but the audience is guided towards how it should respond in true Hollywood fashion, with the demands of the plot taking precedence over character development. Yet Larry Gross detected something in Mitchum's performance which was unheard of in Hollywood: 'He projects the alarming possibility that evil has its authentic moments of satisfaction and even genuine rewards.'[21] This was enough to deter family audiences. It is more characteristic of Hollywood that the Preacher finally pays for his crimes.

Laughton's exuberant acting style harked back to his early days in the theatre. It was outside the norms of Hollywood, so it comes as no surprise that his most acclaimed cinematic performances were in the fantasies, *The Private Life of Henry VIII*

(Alexander Korda, GB, 1933) and *The Hunchback of Notre Dame* (William Dieterle, US, 1939). His interest in abstract staging was sparked by his early theatrical work with Komisarjevsky.[22] *The Night of the Hunter* can be seen as the coming together of these two aspects of his character, even if it was out of step with the prevailing realism of the 1950s. It might have found more success among the British melodramas of the mid-1940s, which attracted a ready audience for their rich vein of fantasy.

Even Callow has to concede that *The Night of the Hunter* has faults, notably in that opening sequence when Miss Cooper is seen recounting Bible stories to a group of smiling children. He judges the visual and musical sentimentality to be of the order of a mass-produced Christmas card.[23] Miss Cooper reads the biblical passage beginning 'Beware of false prophets which come to you in sheep's clothing' (Matthew 7:15). Her voice forms a commentary over the next scene, in which children find a woman's body. A reasonable assumption is that these are the children whose faces we have just seen and that they have found Miss Cooper's body. Until she reappears an hour into the film, there is no way of knowing that this assumption is erroneous and that she has a role in the story. After the body is discovered, the Preacher is seen driving along a country lane and talking to God in conversational terms. The inference is that he has murdered the woman, though the reason is unclear. When he is brought to trial, it is for stealing a motor car rather than murder, so no link with the murder is established. Ben Harper is in court for murder, so is the murdered woman his victim? Ambiguity may be a virtue, but it should not be confused with poor storytelling. Disparate plot strands can be juxtaposed if their significance subsequently becomes clear to the audience, but here such clarity is missing. Nothing can be inferred from the preceding scenes, in contrast to the principles underlying Eisenstein's intellectual montage. Callow is willing to dismiss such flaws as an opening stumble, but they pervade the film. Why should the Preacher show an interest in Ruby, unless he suspected in advance that Rachel Cooper was looking after Pearl and John? How did he come upon that particular town? Answers are not forthcoming, because poetics take precedence over plot, but the logic of the narrative requires that things more or less hang together.

The Night of the Hunter comes out of Mark Twain's *The Adventures of Huckleberry Finn* (1884) and the Brothers Grimm, by way of Nicholas Ray, who tapped the same vein of tortured romanticism in *They Live by Night* (US, 1948), which was based on the same novel by Edward Anderson as Altman's *Thieves Like Us*. Grubb's novel became a minor classic, though it was criticized for its poetic language.[24] If this is a flaw in the film, Laughton must take the blame for retaining it. The film's legacy can be seen in the work of Tim Burton, as well as in Terrence Malick's *Days of Heaven* (US, 1978) and *Undertow* (David Gordon Green, US, 2005), which Malick wrote and produced. One of Charlie Keil's conditions for greatness is satisfied by the way *The Night of the Hunter* has influenced later works, but striking a chord with viewers, his other condition, is more subjective.[25] For me, the film fails on this count.

–10–

Lawrence of Arabia (GB, 1962): An Englishman in the Sun

Production companies: Horizon Pictures/Columbia
Producer: Sam Spiegel
Director: David Lean
Source: T. E. Lawrence (writings: *The Seven Pillars of Wisdom*)
Screenplay: Robert Bolt, Michael Wilson
Photography: Freddie Young
Art Director: John Stoll
Production Designer: John Box
Music: Maurice Jarre
Editor: Anne V. Coates
Cast: Peter O'Toole (T. E. Lawrence), Omar Sharif (Sherif Ali), Alec Guinness (Prince Feisal), Claude Rains (Mr Dryden), Anthony Quinn (Auda abu Tayi), Arthur Kennedy (Bentley), Jack Hawkins (General Allenby)

Synopsis

A young man crashes his motorcycle in an English lane and is killed. This is our introduction to Lawrence. Mourners at his funeral voice contradictory views about him, while professing not to understand him. The rest of the film retraces his exploits during the First World War.

Lawrence is a young British officer engaged in a desk-bound job in Cairo. The diplomat, Mr Dryden, persuades General Murray to second Lawrence to the British Arab Bureau. The purpose of the mission is to find Prince Feisal and gain his support. Lawrence takes an Arab guide and learns to ride a camel in his quest for the nomadic prince. In the desert, he encounters the Bedouin leader Sherif Ali, who claims ownership of a well and shoots the guide for drinking from it. This is Lawrence's introduction to Arab politics.

When the Turks bomb Prince Feisal's camp, Lawrence supports the Arab desire for retaliation. His senior officer, Colonel Brighton, disapproves of Lawrence's unconventional methods and urges caution. Lawrence ignores him and joins forces with Sherif Ali to attack the Turks at Aqaba, from where supplies can be brought to the prince. The raiding party crosses the Nefud desert to approach the port from the undefended landward side. When a Bedouin is lost during the trek, Lawrence turns back to find him, against Sherif Ali's advice. The rescue is successful and Lawrence gains the respect of the Arabs, signified by Sherif Ali presenting him with Arab dress.

Another tribal leader, Auda abu Tayi, is enticed with the promise of gold to join the attackers. The tribes fall out within sight of the port and one of Auda's men is killed. To avenge tribal honour and keep the warring tribes together, Lawrence is forced to shoot Gasim, the Beduin whose life he saved.

Aqaba is captured. Lawrence reports to headquarters in Cairo, but he is alienated from his fellow officers. Allenby assures him that Britain has no ambitions in Arabia and persuades him to return to the desert and continue gaining the support of the Arabs.

An American journalist, Bentley, wants to bring America into the war and uses Lawrence as a hero figure, photographing him against the backdrop of a train the Arabs have sabotaged. Auda loots the train, to the disgust of Colonel Brighton. In a further sabotage attempt, Lawrence's servant Farraj is injured. To prevent him from falling into enemy hands, Lawrence has to shoot him.

While disguised as an Arab in Deraa, Lawrence is captured and beaten by the Turks, who throw him back on the street. This fuels his bitterness, but Allenby will not let him resign. Lawrence seeks vengeance and to Bentley's disgust enthusiastically joins in the massacre of the retreating Turks.

The British fight their way to Damascus, the Arabs taking the right flank. When Allenby arrives, Lawrence and the Arabs are already there. An Arab National Council has been established, but it is ridden with internecine disputes. The British stand back as chaos ensues. Dryden reveals that the French and the British have agreed to divide Damascus between them. A disillusioned Lawrence is promoted and returns to England, his work done.

Cultural Context

The genesis of *Lawrence of Arabia* is as labyrinthine as its scenario, though it is hardly unique in this respect. The script by Michael Wilson was disliked by Lean and the original screen credit went to Robert Bolt, who wrote the second version.[1] Alec Guinness played Lawrence on stage, but because he was too old to repeat his performance by the time the film was made, the role went to the unknown Peter O'Toole after Marlon Brando and Albert Finney turned it down. The film's original running time of 222 minutes was trimmed by 20 minutes for general release and by a further 15 minutes for its 1971 re-release. The 1989 restoration by Robert Harris reinstated the deleted scenes and included previously unseen material. The length was 223 minutes, which Lean re-edited to 216 minutes for the version seen today.[2]

Variety hailed the film as a vivid box-office success on its first release, despite occasional sluggishness of action and the looseness of the screenplay.[3] *The Times* described it as an adventure story told in visual terms, but 'in the last analysis, however, *Lawrence of Arabia* remains a film for the eye rather than the mind.'[4] In *Film Quarterly,* Roger Sandall was less circumspect: 'The acting, dialogue and direction are all so uniformly elephantine one feels that the film can't have been directed in the usual sense at all.'[5] For Bosley Crowther of the *New York Times,* 'It is such a laboriously large conveyance of eye-filling outdoor spectacle … that the possibly human, moving T. E. Lawrence is lost in it. We know little more about this strange man when it is over than when we began.' Lacklustre dialogue compounded the failure: 'Seldom has so little been said in so many words.'[6]

With the film's re-release in 1971, enough time had elapsed for it to be assessed in the context of Lean's career. Steven Ross took a positive view: 'Lean's films reveal a consistently tragic vision of the romantic sensibility attempting to reach beyond the restraints and constructions of everyday life.'[7] The restoration in 1989 generated another flurry of critical interest. Desson Howe of the *Washington Post* was willing to overlook Bolt's 'occasional patches of desert', O'Toole's nervous twitchings, Anthony Quinn's fake nose and Guinness's mascara, because 'Like *Gone with the Wind* or *Ben Hur, Lawrence* is too emotionally overpowering for critical reservations.'[8] Chris Dashiell in *Cinescene* takes a more analytical route to the same conclusion: '[Lean] used the mythic mode to explode the myth. That's what ultimately makes the film a masterpiece that will endure, long after other epics have become outdated.'[9] Others remain cautious. For Rita Kempley of the *Washington Post,* 'It's rather like wandering the desert with the children of Israel. There's a sameness to the grandeur that so intoxicated Lean, Harris and the hero.'[10] Jonathan Rosenbaum is equally wary: 'The ideological crassness of De Mille and most war movies isn't so much transcended as given a high gloss: the film's subject is basically the White Man's Burden.[11] Such judgements have barely dented the film's reputation. In a 2004 *Sunday Telegraph* poll, 230 actors, directors and writers voted *Lawrence of Arabia* as the best ever British film.[12] In a *Variety* poll from 2005, five out of ten leading American critics included *Lawrence of Arabia* among their ten best films.[13] Rosenbaum was among the dissenters. The film has kept its place in the affection of the public, rating thirty-second among the top 250 films on the IMDb Web site.[14]

Subjective Impression

Once beyond the establishing scenes set in Britain, the main impression the film makes on me is of the epic scale of both film and desert. This is reinforced by the grandeur of the music. Lawrence, too, seems larger than life, oratorical poses and flowing robes making him into a Jesus figure. He begins his army career as an ineffectual-seeming character, out of place in the desert. Nor does he take to the discipline of the army, as his first encounter with Colonel Brighton demonstrates. Lawrence's values are tested when his guide is shot at the well and later when he has to choose between Brighton's caution and the Arabs' wish to attack the Turks. Greater tests come when he has to sacrifice Gasim and Farraj, particularly as this means killing them himself. He embraces the alien world with enthusiasm, choosing to wear Arab robes even when mixing with his fellow officers. He becomes intoxicated by violence, relishing the attack on the retreating Turks. At the same time, he seems appalled at how he is changing, so that Allenby has to command him to continue his work. The film is long, but it cannot encompass such a conversion.

Initially I am supportive of Dryden and the British position. The Arab values seem alien to the British, an example being Sherif Ali's willingness to shoot Lawrence's guide. Auda abu Tayi is a mercenary who shows a similar disregard for life. Only Prince Feisal comes across as reasonable and thoughtful. As the film progresses, my sympathies change. Dryden is revealed as duplicitous. I come to appreciate the Arab position, even if the internecine fighting in Damascus stops me from supporting it. The trouble is that I feel manipulated. The characters do not evolve, which would prepare me for the change. They are stereotypes, which contributes to my sense of disappointment. Lawrence is the exception, yet he leaves me with similar feelings of dissatisfaction. Initially he engages my interest as a man out of his element. I can understand his frustration at the conventional attitudes of his fellow officers, while being intrigued by how an aesthete becomes transformed into a man of action. He progresses from liaison officer to a leader in battle. This allows him to remain a maverick, happier among the warring Arab tribes than in the regular army. Yet my interest in replaced by frustration as his character changes. He seems driven by an obsession which I cannot understand and which the film-makers barely probe. The gulf between the Lawrence who crashes his motorcycle and the Lawrence who is driven across the desert for the last time is too great to leave unexplained. Even the Lawrence of the desert hardly emerges as a rounded character. I want to understand his emotional pilgrimage, but so much is abandoned in favour of spectacle that I question whether film-making on a grand scale is the place for character studies.

Analysis

This film engenders contradictory opinions, but there is agreement on the quality of Freddie Francis's cinematography. The desert becomes a character, expressing its changing moods in swirling sands, storms and lengthening shadows. Cinematography transforms the film into a spectacle, particularly when seen on the big screen, but any good cinematographer with 70mm Panavision and desert locations at his disposal could hardly fail. One test is to consider how the film fares when viewed on a television screen. If it fails to hold the attention, the suspicion is that spectacle has become an end in itself, which is no qualification for greatness.

The other aspect of the film which garners general approval is Maurice Jarre's score. The young and untried Jarre was the default candidate after a clutch of composers including William Walton turned down the project and Lean rejected the efforts of Richard Rodgers.[15] The opening bars have become inextricably associated with vistas of unending desert, but this derives from the film's reputation as much as the music's intrinsic quality. Jarre opts for grandeur over pseudo-authenticity. The effect is undeniably impressive, but the lack of contrast or thematic development means that it becomes less so by the fourth appearance of the opening theme. After two hours, the score is likely to be taken for granted. Reliance on music and cinematography is justified if they contribute to the drama, but music is absent at crucial moments, raising the suspicion that its function is to bolster the stretches where dramatic tension sags. In mitigation, any composer would be hard put to fill three hours of screen time with original material. Lean and Bolt seem to sense the danger, for the endless vistas awash with full orchestral accompaniment give way in the second half of the film to more dialogue and personal conflicts. Ironically, it is this section which is generally considered less successful.

The script has prompted varied responses, though many commentators detect weaknesses in structure and dialogue. One problem becomes apparent in the opening scene, when a man on a motorcycle speeds down an English country lane to his death. On the film's first release, most of the audience probably had a folk memory of Lawrence and some knowledge of his fate. Today, the opening might prove baffling. What was Lawrence doing there, assuming the cyclist was Lawrence? What was his state of mind? Where was he going? The film offers no clue as to whether his death was an accident or the consequence of deliberate risk-taking. If the truth will never be known, at least the film-makers could offer their interpretation. The dramatic purpose of the opening sequence is to allow characters to talk about Lawrence after the memorial service, with his desert exploits being presented as an extended flashback. This distances the audience from Lawrence: we see him through other people's eyes, though we are not sure whose. Harold Pinter handled the same device more subtly for Joe Losey in *Accident* (GB, 1967) and *The Go-Between.*

The final sequence of *Lawrence of Arabia* is equally unsatisfactory. Lawrence is seen returning to England, having been granted his wish to leave the desert. His subsequent search for obscurity in the ranks and the contradictory need to publicize his ideas in his writings are ignored. The film makes no attempt to understand Lawrence, or to portray his life in any realistic sense. Incidents from his life are used as an excuse for some epic desert scenes.

The politics of the Middle East have never been simple, and Lawrence's desert wanderings only make sense in the context of British military strategies and political aims. One strategy for dramatizing a confrontation is to omit the politics and concentrate on the fighting, which is the approach adopted in *Zulu* (Cy Endfield, GB, 1962). Bolt and Lean try to have it both ways, providing enough exposition to slow the film, but not enough to clarify the politics. Why the Turks are fighting the Arabs is no more explained than the nature of British involvement. Nor is it clear why there is a Franco-British agreement to divide the spoils, when the French never figure in the film. This is another case where more background knowledge could be assumed of a 1962 audience than a generation later, though six years after the Suez debacle, British audiences were unlikely to be sympathetic to the Arab cause.

Whatever incidental pleasures the music and visual images provide in filling the longueurs, they cannot disguise that fact that *Lawrence of Arabia* is a long film built around a slight script. This puts stresses on the film's structure. Bolt's way of expanding his material is by repetition. Crossing the Nefud desert to Aqaba is signposted as a perilous undertaking. When Aqaba is captured, reporting the matter to headquarters entails crossing the Sinai desert, a journey which is also defined as perilous. Crossing one desert might be interesting; facing the hazards a second time risks boring the audience. The film reprises other incidents, including sabotaging a train, the Arabs' proprietorial attitude to wells, and Lawrence's reluctance to kill somebody he knows. The result is a convoluted plot which offers meagre justification for the film's inflated proportions.

The dialogue is equally problematic, veering between banality and aphorism. When Lawrence crosses the Sinai desert with his two servants, there is a close-up of his compass lying on the sand. The shot is rendered superfluous by his comment: 'My compass! No matter. If we ride west, we must strike the canal.' The remark explains where Lawrence is going, while giving no insight into his character. It is representative. The crassness of Bolt's dialogue contributes to making the stretches of exposition so tedious. When the Arab National Council in Damascus is faced with a fire and the British refuse to help, there should be heightened tension. Instead the showdown fails to engage the attention, the actors shuffling uncomfortably with nothing interesting to say.

Aphorisms abound, making Bolt's dialogue resemble a parody of Oscar Wilde. This applies particularly to Prince Feisal. Guinness was a master of the gnomic utterance, which arouses the suspicion that he was indulging in self-parody when faced with such lines as: 'No Arab can love the desert. We love water and green trees. There is nothing in the desert. No man needs nothing.' This is said when the prince meets Lawrence for the first time. Their conversation soon degenerates into cliché:

Lawrence: Yet you were great.
Feisal: Nine centuries ago.
Lawrence: Time to be great again, my lord.
. . .

Feisal: To be great again it seems we need the English, or—
Lawrence: Or?
Feisal: Or what no man can provide, Mr Lawrence. We need a miracle.

This might be Bolt's attempt to suggest a florid Arab syntax, but all the characters become infected with the same mannerism. On the capture of Aqaba, General Allenby proclaims: 'With Lawrence, mercy is a passion, with me it is merely good manners. You may judge which motive is the more reliable.' When Lawrence learns of his betrayal by the politicians, Dryden declares: 'And a man who tells lies, like me, merely hides the truth, but a man who tells half lies has forgotten where he put it.' Dialogue can hardly get more portentous. The surprise is that Roger Ebert considers it 'so spare it sounds like poetry'.[16]

Nor is there any consensus about the performances. The film is unusual for a prestigious production in having newcomers in the lead roles. O'Toole's Nordic good looks distinguish him from the Arabs. In David Thomson's words, 'he played [Lawrence] with a desperate intensity as unrevealing as it was uncharacteristic of the director.'[17] Some of the failure is attributable to the script, but Lean must take responsibility for O'Toole's matinee-idol performance. Omar Sharif slots into the ensemble more easily, his friendship with Lawrence emerging naturally. He is believable as a proud Arab leader. Anthony Quinn takes an exuberant approach to Auda, eschewing authenticity and playing him as a loveable rogue. If Lean tried to rein him in, the attempt failed, but at least the result is never dull. Guinness is the antithesis of Quinn, underplaying rather than overplaying and disappearing into his role rather than imposing his personality. His performance gives the prince a veneer of Britishness which distinguishes him from his headstrong companions, but he seems too passive and urbane for a regal figure, making the prince into a philosopher rather than a leader. Feisal the wily politician emerges too late, when the Western powers carve up Arabia.

The character of Lawrence is central to the film and its signal failure. The junior officer in Cairo is portrayed as a foppish young man with quirks of speech and gesture which are accentuated as the film progresses. Initially he is wary of violence, as evinced by his reluctance to shoot Gasim and Farraj. Looting leaves him unconcerned, so long as Auda remains on his side. Then comes the beating, after which Lawrence demonstrates his intoxication with violence by shooting as many Turks as possible during their retreat, to the point where he has to be restrained by his companions. This metamorphosis in his character goes unexplained. The suggestion that he was raped as well as beaten at Deraa might account for his subsequent bitterness and anger, but the film offers no evidence for this. In mitigation, this was not an appropriate topic for an epic in 1962: a mass audience was needed for the film to recoup its costs, and the family audience was still a significant force.

Also unexplained is Lawrence's growing love of the desert and its people, which parallels his alienation from his fellow officers. His reluctance to lead the Arabs against Damascus suggests a further unexplored change of heart. O'Toole's Lawrence is not so much a complex and haunted man as an eccentric. It is hard to empathize with so superficial a character. Only the three Arab leaders are given opportunities to display much individuality, but as two of these are played by non-Arab actors, their performances raise other issues.

There is a long tradition of actors being blind to race. Only recently have Shakespeare's *Othello* and *The Merchant of Venice* become problematic. Guinness's performances for Lean as Fagin in *Oliver Twist* (GB, 1948) and Godbole in *A Passage to India* (GB, 1984), as well as his Prince Feisal, are open to the charge of being racially insensitive, and the reputation of *Lawrence of Arabia* may suffer in this respect. The paradox is that seeking freedom from racial caricatures allows notions of racial purity to gain credence, so that only Arabs can play Arabs. At the same time, audience responses to performances which are deemed inappropriate are inhibited. Older interpretations stand as exemplars of their times, preventing us from being carried away by the new and ephemeral. To denigrate them is to find common cause with zealots who destroy religious art in the name of principle.

The film's religiosity is striking. As though fulfilling a prophesy, O'Toole wanders the Sinai desert on his way to Damascus, renouncing his own background to fulfil his destiny in uniting the tribes and suffering flagellation in the process. Often photographed from a low level to enhance his stature, he stands like a pre-Raphaelite Jesus (or like Superman) on the wreckage of the sabotaged train, his arms outstretched, the white robes billowing around him, the sheath of his scimitar forming a golden 'J' at his waist.

It might be less contentious to accept Rosenbaum's assessment of *Lawrence of Arabia* as the most homoerotic of epics.[18] It is easy to tease homoerotic symbolism from the film, but whether this was intended by the makers or perceived by the first audiences is another matter. The 'swinging sixties' had not begun by 1962: the Lord Chamberlain still censored British stage plays, while the homoerotic oysters and snails scene in *Spartacus* (Stanley Kubrick, US, 1960) between Laurence Olivier and Tony Curtis was to remain unseen until the restored version of the film appeared in 1991. With its emphasis on the indomitable British character, *Lawrence of Arabia* may be considered as the last of the British war films of the 1950s. Homoerotic readings are a later accretion.

Lean and Spiegel lived through the waning years of Britain's imperialism, albeit on opposing sides. During his epic phase, Lean seemed fascinated by fault lines in the empire. As his final completed work was *A Passage to India,* from the novel by the anti-colonialist E. M. Forster, it should not be assumed that because Lean was a traditionalist, he was also an apologist for empire. He strove to portray Englishness, and Lawrence is the quintessential English hero. It is his heroism which dominates the film and which appealed to audiences.

Responses to the film have changed in a multicultural and post-colonial society. For Marco Lanzagorta, Britain is aligned on the side of right, with the 'Others' being demonized. Rather than the film evoking a nostalgia for empire, Britain is exposed as self-serving, this being symbolized in the characters of Dryden and the generals. Cumbersome moral and social repression is imposed by the 'civilized' imperial cultures of Britain and Turkey. The oppressors are themselves oppressed by social codes and the burden of maintaining their empires. The film reinforces racial stereotypes, the Arabs being portrayed as dirty, violent and primitive. This is exploited visually: as Lawrence's skin darkens, so does his morality, becoming closer to that of the

Arabs.[19] Lanzagorta is on shakier ground in seeing the British as being played by blonds; nor does he consider whether the imagery was intended.

Was Lawrence really a hero and, if so, is the film an accurate portrayal? The cinema has always been cavalier with great men. This attitude has incurred the wrath of critics, with Korda's 1930s biopics of Rembrandt and Henry the Eighth being exceptions. This makes the critical adulation of *Lawrence of Arabia* all the more surprising. Wilson claimed that he wanted to portray a man attempting to shed one identity and assume another, and that his Lawrence was a composite character.[20] Bolt asserted that his script was based on Lawrence's own writing, allowing scope for wish fulfilment on Lawrence's part. This is understandable given that the government records were embargoed and Lawrence's brother insisted on maintaining the image of Lawrence as hero, but it was also a handicap.[21] Bolt and Lean risked creating a hero who was already becoming old-fashioned in 1962. Lean exercised artistic licence by casting O'Toole in the lead—the real Lawrence was neither tall nor handsome—but this was what the myth demanded.[22]

All war heroes accumulate myths, and Lawrence was no exception. He encouraged the process, so that his legacy is a flourishing Lawrence industry.[23] His story follows the classic mythic pattern of the solitary hero wandering a strange land and assuming the role of leader by virtue of his exploits, ridding the country of its enemies before going on his way. As Jeffrey Richards notes, the gods of empire like David Livingstone, Robert Clive and Robert Falcon Scott shared characteristics of dedication to duty, acceptance of loneliness and an inspiring dream, with death as their common destiny, though Lawrence hardly dies so that his people might live as Richards implies.[24] This mythic status makes Lawrence an ideal subject for the cinema, though Korda's attempt to film his life in the 1930s came to nothing. Neither did the 1957 collaboration of Anthony Asquith and Terence Rattigan, with Dirk Bogarde as Lawrence.[25] Lawrence was a dashing war hero for British audiences in 1962. What is hard to disentangle is how far Lean's film enhanced the myth rather than perpetuating it. O'Toole's performance has become synonymous with Lawrence, while Lawrence's exploits are viewed as those of an outsider whose principal battle was with the British establishment rather than Germany and its allies.

Lawrence of Arabia is Lean's homage to that other mythic genre, the Western. It has the look of a Western, particularly when mounted figures circle the base of giant rock formations; it matters not that they ride camels rather than horses. In Lean's version, the hero is a tragic figure, forever seeking his destiny and aware of the perils of his journey. The trouble is that Lean's grandiosity got the better of him. As Damian Cannon puts it, 'Thoughts, dreams and needs remain barely touched in a film which explores [Lawrence's] status as a catalyst and figurehead far more than the man himself.'[26]

It is easy to see why *Lawrence of Arabia* became a popular success. It has something for everybody: epic scale, colour, music, wartime adventure and a larger-than-life hero, as well as the imprimatur of Lean's reputation. These qualities have helped to maintain the film's appeal. Unrest in the Middle East has given Lawrence's activities continued relevance, and it can be argued that current problems are traceable to the settlement at the end of the First World War. Less easily explained is why filmmakers look on the film with continuing affection. Was Lean any more than a craftsman? On one side are ranged his supporters, with Alain Silver being representative (and providing a comprehensive bibliography).[27] He analyses Lean's editing with particular reference to *Oliver Twist* and sees self-centred individuals at the heart of Lean's films. As Silver points out, directors included Lean among their top ten in the 2002 *Sight and Sound* poll, but critics did not. One explanation for the discrepancy is that practitioners admire Lean's ability to tell a story with the camera, while critics have reservations about what he tells.

Opposing the Lean enthusiasts are heavyweights like David Thomson. He acknowledges the director's visual flair but detects a decline setting in after *Summer Madness* (US, 1955): 'Lean became the prisoner of big pictures, a great eye striving to show off a large mind.'[28] Even Lean's supporters might concede that *Ryan's Daughter* (GB, 1970) and *A Passage to India* are small stories masquerading as big films. More contentious is whether *Lawrence of Arabia* comes into the same category. Lawrence was a complex and intriguing figure, but Lean is seduced by the visual opportunities provided by the desert. O'Toole is every inch the star posing against sumptuous backgrounds. Against the production values of an epic, the real Lawrence stands little chance.

–11–

8½ (Italy/France, 1963):
The Director as Superstar

Production companies: Cineriz/Francinex
Producer: Angelo Rizzoli
Director: Federico Fellini
Story: Federico Fellini, Ennio Flaiano
Screenplay: Federico Fellini, Tullio Pinelli, Ennio Flaiano, Brunello Rondi
Photography: Gianni Di Venanzo
Art Director/Production Designer: Piero Gherardi
Music: Nino Rota
Editor: Leo Cattozzo
Cast: Marcello Mastroianni (Guido Anselmi), Claudia Cardinale (Claudia), Anouk
    Aimée (Luisa Anselmi), Sandra Milo (Carla), Rossella Falk (Rossella)

Synopsis

The film alternates between dream sequences and the apparent reality of making a
film. It begins with a silent dream sequence in which Guido is in a traffic jam and
trapped in a car as it fills with fumes. He manages to free himself and float away,
but he is pulled back to earth by a rope attached to his ankle. Medical attendants
are surrounding him when he awakens. He is at a spa and his doctor is prescribing
treatment.

Day one. Guido joins the patients promenading in the crowded grounds of the spa.
Scriptwriter Daumier walks with him, rubbishing Guido's ideas for the forthcoming
film. They encounter one of Guido's old friends who is there with his fiancée, an
aspiring actress who becomes interested once she discovers that she is talking to a
film director. At the railway station, Guido meets his mistress, Carla, who asks him
to find a job for her husband. That night, Guido urges her to make herself up to look
like a whore. He sees his parents in a dream: they are in a graveyard.

Day two. The hotel's reception area is crowded with journalists. In the mêlée,
Guido tries to choose which of three old men will play his father. The film's producer
has a young actress in tow, hoping for a part in the film. At dinner, Guido discovers
that the magician entertaining the guests is another old friend. Guido's thoughts go

back to bath time as a child. He rings his wife, Luisa. In the production office, he is plagued with doubts about the film. That night, he is called to the station hotel where Carla is staying. She is feverish, but she refuses to let him telephone her husband.

Day three. The gardens are populated with priests, triggering memories of Guido's schooldays. Once he played truant to join the local boys who paid the ugly but sensuous Saraghina to dance for them on the beach. The priests found him and dragged him back to face their wrath and his mother's anguish. At the spa, Daumier rubbishes Guido's ideas again. Guido talks about his project to a cardinal who has come for the cure, but no salvation comes from the Church. In town he encounters Luisa, newly arrived from Rome. Accompanied by the producer and Luisa's friend, Rossella, he visits the film set, where a launching pad for a giant spaceship has been constructed for survivors trying to escape an atomic plague. The project is becoming far too complex and expensive for Guido, as he confesses to Rossella. Later that night, recriminations fly between Guido and Luisa in the hotel bedroom as they argue about why their relationship failed.

Day four. While sitting in a cafe with Luisa and Rossella, Guido glimpses Carla. He fantasizes about visiting a brothel, where he encounters all the women in his life. While he watches screen tests for his film, the arrival of the actress Claudia causes Luisa to storm out of the cinema. Guido and Claudia go for a drive and Guido confesses that he has failed. There will be no film.

Day five. Guido has to be dragged onto the film set. He hides under the table while a press conference is underway and tries to shoot himself as the producer admits publicly that the project is cancelled. Guido is sunk in depression. He is about to drive away when another ending presents itself. He sees white-clad figures conjured from his past by the magician. Guido is unable to resist the desire to choreograph events as a band enters an improvised circus ring, followed by a boy who might be a younger version of himself. Curtains concealing the staircase to the rocket launcher are drawn back to reveal all the characters we have seen. They descend into the ring, where Guido joins them as they parade around the perimeter.

Cultural Context

Fellini began his film career as a scriptwriter in the 1940s. In his early work as a director, he followed the neo-realist tradition, though recurring images of the circus, prostitutes and priests provided motifs which are dominant in his later work. *La dolce vita* (Italy/France, 1960) marked the shift to personal concerns and a more flamboyant style which was also evident in *8½*. Laurence Olivier was considered to play Guido, but he was too well known according to Mastroianni, who copied Fellini's mannerisms for the role.[1]

The film did well at festivals but garnered a mixed response from critics. The final sequence attracted particular attention, with Eric Rhode in *Sight and Sound* detecting uncertainty in what to include: 'Both Guido and Fellini show themselves incapable of making the distinction between the truths of the mind and those of behaviour.'[2] Dilys Powell acknowledged that there was a slowing of the plot but felt that such a comment was an impertinence, given the sense of joyful acceptance which the film captures.[3] For the special correspondent of *The Times,* the ending displayed the 'symbolism for the nursery'.[4] The *New York Herald Tribune*'s reviewer opted for a more general condemnation: 'It is an "in" film, a strangely cold and uninteresting one for the nondevout. Dazzled by the technique and the mind in control of it, we watch and listen with fascination, captives for the duration. And at the end we are instantly fired by the sudden realization that the heart has not been touched nor the spirit moved.'[5] Doubts remained, but there is grudging admiration in Desson Howe's *Washington Post* review from 1993: 'If *8½* seems stuck in the early 1960s, it's only superficially so. Somehow, the movie is more than the dated crisis of a navel-contemplating artist. It's about the inability of us all to make sense of our lives, put it all together and come up with something meaningful.'[6]

A similar tone is evident in Hal Hinson's 1993 review for the same paper: 'What we just barely tolerate in this chronologically numbered, blatantly autobiographical opus is the shamelessly over-luscious "Italian-ness" of it ... Also on this list of negatives is [Fellini's] sentimentality and his tendency to substitute his trademark mannerisms for true substance ... Yet, still, what beautiful mannerisms, what lyricism and romance.'[7] Roger Ebert in the *Chicago Sun-Times* also opts for an emotional approach: 'A movie like this is a splash of cold water in the face, a reminder that the movies really can shake us up, if they want to. Ironic, that Fellini's film about artistic bankruptcy seems almost richer in invention than almost anything else around.'[8] Positive views have prevailed, with *8½* maintaining its place in the *Sight and Sound* listings of the best films and being endorsed by the likes of Terry Gilliam, Martin Scorsese and Ingmar Bergman.[9] Although its popular appeal is limited by the Italian dialogue, it appears in 150th position among the IMDb's top 250 films.[10]

Subjective Impression

This is a film which demands a subjective response. Guido appears in every scene. We see events through his eyes as well as sharing his thoughts and dreams. He is a man who cannot find peace, or who only professes to want it. Despite his insistence that he wants to make a simple, honest film, he enjoys the trappings of fame and sophistication. This makes him suspect as an observer. He drifts through relationships with women, old friends and professional colleagues. The worlds coincide as aspiring actresses clamour for roles, but he placates them without making any promises. When the writer points out flaws in the script, Guido barely responds.

The writer's approach is intellectual, while Guido is guided by his emotions, drawing on events and figures from his past. Or does he? We can never be sure what is real and what is fantasy. More importantly, we learn how he copes with an emotional crisis. We discover preoccupations which may or may not coincide with those of Fellini himself: the Roman Catholic Church, the womanizing, irritation with the press and concern about his mother's reactions to everything he does. Such issues assume considerable importance in his low state. Anything can trigger memories: a glimpse of a woman's legs is enough to make him recall Saraghina. Some of these memories become extended sequences, often drawing upon childhood; others are brief, such as the fantasy of Claudia taking a lamp from a window. This occurs when they sit in the parked car and he asks her to turn off the car lights.

Guido has a complex attitude to religion. It has shaped his life, as the flashback to his schooldays and his deference to the cardinal demonstrate, yet his own morality is not beyond reproach. He has sloughed off his beliefs, but not the trappings of religion. He probes the cardinal's acolytes as to whether his film will be acceptable to the Church, but as events pile upon events, he never seeks solace in his religious beliefs.

In the nightmare which opens the film, Guido escapes by floating away, even if he is brought down to earth again. In reality there is no easy escape, though the writer in *Charlie Bubbles* (Albert Finney, GB, 1968) manages it. Guido comes closest to revealing his true thoughts to Claudia, confessing that he is incapable of love. He looks for consolation in work, yet, as he admits, even this seems beyond him. Claudia is the one person who does not harass him, but even on their night drive, the producer pursues them.

Guido emerges from his creative block/low spirits/depression. How his state is defined depends on our attitudes to creativity and mental illness. The film offers us an opportunity to re-examine our assumptions and prejudices. Guido makes an unlikely hero; we have to decide whether he deserves our sympathy. The circus provides him (and Fellini) with a fitting analogy for life: the world is truly a stage. Deeper concerns are cast aside in the gaiety of the moment; the clown can hide despair under his makeup. At least Guido seems happy in the film's final moments. Yet the ending is confusing. Guido moves from attempted suicide to a reconciliation with his wife in a matter of minutes. Or are these alternative endings? We have to be content with the magician orchestrating proceedings like a film director. In a way this is fitting: the magician draws Guido out of his torpor, bringing together everybody who has meant something to him and giving him the impetus to create. What more could a film director want?

Analysis

'I don't believe that rational understanding is an essential element in the reception of any work of art. Either a film has something to say to you or it hasn't. If you are moved by it, you don't need to have it explained to you. If not, no explanation can make you moved by it.'[11]

Fellini's words reveal that he favoured a subjective response to film. If he was none too fond of leaving explanations to critics, this does not put his work beyond criticism. Discussion of *8½* has focused on four aspects: its autobiographical nature, its vein of fantasy, the self-reflexive elements and the ending. Ironically, one of Guido's sternest critics is Daumier, whom he invited to collaborate on the project. No wonder that in one of Guido's fantasies, he has the writer hanged.

It is tempting to see *8½* as barely concealed autobiography, so that criticizing the work merges into criticizing Fellini. It is not clear which was Pauline Kael's target when she wrote that the film was 'a deluxe glorification of creative crisis, visually arresting, ... but in some essential way conventionally-minded'.[12] At least Fellini avoided nostalgia, which is another danger of autobiography. His own pronouncements were contradictory, making it difficult to know how far he was playing to his image. In a discussion of how far film can be autobiographical, David Lavery quotes Fellini's comment about film-making: 'It is a way of realizing myself and giving my life meaning.'[13] Lavery sees Fellini as a protean figure in whom life and film-making cannot be separated. He cites Fellini's own words as evidence: 'I have invented myself entirely: a childhood, a personality, longings, dreams, and memories, all in order to enable me to tell them.'[14] Another way of putting it is that Fellini invented a persona for public consumption. The final phrase of the quotation stresses the communicative aspect of art, which Lavery does not explore. The motifs in *8½* are drawn from Fellini's earlier works. Anyone so fascinated by circuses and religious rituals must be a showman and a showman craves an audience. If he drew on his own life and obsessions, he also dramatized incidents for audiences. Self-dramatization is a matter of temperament. Like Dickens, Fellini was attracted to the theatrical. Both men mined their childhood experiences; both craved an audience. A hallmark of creativity in narrative fiction is the freedom to embroider the past, constructing a scenario which may have little to do with fact so long as it makes a good story. Fellini was blatant in mining his past, so if incidents which are presented as autobiography do not ring true, the audience is entitled to feel cheated. Events need to cohere in a convincing narrative which holds the interest of the audience as much as the creator. Fellini's diversions verge on self-obsession.

Philip Kemp points out that Fellini mined autobiography from the beginning of his film-making career, with *The White Sheik* (Italy, 1952) being set in the world of comic strips in which he found employment on moving to Rome.[15] What distinguishes *8½* from the earlier work is the extensive use of fantasy to convey Guido's inner life. Another of Fellini's comments is apposite: 'For me the only real artist is the visionary because he bears witness to his own reality. A visionary—Van Gogh, for instance—is a profound realist. That wheat field with the black sun is his; only he saw it. There can't be greater realism.'[16] Fellini is proclaiming himself a visionary artist when his audience should be the judges. He makes free with the term realism, but the imagery of the early neo-realistic works is as artful in its own way as anything appearing in *8½*. To quote Fellini again: 'Reality? There are only images of it, after all.'[17]

He fashions a fantasy while assuring us that it is reality. This leaves us uncertain how seriously to take the film and to take him. Not that this situation is unique: the appeal of Laurence Sterne, Lewis Carroll and Luis Buñuel depends on teasing the audience, while the world of fine art has wrestled with the dilemma of what to take seriously since that urinal. J. P. Telotte takes an analytical view of the problem:

> In film after film the blurring or absence of that line [between imagination and reality] produces the moment of "hesitation" between naturalistic and supernatural explanations for events that, Tzvetan Todorov argues, marks all forms of the fantastic genre. Fellini's attitude might also help explain the increasingly reflexive turn of his later films, as works like *Roma, Orchestra Rehearsal* (1979), and *And the Ship Sails On* (1984) play at the borders between the lived and filmed worlds.... These works freely, if at times disconcertingly, acknowledge their filmic nature; they explore the points at which reality and human fantasizings intersect and become something more.[18]

The 'something more' which gives *8½* its emotional appeal is drawn from the same subjective elements which arouse controversy.

Fellini drew on his own experience of Jungian analysis for the film, using dream notebooks kept since 1960 in addition to fantasies of childhood.[19] This provides fertile ground for analysts. The collective will of the Church, the spa and the film crew can each oppress Guido. The anima—the mystical, conservative and female part of the collective unconscious—is represented most obviously by the seductive charms of Saraghina, whom the priests consider to be a devil. The other character who operates on this level is the mind reader in the restaurant. Alan A. Stone points out that the message 'asa nisi masa', which she scrawls on the blackboard after reading Guido's mind, is 'anima' with pig-Latin tags attached. Stone accepts a psychoanalytic reading but concludes that 'It makes "sense" of the film in a way that suggests self-conscious obscurity and condescending ambiguity rather than passionate inspiration.'[20] This implies calculation on Fellini's part, which Stone regards as reductive. He reviews other interpretations of the film: as a recreation of Dante's purgatory, a psychiatric drama with Guido as a victim of bipolar depression and as a visual equivalent of stream-of-consciousness writing, with fantasy, memory and reality being interwoven. Stone argues that the work soars above these simplistic interpretations: 'Like all sublime art, Fellini's improvisations surprise and convince almost in the same moment.'[21] This does not prevent Stone from conceding that Kael's negative review marked the beginning of Fellini's 'creative implosion', as aesthetic ambitions and the abandonment of storytelling lost him his audience.[22] But this is an instance of judging the film not on its own merits, but on the basis of the director's career.

An alternative assessment of Stone's position is that he baulks at Fellini's abandonment of realism in favour of a wholehearted commitment to fantasy. Stone is more nuanced than this suggests, accepting that Kael is too dismissive, while many of her colleagues oversimplify. The gist of his criticism is contained in one sentence: 'The film is certainly self-centered, perhaps even disrespectful of its audience, and there is also in it the narcissistic confusion of self-absorption and creativity.'[23] When a director achieves enough fame and prestige to dictate terms, there is a danger of film-making to satisfy the ego. Fellini's previous film, *La dolce vita,* marked his ascent to directorial stardom, allowing him to realize his aspirations with minimal compromise. This was the first of Fellini's films with the marked reflexive element noted by Telotte. Focusing on the process of film-making as in *8½, Day for Night* (François Truffaut, France/Italy, 1973), or *The Caiman* (Nanni Moretti, Italy/France, 2006) risks being called too clever by half. The device works if the viewer gains insight into the creative process and is not left feeling tricked. Opinions on *8½* remain equivocal. As with *Lawrence of Arabia,* film-makers appreciate the director's technical bravura more than critics if the 2002 *Sight and Sound* listings of the best films are any guide.[24] An example of critical caution comes from J. Hoberman of New York's *Village Voice:* 'The movie's major flaw remains its romantic, self-serving portrait of the artist as a big-time moviemaker.'[25] Robin Wood has similar qualms. After dismissing criticism of the film's fantasy elements, he continues:

> In *8½* one is constantly troubled by doubt as to whether we are meant to find the hero, with the arrested infantilism apparent in his relationships both with wife and mistress, so distasteful. Furthermore, Fellini here trades too much on our awareness of his large measure of self-identification with his hero, whose alleged genius remains for the spectator merely alleged.[26]

This is an attack on both the characterization of Guido and the self-regarding elements of the film. In Guido's (and Fellini's) defence, an Italian male sensibility may look upon his actions differently; the surprise is that the film has drawn little fire from feminists.[27] A counter-argument to the accusation of being self-regarding is that Fellini outlined the scenario of *8½* to his colleague Brunello Rondi in 1960. It would be misleading to see the film as a hastily concocted account of his own creative block when at this early stage the hero had no specific occupation.[28]

As already noted, the film's ending elicits equally conflicting views. Marilyn Fabe agrees with the emphasis on self-identification but discerns a final symbolic triumph of the imagination.[29] For Ted Perry, the camera draws back to render Guido less significant, thereby incorporating him into the community.[30] There is enough ambiguity to encompass both interpretations, yet are they both too easy? No relationship is resolved and our hero has not changed. As Stone points out, Guido seems closer to whistling in the dark than showing genuine elation.[31] For some viewers, the ending comes as an affirmation of life; for others, it is a conceit too far. I find it incoherent, but its most serious weakness is the absence of any emotional resolution. There is a need to draw together Guido's uncertainties in an emotional catharsis, so that we glimpse where he is going. Instead, Fellini resorts to displaying his trademark tropes in pick-and-mix fashion, as though he is as uncertain as everybody else what is happening.

This is a tantalizing film. It can appear modish and dated on first viewing, yet the issues which it encompasses are timeless. As Fellini realized, many of the criticisms result from the film being analyzed rather than experienced. His skill as ringmaster of his characters cannot be denied, yet, as the *New York Herald Tribune* critic noted, there is a coldness at the film's heart. I can sympathize with Guido and I can be entertained, but I am not moved. This is a film which elicits admiration rather than laughter or tears. Where it should be self-deprecating, it is self-regarding. The opening has a sense of mystery which is not sustained. Those white-faced figures in the final scene belong in a masque, which the film resembles. We are kept at a distance, as though Fellini is too much of a showman to let his true feelings show. Yet this is a film about relationships and creativity. We need to appreciate what is in Guido's mind, and it is here that the film ultimately disappoints.

2001: A Space Odyssey (GB/US, 1968): The Long Voyage to Destiny

Production company: MGM
Producer/Director: Stanley Kubrick
Screenplay: Stanley Kubrick, Arthur C. Clarke
Source: Arthur C. Clarke (short story: 'The Sentinel')
Photography: Geoffrey Unsworth
Production design: Tony Masters, Harry Lange, Ernie Archer
Art Director: John Hoesli
Editor: Ray Lovejoy
Cast: Keir Dullea (Dave Bowman), Gary Lockwood (Frank Poole), William Sylvester (Dr Floyd), Douglas Rain (voice of HAL)

Synopsis

The opening 'Dawn of Man' section portrays a world where animals and apes compete for food. One ape is disturbed at night by the coming of a monolith. The others crowd around, fearful yet curious. Daylight again and the tribe discovers that bones can serve as weapons. A bone is thrown into the air, where it spins. A cut transforms it into a spacecraft.

In the second (untitled) section, Dr Floyd is in a spacecraft visiting a space station orbiting Earth. There he attends a meeting with Russian scientists, who quiz him about an epidemic occurring at the Clavius station on the moon. He refuses to discuss the issue with them, but later he attends a briefing at Clavius, where the epidemic is revealed to be a cover story. The sudden appearance of a monolith is the real cause of the security alert. He joins a party visiting the strange object. They treat it like a tourist attraction, until it emits a high-pitched noise which makes them recoil in discomfort.

The third section, 'The Jupiter Mission', takes place eighteen months later. Astronauts Frank Poole and Dave Bowman are on a voyage to Jupiter, accompanied by three colleagues in suspended animation. The onboard computer, HAL, predicts the imminent breakdown of a component. It works normally when it is retrieved and tested, leading mission control to advise that the computer prediction is wrong. HAL recommends that the component be put back into use so that when it fails, the fault can be located. The two astronauts are undecided what to do. They go into a communications pod where HAL cannot monitor their conversation and decide that the computer is unreliable and should be disconnected. HAL reads their lips through the observation window and severs Frank's oxygen supply when he goes outside the ship to put back the component. Dave takes out another pod to retrieve Frank's body, giving HAL the opportunity to turn off the life support systems of the other three astronauts. When Dave returns, HAL refuses to let him re-enter the ship on the grounds that he might jeopardize the mission. He gains entry through an emergency hatch and disconnects the computer.

In the final section, 'Jupiter and beyond the Infinite', Dave continues with the Jupiter mission and is drawn into a new dimension. In a period bedroom, he confronts himself as an old man. The monolith is seen again. In the final frames, a foetus looks down on the solar system.

Cultural Context

The film was developed from a short story by Arthur C. Clarke, which itself owes a debt to Olaf Stapledon's novel *Star Maker* (1937). Clarke and Kubrick worked on the screenplay together, at the same time as developing the scenario into a novel which was published under Clarke's name. A hostile response at the film's premiere in New York caused Kubrick to cut nineteen minutes and introduce inter-titles between the sections. This is the version seen today. Renata Adler of the *New York Times* is representative of initial critical bafflement: 'The movie is so completely absorbed in its own problems, its use of color and space, its fanatical devotion to science fiction detail, that it is somewhere between hypnotic and immensely boring.'[1] Pauline Kael found it 'a monumentally unimaginative movie', while Andrew Sarris called it a disaster.[2] One of the most rapid conversions came from Joseph Gelmis of *Newsday*. His initial review described the film as disjointed and pretentious, with characters who were standardized, bland, anti-dramatic and self-defeating. In a reassessment two weeks later, he still found the characters uninteresting and anti-dramatic, but his analysis of their significance had changed: 'It is precisely this cumulative weight of having experienced a kind of living hell with Keir Dullea [Dave] that makes the symbolic rebirth of his automaton Everyman of the 21st century so profoundly stirring and such a joyous reaffirmation of life.'[3] A second viewing failed to impress John Russell Taylor of *The Times:* 'I found the beginning as long drawn out, and the end as wilfully obscure, as before.'[4] Roger Ebert was in two minds at the time of the film's initial release: 'The fascinating thing about this film is that it fails on the human level but succeeds magnificently on a cosmic scale.'[5] His qualms were relegated to the background by 1997:

> The genius is not how much Stanley Kubrick does in *2001: A Space Odyssey,* but how
> little. This is the work of an artist so sublimely confident that he doesn't include a single

shot simply to keep our attention. He reduces each scene to its essence, and leaves it on screen long enough for us to contemplate it, to inhabit it in our imaginations. Alone among science-fiction movies, *2001* is not concerned with thrilling us, but with inspiring our awe.[6]

This was indicative of received opinion, with the Online Film Critics Society voting the film into first place among the top 100 sci-fi movies.[7] Stephen Hunter of the *Washington Post* was in a minority: 'Now seen in the actual 2001, it's less a visionary masterpiece than a crackpot Looney Tune, pretentious, abysmally slow, amateurishly acted and, above all, wrong.'[8] The public was won over more quickly than the critics, and the film ranks eightieth among the top 250 films on the IMDb Web site.[9]

Subjective Impression

This is a confusing and baffling film, in part because it has no emotional core. The first half hour has no dialogue; the only living things to be seen are apes and prowling animals. Kubrick gives us a geographical and cinematic world without landmarks. There is nobody to empathize with, making it difficult to identify what is important, or to speculate on what might happen.

People are introduced in the second section, but the emphasis is still on spectacle. The sequence inside the space shuttle resembles a slow-motion ballet, yet the movements never express feelings. The characters are dehumanized by their surroundings, functioning as servants of technology. This is emphasized by their bland dialogue and absence of facial expression. A few chinks of humanity shine through. Dr Floyd speaks to his daughter on the videophone, but the conversation is stilted and he has to explain why he cannot be with her on her birthday. Later he shares a meal with two astronauts as they travel to the monolith. These occasions are the closest the film comes to revealing the characters' private lives, yet we learn nothing of their thoughts or feelings except that Floyd is wary of the Russians.

The journey to the moon ends with the image of the shuttle descending slowly into the airlock on a platform supported by six arms. The craft is shaped like a human head and bathed in red light. After Richard Strauss's *Also sprach Zarathustra* in the opening sequence, Kubrick's image evokes for me the scene from Strauss's opera *Salomé* in which Salome holds John the Baptist's head on a platter. Here it signifies nothing so much as the deification of the machine.

On the Jupiter mission, the talk between the two astronauts never strays beyond immediate technical concerns. Their faces are expressionless. Frank's death fails to move me because of this lack of humanity. By contrast, the machines take on human characteristics. The pods with lights on either side resemble faces. HAL watches the astronauts and responds in a human way, expressing doubts about the mission, playing chess with Frank and praising Dave's sketches, albeit in an expressionless voice. Yet HAL cannot have a relationship with the men. Ultimately the mission comes first, even if this necessitates dispensing with humans. But HAL is vulnerable to human intervention, despite its decision-making ability. The computer is programmed by humans and can be disabled by them.

The final section dispenses with dialogue as Dave, clad in his spacesuit, wanders through what looks like an expensive hotel suite. Yet the surroundings are unreal. The white-tiled floor glows, recalling the white-tiled ceiling of the space station seen on Dr Floyd's arrival. An old man with his back to the camera sits at a table. His immobility makes it difficult to arouse much curiosity until we realize that this is Dave in later life. He is the only character who can gain any insight and speculate on the possibilities which life offers. There is a quasi-religious message of death and renewal signified by the foetus appearing in the final frames to the accompaniment of Richard Strauss's music reprised from the opening scene. The sense of mystery is powerful.

Kubrick's intention might be to make emotional engagement with this film difficult. The spacemen appear devoid of feeling and their world is as alien to us as the presence of the monolith is to them. The slow pace reinforces this impression of dehumanization, ironing out the tempo variations which would normally accompany changes of mood. The effect is hypnotic once the pace is accepted. Music establishes the atmosphere in scenes without actors. The opening bars of *Also sprach Zarathustra,* when allied to the emergence of the sun at the beginning of the film, creates the expectation that something overwhelming is about to happen. The music arouses awe at the natural world. The space station is seen to the measured rhythm of Johann Strauss's Blue Danube waltz, with its associations of rippling water and the leisured classes of the Austro-Hungarian Empire. We accept the juxtaposition and make links because we have no action to focus on. In the final section, tonality breaks down, adding to our sense of being adrift in a place without certainty.

I began by disliking *2001;* I came to admire it, though my reservations about its coldness remain. As with Kubrick's other films, I feel manipulated rather than having been offered a revelation. Kubrick's treatment cannot be readily approached on an emotional level, yet the music invites an emotional reaction, most obviously by cueing our responses. The ending hints at a transcendental message which goes beyond warning about the perils of science. Kubrick's vision can be seen as naive or complex, which is the essence of ambiguity, yet I cannot convince myself that this is enough to make my journey worthwhile. Music touches the sublime, but it cannot compensate for what is missing from the film.

Analysis

Undeniably this is an ambitious work; differences of opinion hinge on how far Kubrick achieves his ambition. Problem areas for commentators are the film's structure, the obscurantism, the banal dialogue, the dominance of the machine, the role of humour and the use of music.

The structure has more than academic significance, as Alexander Walker makes clear:

> The way the usual time sequence of narrative cause and effect have been thrown out of the film is only the first of many things that unsettle a conventional audience.... For finding the meaning is a matter not of verbalizing but of *feeling* it in the images drawn from past and future time, in the involvement with the experience of space, and in *apprehending* what is happening rather than being fed cut-and-dried information. It is a whole new concept of cinema. [Walker's italics][10]

This is a bold statement which deserves challenging. Events follow a temporal sequence, so Walker has to concede that narrative structure is not completely abandoned.[11] Logically, the 'Dawn of Man' section opens the film. The voyage to Jupiter takes place because of Floyd's encounter with the monolith, or so HAL suspects. Narrative breaks down as Bowman reaches his destination. The problem until this point is not the lack of narrative, but the weakness of the links between sections. The most successful transition is from the 'Dawn of Man' section to Floyd's journey to the space station, the cut from bone to spacecraft recalling the transformation from bird of prey to fighter aircraft in Powell and Pressburger's *A Canterbury Tale*. Elsewhere, inter-titles make an uneasy afterthought, emphasizing Kubrick's abrupt changes of direction and doing little to clarify the action. The monolith launches the narrative and provides a motif linking the inner sections. Its place in the outer sections is so tenuous that it could as well be another afterthought. The conjunction of Earth, moon and sun performs a similar function.

Walker maintains that audiences need to feel the images and apprehend what is happening rather than being fed information, which is an implicit acceptance of the subjective approach. Cinema has evolved ways for audiences to anticipate what they will see, including genre (we know what to expect from a Western), the star system (we know what to expect from John Wayne) and the grammar of editing (the purpose of intellectual montage is to suggest connections). Rather than accepting that *2001* introduces something new into cinema, it can be questioned whether Kubrick is transgressing conventions or failing to exploit them successfully.

One pointer to obscurantism is the difficulty of trying to summarize what happens in the film. Should a viewing need to be supplemented with details from the novel and interviews with the director? Most commentators mention the star-child seen in the final frames, but this name cannot be gleaned from watching the film. Similarly, the relationship of Dave to the old man has to be inferred. Kubrick did not help matters by refusing to discuss the ending on the grounds that it was highly subjective. He conceded that God was at the heart of the film, but this does nothing to introduce clarity.[12] An emphasis on technology obscures the fact that rebirth is a concept common to all religions. Kubrick looks back not only to the first use of tools, but to society's earliest stories. As he provides no accepted religious context, the film invites a range of religious and quasi-religious interpretations. There is room for Tim Hunter to claim it as anti-Christian and anti-evolutionary for proposing that man is controlled by an ambiguous and capricious extraterrestrial force.[13]

The film's philosophical origins are equally elusive, with suggested inspirations including Yeats's poem 'Sailing to Byzantium' and C. S. Lewis's Ransom trilogy.[14] Given that Richard Strauss's music takes its title and ethos from Nietzsche's *Also sprach Zarathustra,* it is reasonable to assume an association between the film and Nietzschean philosophy. Nietzsche borrowed from Zoroastrian mythology, in which Zarathustra rises on the first day of the new millennium; the film's ending can be seen as a reworking of this idea. In examining these links, Leonard F. Wheat stresses the film's allegorical nature, identifying a triple allegory involving Nietzsche, Homer's *Odyssey* and Clarke's merging of man and machine.[15] Wheat has been criticized by Carl Freedman for making too much of these links, which prompts the question of what is left if Nietzsche, Homer and Clarke are excluded.[16] Does the film still lodge in the mind if it is shorn of its mythological connotations, or does its paucity of ideas become apparent?

The disparate sections of *2001* never add up to a coherent whole. Too often plot lines are taken up and discarded. The appearance of the Russians betokens a political dimension which never develops. How do the populace live and do they believe the cover story of an epidemic at Clavius? We are never told, so the political and economic implications of the Jupiter voyage remain unknown. Dr Floyd disappears from the narrative abruptly, arousing the suspicion that he was only there to further the plot. Loose ends cannot be disguised by the inventive use of music.

The banal dialogue is often cited as a failing, but if banality serves an artistic purpose, does this make it acceptable? Kubrick is quoted by Jerome Angel as saying: 'I tried to work things out so that nothing important was said in the dialogue.'[17] He succeeded in this unusual aspiration. Speech occupies a mere forty minutes of the film's running time and is absent in two of the four sections, so it is downgraded in quantitative as well as qualitative terms. It has to be conceded that *2001* is predominantly a feast for the eyes, but this is no justification for Kubrick's denigration of dialogue. He gets tentative support from Richard I. Pope: 'Maybe Kubrick is saying that "current" everyday usage of language is pretty boring; we just don't see it as such because we're busy using it. In *2001,* he is just—(im)possibly—"showing" us this.'[18] The snag is that this line of reasoning offers a licence for presenting any trite material under the guise of showing life as it is. Everyday language may be boring, but film dialogue can never be a realistic representation given the compression and the dramatic and stylistic decisions involved. Two men would not spend weeks together without discussing sex or sport, but at least forenames are used, which is an advance on Dr Floyd's story. Given the film's philosophical aspirations, it is hard to consider the leaden dialogue as anything other than a failing. Mediocrity draws attention to itself, distracting audiences and disrupting their involvement in the fantasy being laid before them. Matters are made worse in *2001* by the space suits, which obscure the actors' body language, while the lighting and camera angles smooth away facial expressions. It is not surprising that HAL displays more emotion than the humans. As the science fiction writer Ray Bradbury puts it: 'The freezing touch of Antonioni, whose ghost haunts Kubrick, has turned everything here to ice.'[19]

The relationship between man and machine has a long pedigree in the cinema and has been the subject of divergent approaches. The societal view represented by *Metropolis* (Fritz Lang, Germany, 1927), *À nous la liberté* and *Modern Times* focuses on the regimentation associated with the factory system. The characters in *2001* are dependent on technology, from the voice recognition system which validates Floyd's identity to the zero gravity toilet which so fascinates him. Technology sustains life, but it also constrains the astronauts, the one-way video transmission from Frank's parents and the bland food being examples. The alternative cinematic approach to the man-machine conundrum is psychological, with the machine assuming human powers. *Frankenstein* (James Whale, US, 1931) spawned a host of imitators. Kubrick and Clarke attempted to combine both traditions. The ideas they used were common currency: in 'A for Andromeda' (Michael Hayes, BBC TV, 1961), a signal from space provides instructions for building a computer. The computer in *2001* assumes a surveillance role, monitoring Dave and Frank's conversations. HAL can make decisions, most dramatically when it turns off the hibernating astronauts' life support systems. Kubrick seemed ambivalent about this battle of wills, removing dialogue which would have revealed HAL's growing sense of paranoia.[20] Computers might have the power of life or death, but when Dave disconnects HAL, it is a pyrrhic victory for mankind which dodges the question of how he continues with his mission unaided. Kubrick illustrates how technology may change us and potentially overwhelm us, but this was hardly new. Claudia Zimny concurs with Frederick Nelson in defending the film's dehumanization on the grounds that Kubrick is breaking with the illusion of psychological depth. She disagrees with Nelson's contention that Kubrick shows the insignificance of the individual when confronted by space. For Zimny, insignificance is the consequence of depriving characters of their humanity, as the relationship of the tool and its creator is reversed with increasing technological sophistication.[21] Kubrick risked alienating critics and audiences. The risk came off in the sense that the film is still talked about after forty years. The cost in Bradbury's terms is turning everything to ice.

In the view of Don Daniels and F. Anthony Macklin, *2001* is a satire.[22] *Dr Strangelove* demonstrates that Kubrick could tackle black comedy, though for *2001* he had a strong and idiosyncratic script collaborator in Arthur C. Clarke and no Peter Sellers in the lead. There are moments of sly humour in the second section, such as the Orbiter Hilton Hotel logo glimpsed in the background as Floyd talks to the Russians, but these are so fleeting that they cannot transform the film into satire. The interchange between HAL and the two astronauts on the voyage to Jupiter could be considered satirical as they defer to the computer, but again these moments are fleeting and the actors do not play the scenes for humour. To do so would humanize the characters, which Kubrick resists. Humour seems incompatible with his aims. A comparison is with Buñuel, who blends visual style and black comedy while exploiting dialogue and showing more respect for his actors.

Music cannot help introducing feeling into the film. Alex North's original score was rejected by Kubrick, who opted for an eclectic mix of pieces. Trying to pin precise feelings to music is notoriously difficult, though Jenefer Robinson makes a valiant attempt.[23] As she cautions, the emotions expressed by music may be different from the emotions it arouses. She cites the example of 'Jingle Bells', which makes her sad because it reminds her of Christmases of yesteryear while not being intrinsically sad.[24] Context is crucial. Music may have a more direct physiological effect on the emotions than other stimuli.[25] The complicating factor in film is that the director intervenes between audiences and performers by matching music to image. This is evident in the pacing of *2001*. A Strauss waltz is not an obvious accompaniment for space vehicles, but the tempo matches the slow-motion movements of the people inside the shuttle. Weightlessness is seemingly not a problem elsewhere. The waltz also suits the slow rotation of the circular space station and the elaborate choreography of the docking procedure. How the mood would change if these were set to another piece of river music: Schumann's *Rhenish* Symphony.

As Dave travels into a different dimension in the final section, a sense of timelessness is required. Ligeti's *Requiem* and *Atmosphères* are appropriately indeterminate in pitch and rhythm. It is in the 'Dawn of Man' section with the ambient sounds of the savannah as accompaniment that pace becomes problematic. *Also sprach Zarathustra* heard over the opening credits portends something grandiloquent, yet once the prop of music is removed, Kubrick seems not to trust his audience and shifts restlessly from image to image. This prompts the question of how other sections of the film might fare without music. One answer is implied by Roger Ebert in his 1997 review: 'The classical music chosen by Kubrick exists *outside* the action. It uplifts. It wants to be sublime; it brings a seriousness and transcendence to the visuals.' [Ebert's italics][26] Music brings an emotional dimension to the visuals. Timothy E. Scheurer concludes that Kubrick uses music to honour the conventions of science fiction, underscoring the conflict between the stable and rational (conservative, classical) and chaos and destruction (avant-garde, atonal) in order to articulate the emotional core of the film.[27] This links music and visuals in a common purpose, though whether Kubrick succeeds in articulating the emotional core of *2001* by relying on music is an open question.

The film can resemble a sacred text, which believers pore over endlessly in the hope of finding fresh revelation. Kubrick did nothing to dissuade them in one of his rare pronouncements quoted by Scheurer:

Man must strive to gain some mastery over himself as well as over his machines. Somebody has said that man is the missing link between primitive apes and civilized human beings. You might say that that idea is inherent in *2001*. We are semicivilized, capable of cooperation and affection, but needing some sort of transfiguration into a higher form of life.[28]

Clarke is equally enigmatic: 'If you understand *2001* completely, we failed. We wanted to raise more questions than we answered.'[29] This is a reasonable response providing the film does raise questions, but as with any cultural icon, *2001* can be elevated beyond criticism, the justification being that non-believers do not understand its nuances. In an otherwise thoughtful essay, Adam Dobson slips into this position in discussing the film's final section: 'Despite our tremendous experience as spectators, we lack the means to understand the sequence in the same way that Bowman's tremendous experience as a scientist leaves him ill-equipped to understand the complexities of the universe.'[30] This allows us to share Dave Bowman's bafflement, but if an audience cannot be expected to understand the film, who can?

2001: A Space Odyssey was released at the height of psychedelia, when the space race was in full swing (the edgy relationship between the two superpowers is touched on in the film's second section) and Western youth experimented with drugs, including LSD. Mysticism was in the air, the lyrics from Procol Harum and the Beatles being heavy with significance, even if nobody understood them. Had *2001* had been released in the more prosaic era of Thatcher and Reagan, it might have fared less well. Shrewdly or serendipitously, Kubrick's work appealed to science fiction enthusiasts, to supporters of the alternative society who appreciated the mystical imagery and to fans of television series such as *The Avengers* (ABC TV, 1961–9), which played with fantasy and mind control. The popularity of *2001* with the public was aided by Kubrick's reputation—*Lolita* (GB, 1962) had made him notorious—and the novelty of Cinerama presentation, though technical constraints limited screenings of the Cinerama version to major urban centres. As *2001* became a cultural phenomenon, critics reassessed their initial reservations.

The film remains popular with audiences and critics. The difference is that today most people see *2001* in their homes, where the visual and aural effects are diminished. In Walker's terms, finding the meaning is a matter of feeling the images, or what Robinson would term making an affective appraisal. Is the film's success attributable to its power in making people follow their feelings, or is it sustained by its reputation as a ground-breaking film? However encouraging to find an ambitious and difficult work remaining popular after forty years, the puzzling aspect is what audiences derive from it. The film aspires to myth—Kubrick called it a mythological documentary—yet those feelings and foibles which make mythic heroes into real people are absent.[31] The film's epic scale and bravura use of technology disguise well-worn ideas. Only the final section is challenging in its abandonment of narrative, and underground film-makers had already exploited this innovation.[32] Kubrick's achievement was to repackage myths and reuse cinematic conventions in a way which made them popular and intellectually respectable.

–13–

The Godfather (US, 1972): Keeping It in the Family

Production companies: Alfran/Paramount Pictures
Producer: Albert S. Ruddy
Director: Francis Ford Coppola
Screenplay: Francis Ford Coppola, Mario Puzo
Source: Mario Puzo (novel: *The Godfather*)
Photography: Gordon Willis
Production Designer: Dean Tavoularis
Art Director: Warren Clymer
Music: Nino Rota
Editors: William Reynolds, Peter Zinner
Cast: Marlon Brando (Don Vito Corleone), Robert Duvall (Tom Hagen), Al Pacino (Michael Corleone), James Caan (Sonny), Diane Keaton (Kay Adams). Sterling Hayden (Captain McClusky)

Synopsis

The Second World War has ended. Don Vito Corleone is in his office receiving members of the New York Italian community anxious to enlist his help. With him is Tom Hagen, whom the Corleone family adopted as a child and who is the Don's lawyer and confidant. Music comes from the garden, where the wedding celebrations of the Don's daughter, Connie, to small-time bookie, Carlo, are taking place. The crooner Johnny Fontane arrives to entertain guests. Among them is Michael, the youngest of Don's three sons, who has distanced himself from the family's criminal activities and is home after army service. He recounts to schoolteacher Kay Adams how Johnny was turned down for a lead role in a film because of his philandering. The Don was disgusted by such behaviour, but as Johnny's godfather he felt bound to pressure the producer, Jack Woltz, who awoke one morning to find the severed head of his prize racehorse in his bed as a warning.

The extent of the Don's criminal empire is revealed at a business meeting. To avoid upsetting his political contacts, he refuses to protect Sollozzo 'The Turk' in his drug-dealing activities. The Don survives an assassination attempt when his bodyguard Paulie is off sick. The Don's middle son, Fredo, is driving, but proves ineffective at handling the situation. The oldest son, the hot-headed Sonny, has Paulie killed for neglecting his duty. Sollozzo is revealed as the instigator of the murder attempt.

When Michael discovers from a newspaper headline what has happened, his sense of family loyalty is rekindled. On visiting his father in hospital, he discovers that the guards have been withdrawn on police orders. He pre-empts another attempt on the Don's life, shoots Sollozzo and the policeman shielding him and escapes to Sicily. There he marries a local girl, but before they can move to a safer location, she is blown up by a bomb intended for him. In New York the feuding continues, with Sonny being killed in an ambush. The Don tries to halt the internecine war by calling a meeting of family heads. A truce is agreed, the price being that the Don has to accept the trade in narcotics which the families will control.

Michael returns to New York and seeks out Kay, who accepts his proposal of marriage. The Don cedes the business to Michael, who determines to make it legitimate and move operations to Las Vegas. The ailing Don warns his son that whoever comes to arrange a business meeting with the other families will betray him.

The predicted invitation comes at the Don's funeral. Michael is set on revenge. He is godfather to Connie and Carlo's child, and the killing of his opponents takes place during the christening. Carlo is garrotted when he admits his treachery. Michael's course is set.

Cultural Context

Paramount took an option on Mario Puzo's novel before it became a best-seller. The project was thrust upon a reluctant and untried Francis Ford Coppola after Elia Kazan, Arthur Penn, Peter Yates and Fred Zinnemann turned it down, the most frequently cited reason being that the story glorified the Mafia.[1] Paramount made a shrewd investment: the rights cost US$50,000 and box-office takings amounted to US$86 million by December 1977, making *The Godfather* the company's most profitable film till that date.[2] It remains the top-rated film among IMDb voters.[3] Critics were initially less enthusiastic. Among the doubters were Judith Crist, who dismissed the film as immoral, Stanley Kauffmann, who complained of its implicit endorsement of Mafia methods and excessive length, and Arthur Schlesinger Jr, who wrote in *Vogue* that *The Godfather* had 'swelled into an overblown, pretentious, slow and ultimately tedious three-hour quasi-epic'.[4] John Russell Taylor of *The Times* displayed less strong feelings: 'It is exactly the kind of holding, not too demanding entertainment you would love to drop into by chance and see at your local.'[5] A. D. Murphy of *Variety* was equally tepid, finding the film overlong and occasionally confusing. His conclusion was that 'While never so placid as to be boring, it is never so gripping as to be superior screen drama.'[6] Vincent Canby of the *New York Times* was more enthusiastic:

> Taking a best-selling novel of more drive than genius (Mario Puzo's *The Godfather*), about a subject of something less than common experience (the Mafia), involving an isolated part of one very particular ethnic group (first-generation and second-generation Italian-Americans), Francis Ford Coppola has made one of the most brutal and moving chronicles of American life designed within the limits of popular entertainment.[7]

In 1992, *The Godfather* joined the *Sight and Sound* list of the best films, since when it has retained its popularity with professionals and public alike. In 2006, it came second among the top screenplays chosen by the Writers' Guild of America, being beaten only by *Casablanca*.[8] Desson Howe of the *Washington Post* is representative of current critical opinion: 'With Puzo, [Coppola] forged an epic tragedy about America, capitalism, family greed, treachery and love. He showed us—with almost Shakespearian gravitas—the errors of hasty vengeance and the wisdom of assured leadership. He gave us a great American picture, full of incredible images and lasting moments.'[9]

Subjective Impression

The film opens with a man seeking justice for his daughter after her attackers have received a suspended sentence. The camera draws back from his face to reveal the back of the seated man he is addressing. When the shot switches to the visitor's viewpoint, we see the face of the seated man, who is stroking his cat like a James Bond villain. This is Don Vito Corleone. Though he is old, he has the demeanour of a man with power. At first he gives a show of reluctance, complaining that the visitor has been disrespectful by not showing friendship before. Only when the visitor kisses his hand does he agree to help.

The scene establishes the themes of tradition, family bonds, friendship and respect, as well as the less desirable trait of a disregard for the processes of law. This is a world of darkness, both morally and physically, with interiors so gloomy that it is difficult to distinguish the characters. It is easy to sympathize with the father who sees his daughter's attackers walk free, but the juxtaposition of law and vengeance makes me uneasy.

It becomes clear that rather than being a benign father figure, the Don oversees a corrupt empire. This makes me feel ambivalent about the wedding. The Don is a proud father, yet he cares nothing for people outside his own circle. He has no scruples, only declining to help a drug dealer because that might jeopardize his political contacts. Nor does Sonny show any compunction about using violence, in spite of his concern to keep his own children safe.

The wedding provides an opportunity to introduce the main characters, including Michael, a war veteran who is still in uniform. His partner, Kay, is not Italian. These signifiers and the tenor of Michael's conversation reveal how far he has drawn away from his family. Over the course of the film, he receives an emotional education as he is sucked into the family's closed, corrupt world after the murder attempt on his father. The decisive moment comes when he ignores the voices of caution and shoots Sollozzo and Captain McClusky. His motive might be filial love, revenge or honour; the change in his character is never satisfactorily explained. While Michael shelters in Sicily until the fuss dies down, he is attracted to a local girl. He does not woo her as he did Kay, but uses the threat of force against her father to gain her hand in marriage. Michael is assuming the Don's methods. With the murder of his bride, his course of revenge is set.

When Michael proposes to Kay, he assures her that he will make the family business legitimate. This is patently untrue, for Michael systematically eliminates all his opponents once he is freed from his father's restraining hand. There is an inevitability about his actions, as though family duties cannot be evaded. His final gesture is to close the door on Kay, so that a meeting can take place. The business of crime excludes women.

Kay only appears in a few scenes, but she too receives an emotional education. The Michael she knows at the beginning of the film is like any other soldier glad to be home from the war, but family loyalties prove too strong for her to overcome. She is dropped peremptorily when the Don is shot and only taken up again after Michael's Italian wife is killed. We are left to speculate why she accepts his proposal. The next time she is seen, the couple have a child. In the film's final moments, she has to confront how much her husband has changed. Her expression is our only guide to her feelings.

Don Vito Corleone has to come to terms with change as the gangs move into narcotics and Michael talks of moving operations to Las Vegas. The old man cedes control of his empire gracefully, never criticizing Michael once the decision is made, even when Tom Hagen is sidelined. Instead, the Don's attention becomes focused on his grandson, who is the only person present when he dies. This is a man learning to accept the limitations of age.

Religious imagery pervades the film, even if religious values are absent. The Don's first supplicant kisses his hand. Sacrificial killings, from a severed head of a racehorse to human victims, convey Old Testament messages about loyalty and revenge. Michael is the prodigal son. When he assumes the Don's mantle, he becomes a Christ-like figure surrounded by his disciples, not knowing which one will betray him. The film is framed by religious ceremonies—a wedding at the beginning and a christening at the end—even if the killings turn these into a parody of religion. Those darkened hues of the interiors forge another link with the past, recalling not only Dutch paintings, but the mercantile class who were often their subject. The Don could belong among them.

It is easy to look back with nostalgia to a time when the individual turned to the family and the community for support. The film reveals the costs of clinging to tradition in a modern society. Initially I applaud Michael's desire to be free of the family's stultifying closeness and I feel repelled by the Don; by the end of the film, I understand the Don's situation, even if I cannot like him. In a sense Michael does break free, but only by transforming a family enterprise based on crime into a criminal empire dependent on profits like any other company. There is nobody in the film I care about apart from the women, and they are little more than onlookers.

Coppola might have intended audiences to find a wider resonance in this film, perhaps about the state of the family in an industrial society, or the accretion of power in America. The continuing popularity of *The Godfather* suggests that audiences derive something which goes beyond the story of a criminal family, but I soon tire of this unpleasant, hermetically sealed world. The simplistic message that the family looks after its own is taken to inordinate length. I can detect no assimilation of Italian cultural values into American society. Instead there is cloying nostalgia for a world which is better left behind.

Analysis

A comprehensive assault on the first two *Godfather* films came from Jack Shadoian in 1977, before they achieved eminence. He detected a new vigour and a modernist emphasis in the evolution of the crime film, yet rather than being praiseworthy, the aspects which he identifies appear as indictments.[10] Three of these are relevant, embodying my own reservations about *The Godfather:* the issue of length, the emphasis on style and the effect on the audience.

'Both films lack the genre's typical brief efficiency. Together, they are a rhythmically ponderous domestic epic about the consequences of American capitalism on family life.... We watch a pageant and are kept detached.'[11] It is hard to disagree that the films lack forward momentum, a fault which is already apparent in the wedding scene, where Coppola seems unwilling to abandon the festivities (six years later, Michael Cimino was to display a similar reluctance in *The Deer Hunter*). The emphasis on ceremonies establishes the stately pace and mires the film in an unchanging past. Having settled on a leisurely rhythm, Coppola only varies the tempo for moments of violence. One consequence is excessive length, which accentuates the difficulty of holding together a discursive plot.

Shadoian's reference to rhythm invites comparison with music, but caution is needed in making the analogy. The triple rhythms of Nino Rota's score, which underpin *The Godfather,* recall Verdi, leading Naomi Greene to seek links with *Rigoletto* and with Mascagni's *Cavalleria Rusticana,* which is set in Sicily.[12] What distinguishes Verdi from Coppola is that Verdi engaged with society: he was a member of parliament as well as being a composer committed to tackling political themes. Censorship meant that issues had to be presented in historical guise, but audiences got the point. Coppola faced no such strictures, but he still opted for the distancing effect of the past. In place of political realities, *The Godfather* offers a series of lyrical set pieces bathed in sepia hues and linked by stretches of dialogue. Periodic bouts of violence make poor substitutes for Verdi arias. Bernardo Bertolucci integrates *Rigoletto* into *The Spider's Stratagem* (Italy, 1970) more successfully, letting the action evolve in parallel with an operatic performance. And he uses genuine Verdi.

Shadoian's second criticism is that 'Both [*Godfather*] films have a generally petrified air, a lifelessness that keeps us at a distance. Even private emotions are treated ceremoniously by style … The past is projected … as a tableau…. What used to be accomplished by voice-over narration is now embedded within directorial attitude and photographic style.'[13] The abstractions arise from a lack of differentiation between the male characters, who are there to display clan loyalty and macho posturing rather than individuality. The directorial attitude detected by Shadoian shows itself in the self-consciousness which can afflict Merchant-Ivory films. Shots feel posed for the camera. One scene in *The Godfather* which escapes the director's deadening hand is the Don's death, which Brando improvised in order to coax a natural response from the child actor.[14] Would that there were more such moments.

The photographic style might be characterized as Technicolor noir, borrowing from gangster films of the 1930s and only shaking off the prevailing gloom for the wedding scene, the Don's death and some tourist views of Sicily. Greene makes clear how this affects the wedding: 'What strikes us most about this sequence are its formal qualities (the sunlight wedding contrasting with the dark interiors) which create a kind of subtext reinforcing the film's themes of claustrophobia and power.'[15] Colour could be used to subvert or parody the gangster genre, but Coppola does neither. Humour is missing from his world. Nor does he redefine his chosen genre like Sam Peckinpah in *Junior Bonner* (US, 1972), or Ang Lee in *Brokeback Mountain* (US, 2006). *The Godfather* seems conventional beside them. The gangster genre is predicated on black and white photography; by comparison, Coppola's use of colour creates a mannered opulence, leading to what David Thomson terms a 'lustrous suppression of vitality'.[16] Coppola's emphasis on directorial attitude and photographic style serves to conceal rather than clarify when the film is set. The focus is so much on the family that they exist out of time, like characters from *Hamlet*. The crooner at the wedding, the men's clothes and those dark interiors with Venetian blinds which resemble prison bars betoken another era, though it is only when cars are seen that the period can be identified precisely. This vagueness is an aspect of the film's distancing from the audience, noted by Shadoian. By cocooning the subject matter in the costumes and props of a mythical past, Coppola neutralizes any relevance to today. Events take place in a never-never land where the public never ventures and the audience are voyeurs. So that Michael can be lured back to the family firm as the Don's successor, Coppola and Puzo make the older brothers flawed and undercharacterized, allowing them to be conveniently sidelined. There are hints of real life beyond the gates of the Corleone mansion—the crooner Johnny Fontane resembles Frank Sinatra, while Harry Cohn might be the model for producer Jack Woltz—but this is drawing from the outside world rather than reflecting upon it.

If the film's style seems familiar, Clarens suggests a source: 'Coppola's Don Corleone appeared at times as a kindred soul to Visconti's Sicilian prince in *The Leopard,* both symbols of an order about to pass. Visconti's original choice for his princely hero was Laurence Olivier; so was Coppola's for the godfather.'[17] Coppola appropriates Visconti's seedy glamour, but Visconti is a treacherous master, whose opulent facades can conceal the lack of anything important to say.

Shadoian's third point echoes this: 'There is a profound mood of uselessness in the audience ... [which] never quite feels that it is either being instructed about the workings of the Mafia or that it is emotionally embroiled in the high drama of its participants. The material seems to be treated indirectly; it does not have an organic self-sufficiency.'[18] Rather than engaging with the characters, the audience is invited to watch them posturing at the director's whim. Some of the strategies which contribute to this indirectness have already been considered: the deliberate pacing, setting events in the past, stylization which turns proceedings into a tableau, superficial characterization and music which gives the illusion of watching an opera. Michael is at the centre of the film, yet we learn nothing of why he was so determined to escape from his family (was there a family rift?), his war service (does a war veteran need lessons on using a gun from a hoodlum?) or his relationship with Kay (does she try to change him?). And how could Jack Woltz fail to wake when intruders put a horse's head into his bed? This incident dramatizes the Don's character but points up the falsity of the story. The mobsters conform to type, putting the Corleone family first and being ready to kill for it. They are interchangeable, with only Fredo breaking the mould by weeping when his father is shot and getting no sympathy for his weakness. Coppola's degree of control gives the actors little scope to develop their roles, despite the film's length. We marvel at the characters' nastiness, but they are forgettable. The exception is Brando, whose overblown performance lingers in the mind as a grotesque. *Chinatown* (Roman Polanski, US, 1974) is equally stylized and also set in a time just out of memory, the difference being that its characters are fallible human beings who have the ring of authenticity.

The passivity engendered in the audience makes *The Godfather* a profoundly conservative film, endorsing John Russell Taylor's view that this is well made but undemanding entertainment. Without emotional involvement, audiences need not take a moral stance. As Thomson puts it, '*The Godfather* is a supreme American film, but it is not good enough. Worse than that, it resists the potential that makes all imaginative work hopeful: that the public may pursue a more searching sense of themselves and their lives.'[19] A great film need not be crusading, but it needs to proclaim its vision if it is to lodge in the mind. *The Godfather* fails by this criterion.

For Clarens, previous gangster films such as *Pay or Die!* (Richard Wilson, US, 1960) adopted an external legalistic viewpoint and an attitude tinged with outrage.

'*The Godfather* reversed this viewpoint, looking from inside the underworld out into a hopelessly corrupt society from which tradition, loyalty, honor, and respect for one's elders had almost totally vanished. This daring dramatic device would ruinously have failed had the outside, straight world been allowed to intrude.'[20] Keeping outsiders at bay adds to the film's introspection, though whether it is essential to the story is debatable. *The Godfather* marks a shift of viewpoint from previous gangster films, but not necessarily in the way that Clarens perceives. In Roger Corman's view, 'Coppola gives us the inherently American story of the aspirations of the outsider,' while Steve Erickson calls the Statue of Liberty the femme fatale of the *Godfather* trilogy.[21] The innovation of offering the immigrant's viewpoint led to the philosophy of the ghetto rather than the potential of the new world. Because the wider society is never seen, its flaws have to be inferred, allowing it to be presented in any way which suits the argument. The Corleones could be a microcosm of any corrupt society. The film is too self-regarding to comment on the outside world, while the values it espouses, such as family bonds, are perversions of Western values when family honour matters more than individuals. Again the comparison with *Chinatown* is illuminating. *Chinatown* looks outwards. Corruption is seen to affect society in the most basic way by threatening its water supply, while Jack Nicholson takes the mythic role of the avenger, intent on rooting out evil. *The Godfather* looks inwards to a world where corruption is endemic. The final scene of each film crystallizes the difference. In *Chinatown* it takes place in the street, where the blaring car horn attracts the populace; *The Godfather* ends with a door being slammed, shutting out not only Kay, but the audience.

Despite American society being conspicuous by its absence, the film parades its American credentials as blatantly as *Citizen Kane*. The first words heard are 'I believe in America.' Yet the visual style owes as much to European sensibilities as American film noir, the music harks back to Italian opera, and the values espoused by the characters are drawn from their spiritual homeland of Sicily. More precisely, the values are those attributed to the Mafia by Puzo, which Coppola translated to the screen as romanticized thuggery. The Italian American Civil Rights League objected to the making of the film and got the sole reference to the Mafia deleted from the script. Misgivings evaporated when *The Godfather* was taken up enthusiastically by gangsters.[22] Given the way the *Godfather* trilogy has provided them with role models, it is hard to distinguish the reality behind Puzo's story from myths which the films generated.[23] In this sense, the *Godfather* trilogy has become a monster beyond Coppola's control.

David Ray Papke arrives at a similar conclusion using the legalistic model, which Clarens rejects as inappropriate. Papke contends that Coppola's purpose was to challenge the myth of America as a pluralistic society living by the rule of law. The trouble was that audiences wove mythic meanings of their own into the *Godfather* films, so that they saw it as valorizing the self-made man and celebrating the family and authoritarian power.[24] The implications go beyond the scope of Papke's article. Are audiences repelled by what they see, or appreciative of the Corleones' strengths? Do they view the film as historical fiction, historical fact, or a comment on 1970s

America? Do they feel that it has continuing relevance? And what do audiences in other countries take from *The Godfather?* Does it confirm their prejudices of an America infiltrated by the Mafia? Do they believe that the values portrayed are those which most Americans espouse? Such is the state of audience research that these questions remain unanswered.

The continuing popularity of *The Godfather* is remarkable. IMDb voters under 18 give it an average rating of 9.0 out of 10, the same as that given by voters aged 45 and over.[25] This suggests that concern about the dwindling attention span of young people is unfounded. The film is misogynistic, it has no hero or likable leading characters and its moments of drama are few. Taken together, these factors make for an unlikely box-office success. *The Godfather* is fêted in the avowedly Christian United States, yet it is predicated on wielding violence and amorality to maintain power, while the disparity between the trappings of religiosity and the family's activities arouses few qualms. For Camille Paglia, the symbolism of food in the film exemplifies its pre-Christian Sicilian ethos.[26] If this view were widely accepted, with the film being seen as a rejection of Christian values, this might dent its popularity. Clarens makes a similar point: 'Could *The Godfather* have pleaded less openly for peaceful coexistence with the underworld or seemed less accepting of things-as-they-are and still have become in its time the most successful film ever?'[27] In the view of Charles T. Gregory, 'There are two ways out: understand the violence inside yourself and the wrongness of changing sides or denounce the film as violent, manipulative and exploitative.'[28] The first option turns the film into a morality tale; both put the onus on audiences to indulge in soul-searching. But is this too easy? Film-makers cannot control the reception of their work, but they determine its mood, content and context. This film's greatest defect is that Coppola lulls audiences into not thinking through the implications of what he is presenting. He cannot be absolved from this.

The esteem in which critics hold *The Godfather* is a greater puzzle than its success with the public. Even Thomson has mellowed, admiring the film's emphasis on order.[29] One approach is to treat the work as akin to opera, with the combination of deliberate pacing, music, visual style and revenge tragedy amounting to a multifaceted experience. This clarifies the form without resolving the issue of quality. Greene defines the *Godfather* trilogy as a cinematic melodrama sharing the characteristics of nineteenth-century opera, but her conclusion is dispiriting: 'The result is that spectacle encourages us to lament the past, to forget history, and to luxuriate in spectacle for its own sake.'[30]

Artists have long been fascinated by evil, from the novels of Dostoevsky to Michael Powell's *Peeping Tom* and Oliver Hirschbiegel's *Downfall* (Germany, 2004). It could be said that entertainment exploits evil, while art tries to understand it, even if the dividing line is blurred in the case of Alfred Hitchcock and Michael Reeves. Coppola might bring a Catholic sensibility to *The Godfather,* but he lacks the combination of objectivity with compassionate understanding found in the works of Robert Bresson or Ermanno Olmi. Instead he connives in an acceptance of evil, a position which is seductive, morally dubious, superficial and ultimately dangerous.

−14−

Raging Bull (US, 1980): The Drama
of the Fight

Production companies: Chartoff-Winkler Productions/United Artists
Producers: Robert Chartoff, Irwin Winkler
Director: Martin Scorsese
Story: Jake La Motta, Joseph Carter, Peter Savage (*Raging Bull: My Story*)
Screenplay: Paul Schrader, Mardik Martin, Martin Scorsese, Robert De Niro
Photography: Michael Chapman
Art direction: Sheldon Haber, Alan Manser, Kirk Axtell
Production Designer: Gene Rudolf
Editor: Thelma Schoonmaker
Cast: Robert De Niro (Jake La Motta), Cathy Moriarty (Vickie La Motta), Joe
    Pesci (Joey La Motta), Frank Vincent (Salvy)

Synopsis

1964. A middle-aged Jake La Motta is rehearsing his speech for a celebrity appearance in a nightclub. The film follows his career chronologically in a series of extended flashbacks, beginning with a fight in 1941 which has been rigged by the
Mafia. The audience erupts with displeasure when Jake loses. Joey is his manager as
well as his brother and is just as unhappy with the result. Later, a squabble between
Jake and his wife, Irma, is interrupted by Joey with a warning from the Mafia that
Jake should be cooperative. Salvy is the Mafia's messenger and watches the two
brothers sparring at the gym. Jake is angry that Joey has acquiesced to the Mafia and
hits him viciously.

Jake is fascinated by Vickie, whom he glimpses with Salvy and his friends at the
local swimming pool. The brothers attend a church dance in the hope of seeing her.
She is there, but Joey does not get an opportunity to talk to her. Irma is angry at being
left at home, which provokes another row. The next day, Jake encounters Vickie at
the swimming pool and invites her for a drive. They make love in the flat he bought
for his father.

Ensuing scenes are interspersed with further glimpses of Jake in the ring. He
divorces Irma and marries Vickie. In their bedroom he draws back from her, putting

the forthcoming fight first. It is his third bout with Sugar Ray Robinson. The judges award the match to Robinson, despite an indifferent performance. Joey is angry that the fight has been rigged, while Jake feels jinxed.

1947. When Vickie remarks on the good looks of Jake's opponent, Janiro, the overweight Jake is jealous. His suspicions are fuelled when Salvy kisses her at a nightclub, prompting him to ask Joey to watch her. Vickie confides to Joey the problems which Jake's jealousy is causing, but Joey is unsympathetic. His links with the Mafia have strengthened, and he advises Jake to lose the fight. Jake dismisses the suggestion but loses anyway. He becomes suspicious that Vickie is too close to Joey and turns on them, though afterwards he is filled with remorse. He is out of condition and loses his next fight, which is with his old adversary Sugar Ray Robinson.

1956. Jake is seen performing in his seedy Miami nightclub. He emerges at dawn to find Vickie outside. She announces that she is leaving him. To add to Jake's woes, he is imprisoned for allowing underage prostitutes into his club. He is next seen after his release, introducing strippers in a New York bar. In the street outside he encounters Joey, who turns down his attempt at reconciliation. In a reprise of the opening scene, Jake is seen rehearsing for his stage show before a mirror.

Cultural Context

De Niro introduced Jake La Motta's autobiography to Scorsese, who shelved it in favour of *New York, New York* (US, 1977). De Niro had faith in the idea and hired Mardik Martin, who scripted Scorsese's *Mean Streets* (US, 1973). Scorsese demanded changes which were unacceptable to De Niro. Paul Schrader worked with Scorsese and De Niro on *Taxi Driver* and was recruited to rewrite the script. His version put greater emphasis on the brothers' relationship. Scorsese was receptive and worked with De Niro on revising Schrader's script.

The visceral violence of *Raging Bull* caused controversy. Pauline Kael was scathing: 'By removing the specifics or blurring them, Scorsese doesn't produce universals—he produces banality. . . . Scorsese is putting his unmediated obsessions on the screen, trying to turn raw, pulp power into art by removing it from the particulars of observation and narrative. . . . He aestheticizes pulp and kills it.' De Niro's performance she likened to 'a swollen puppet with only bits and pieces of a character inside'.[1] Roger Ebert took the opposite position: '*Raging Bull* equates sexuality and violence because one of the criticisms of this movie is that we never really get to know the central character. I don't agree with that. I think Scorsese and Robert De Niro do a fearless job of showing us the precise feelings of their central character, the former boxing champion Jake LaMotta.'[2] The trade press was more cautious. Joseph McBride in *Variety* was impressed by the boxing scenes and concluded that the film 'should do well in class situations, but may flounder in the mass market due to the offputting character'. The problem was that 'the director excels at whipping up an emotional storm, but seems unaware that there is any need for quieter, more introspective moments in drama.... Scorsese never makes credible why a woman should put up with such incredible abuse for so long. The inarticulate performance of newcomer Moriarty ... never adequately fills in the blanks of the character.'[3]

In Britain, the Rank organization refused to distribute the film. Critics were less hostile. Philip Oakes of the *Sunday Times* found the sense of ritual overwhelming. He concluded that the film 'pulses with unimaginable emotion and blood about to be shed'.[4] Tom Pulleine in the *Guardian* was more guarded: 'The episodic narrative admits a rigorous spareness and refusal to explain.'[5]

Roger Ebert has been consistent in his admiration, as his 1998 review reveals:

> It is remarkable that Moriarty, herself 19, had the presence to so convincingly portray the later stages of a woman in a bad marriage.... *Raging Bull* is the most painful and heartrending portrait of jealousy in the cinema—an *Othello* for our times. It's the best film I've seen about the low self-esteem, sexual inadequacy, and fear that lead some men to abuse women.[6]

Hostility has melted away. Amy Taubin of the *Village Voice* could write in 2000: 'The sense of risk is palpable and the payoff is exhilarating. There's not a single pulled or wasted punch. The film is a perfect match of form and content.'[7] Ty Burr of the *Boston Globe* was equally enthusiastic in 2005 and made a perceptive comment on the film's reception:

> In the final scene, the has-been boxer turned night club impressionist flatly rehearses Brando's speech from *Waterfront,* and the pathos is overwhelming. But for himself, La-Motta could have been a contender with staying power, and he knows it. If you're not moved by that, then Scorsese—and by extension the entire aesthetic of his filmmaking generation—is simply not for you.[8]

The film ranks fourth in the AFI's 2007 list of the greatest American films and seventieth in the IMDb's list of the top 250 films.[9]

Subjective Impression

The film charts Jake's rise to fame and his subsequent decline. It is presented in black and white, like an old newsreel. The emotional response will depend on whether the fight scenes are interpreted as glorifying or condemning violence. Scorsese seems fascinated by it, which I find disturbing. Much is made of Janiro's good looks. The camera lingers on the damage inflicted by Jake, who shows no concern at what he has done. Elsewhere, the violence is romanticized by the ritualistic pacing of the music. If soft porn can shelter under the guise of art, so can violence.

The first scene shows a middle-aged man remembering his lines; in the next, a boxer is seen fighting in the ring. We assume that we are seeing Jake at two stages of his life, but we are left to make the connection. His sexual jealousy and unwillingness to cooperate with the Mafia are revealed. At the close of the film, he is preparing for a performance in which he will read from the works of Paddy Chayefsky, Shakespeare and Tennessee Williams. I have difficulty making connections between these disparate images. They make me curious about Jake's decline, which may be Scorsese's intention, yet I feel uneasy about what is omitted. I want to know about Jake's family. And what happened to his first wife who disappears so peremptorily? This is another film in which inconvenient facts are glossed over.

Scorsese's attitude to his protagonist's jealousy and chauvinism is no clearer. He may have assumed that the sort of men who saw his film did not beat their wives, which is to condescend to his characters. Art should do more than this. Values need testing and their consequences considered.

Jake's final speech reveals his insight: 'I coulda had class. I coulda been a contender. I coulda been somebody instead of a bum, which is what I am.' Yet the speech made to his reflection in the dressing-room mirror dwells on what might have been. There is no sense of looking forward. Jake does not learn. Joey and Vickie learn in the sense that they sever their ties with Jake, but how they have been changed by their experiences remains unexplored like so much in this film.

Jake's fate is subordinated to Scorsese's desire to make an artistic statement. The rise and fall of the unlikable hero is shaped self-consciously, beginning and ending with the older Jake in his dressing room and punctuated by bouts of violence in and out of the ring. The biblical quotation 'Once I was blind and now I can see' (John 9:25) appears in the final frames to hammer home the moral. The film's arc-like narrative structure, the religious props in the homes (noticeable when Jake takes Vickie to his father's flat) and the backlit image of the bare-chested Jake draped over the ropes as he undergoes his mortification betoken a spiritual experience, yet the film fails to elicit a sense of catharsis. Jake remains as much an enigma at the end as he was at the beginning. His journey has brought him loneliness. My only emotion is admiration for some slick film-making.

Analysis

Scathing reviews from Dan Georgakas and David Thomson dating from the film's release cannot easily be dismissed.[10] For Georgakas, the narrative flaws are paramount. He cites the opening scene, which introduces the overweight, middle-aged Jake. This cuts to a flashback of a fight. 'The scene telegraphs the theme of decay which consumes the film, and it's a forthright indication of the director's slap-dash attitude to narrative needs whenever tempted by an opportunity to spotlight De Niro's, or his own, technical flair.'[11] The consequence is that the narrative becomes fractured: 'It is as if scenes were written for acting class, rather than for incorporation into a narrative structure. They allow the actors to shout and weep and move dramatically as often as possible.... But the brilliant pieces do not add up to a coherent whole.'[12] The test is how much each scene contributes to the narrative and on this basis, Georgakas has a valid criticism. One fight is much like another, while Jake's attitude to women is signalled early on and does not change. Scorsese might argue that he is not recounting a narrative, but offering a psychological study of one man's decline. Yet his partial view of the man militates against psychological insights. A narrative is there in the progress of Jake's career; it is just not well done.

Georgakas's second criticism is that the portrait of Jake is superficial. Neither the reason Jake becomes a boxer nor why he refuses to cooperate with the Mafia is explained. Equally baffling is how somebody with boxing as his only apparent interest comes to be giving readings from classic and contemporary writers.

Thomson is equally critical, but more acerbic. He offers two additional criticisms. First, the film is exploitative because the director knows little about boxing: 'The fight scenes are as fanciful as they are brutal. Scorsese settles for closeups cross-cut, turning every fight into a confrontation of movie manner—whereas real fights are relationships that demand the two-shot style.'[13] This echoes Georgakas's criticism that a display of technique is taking over from storytelling. Scorsese emphasizes the violence by concentrating on visible damage, which entails body blows being omitted in favour of damaged faces spurting with blood. Context distinguishes exploitation from art and though Scorsese provides the trappings of a serious film, the substance belies this. The fight scenes may be brief, but they are pivotal, and he revels in every blow.

Thomson's other criticism is that Scorsese knows even less about women than about boxing. This is evident in his portrait of Moriarty: 'Just as the camera treats her like golden meat, so the film begins to furnish the mythology that she is only a body, somehow willing to be scrutinized, and therefore innately promiscuous. That is the real sadomasochistic spasm of pinup photography, and it is thrust in many films that would like to despise the "trashiness" of pinups.'[14] Once again context is crucial, and the film offers nothing with which to counter Thomson's accusation. The camera dwells lasciviously on Vickie at her first appearance, when Jake's response would be more illuminating. Scorsese might argue that we are seeing her as Jake does, but to adopt the character's point of view is a directorial decision, forcing the audience into the role of voyeur. As Vickie ages, albeit unconvincingly, she is relegated to the background, which means that we see little of the couple's home life. Scorsese manages to reveal more about himself than his subject. In common with Coppola and Hitchcock, a streak of misogyny runs through his early films, which makes the strong female roles in *Alice Doesn't Live Here Anymore* (US, 1984) and *After Hours* (US, 1985) all the more intriguing. Moriarty is never allowed to become more than what Thomson terms an icon of desire, which helps to account for the contradictory opinions on her performance: your view depends on your liking for icons.[15]

An alternative approach comes from Francesco Caviglia, who examines the role of the traditional Italian male, which was being usurped by consumerism from the mid-1960s onwards, but which persisted in Italian American society.[16] Similar changes occur in other agrarian societies with a strong religious tradition. There are four characteristics:

1. Self-denial. For Caviglia, *Raging Bull* brings self-denial to paroxysm as Jake spurns his wife's sexual advances and urges his brother to hit him. The consequence can be success or misery, with both being apparent in *Raging Bull.*
2. Violent jealousy. This is evident in Jake's proprietorial attitude towards his wife, which destroys his relationships.
3. The threat from a hierarchical and hostile outside world. This is more noticeable in Italian American films than those emanating from Italy, *The Godfather* being the exemplar. Jake has his brush with the authorities when he is arrested and imprisoned, but how his encounter with the courts and the penal system affects him is glossed over.
4. Familism. *Moral familism* is embodied in the close-knit family. This has admirable qualities, such as care for older relatives, but it can restrict ambition and social mobility. Caviglia suggests that Jake goes to pieces after severing family ties. *Raging Bull* might make more sense if this were the case, but it is difficult to demonstrate, given that the family is never seen. Its absence leaves a void at the heart of the film. That empty flat where Jake takes Vickie on their first date never rings true. The trappings of the traditional Italian family adorn the rooms just as their Catholic values permeate the film, but only ghosts are there. As to Jake's rift with Joey, this is precipitated by Jake's breakdown rather than the rift causing psychological problems. We need to know far more about him to make sense of his alienation.

   More sinister is *amoral familism,* a concept used to explain the lack of economic development in southern Italian villages, their occupants being unable to come together for the common good. This is a world in which organizations like the Mafia flourish. The clannish loyalties and closed communities evident in *The Godfather* and *Mean Streets* are relegated to the background in *Raging Bull.* They might be claustrophobic for audiences and characters alike, but at least they provide context.

Scorsese reprises familiar preoccupations. The loner battling with society in *Taxi Driver* is that model of self-denial, Travis Bickle; *Raging Bull* transposes his implosion to the boxing ring. We seem destined to return to the world of *Mean Streets* as Joey and Salvy walk through the Bronx early in the film, but this theme is abandoned as cursorily as Jake's first wife. Thereafter, the community is sketchily represented by a church dance and a couple of scenes at the swimming pool. Society beyond the Mafia and nightclub audiences remains as invisible as it is in *The Godfather.* It has to be Scorsese's choice to focus on Jake's career to the exclusion of the wider world. This is a risky strategy, given that he fails to make the boxing interesting or the character believable. Michael Bliss concurs: 'What we are supposed to see in *Raging Bull* is the progress of an unreflective, unselfconscious character towards wisdom and self-awareness. Unfortunately, while this is clearly the film's intention, it is at a variance with its effects.[17] A relentless concentration on one person can work in film, as Bresson demonstrates in *Mouchette* (France, 1967). Jake is one-dimensional by comparison. His plight does not move us. He functions as a vehicle for De Niro's virtuoso performance.

Robin Wood, writing in 1986, showed more enthusiasm for *Raging Bull* than Georgakas, Thomson, or Bliss, seeing it as an eloquent sermon on the need for gay liberation.[18] It is easy to discern a homosexual subtext in a film about a group of men, but harder to justify when the only physical contact between them is familial (the bond between Jake and Joey), or professional (the clinches in the boxing ring). The camera never dwells on Jake the way it does on Vickie. More telling is Wood's worry about the film's lack of specificity: 'The meaning the film finally seems to offer its audience—Jake's progress towards some kind of partial understanding, acceptance or grace—must strike one as quite inadequate to validate the project, and actually misleading: the film remains extremely vague about the nature of the grace or how it has been achieved.'[19] Jake confesses in his final speech that he is a bum, revealing his awareness of how far he has sunk, but the audience already knows this. Can his long and bloody journey yield no greater insight? Jake does not find God or anything else during his decline. We never discover whether he even finds consolation.

As Ty Burr perceived, Scorsese's approach to violence divides viewers. One way of considering how the director guides his audiences' reactions is to use the concept of the implied author. What viewpoint does Scorsese want us to adopt? Initially we see a solitary figure shadow-boxing in slow motion. The tone is set by the pseudo-religiosity of Mascagni's score, indicating that we are expected to interpret the tale as a tragedy on an operatic scale. This gives no indication whether we should view Jake with compassion, pity, or contempt. Scorsese's writings and interviews, as well as the biblical quotation in the closing frames, suggest that he intended us to experience La Motta's redemption, yet the film's relish for violence makes a different point.

Richard A. Blake examines the use of blood imagery in Scorsese's films. In *Raging Bull* it is evident in Jake's desire to atone for his sins by inviting opponents and his brother to hit his face, and in the washing of blood from his body.[20] Thomson would probably cite these scenes as evidence of sadomasochism. As Blake notes, the former Calvinist divinity student Paul Schrader 'maintains that a film reaches the transcendent by paring away props to the senses and forcing the viewer to confront the spiritual realities behind the images.... He argues that even plot, character motivation, and long shots can distract viewers from the spirituality of the image on the screen.'[21] Schrader could have been thinking of Dreyer or Bresson. He might be more circumspect today than when he expressed these views as a graduate student.

Harness them to Scorsese's Catholic sensibility and the result is a film of unrelieved gloom which never reaches the spirituality to which Schrader aspired. Thomson is scathing: 'Jake LaMotta's ugly nature has been dumped upon by the trite aesthetics of chic drab photography and FM easy listening.'[22] It should be said that Thomson still has reservations about Scorsese's admiration of immature male role-playing but now views *Raging Bull* as Scorsese's greatest film, which is as intriguing as his volte-face over *The Godfather.*[23]

Having Jake quote from *On the Waterfront* in the final scene sums up my reservations about the film. As Georgakas points out, Brando's character realizes that he has been betrayed by the code he has followed and by his brother; Jake has suffered no such betrayal and has sampled fame: 'In *Raging Bull,* the moment is just homage to another film.'[24] Scorsese's love affair with old films seems stifling. Nor could he escape his Italian American background, which acted as a brake on his choice of subjects at this stage in his career and restricted his outlook. A great director should transcend his material and find a greater range of moods. In *Raging Bull,* Scorsese seems intent on orchestrating our responses rather than letting the work speak. He should trust his material and his audience.

The Piano (Australia/NZ/France, 1993):
Love in a Rough Place

Production companies: Jan Chapman Productions/CiBY 2000
Producer: Jan Chapman
Director/Screenplay: Jane Campion
Photographer: Stuart Dryburgh
Production Designer: Andrew McAlpine
Music: Michael Nyman
Editor: Veronika Jenet
Cast: Holly Hunter (Ada McGrath), Harvey Keitel (George Baines), Sam Neill
     (Alisdair Stewart), Anna Paquin (Flora)

Synopsis

In 1847, Ada and her daughter, Flora, are sent to New Zealand, where the mute Ada
is to marry Stewart. Mother and daughter disembark on a remote beach, where they
spend the night. When Stewart and the hired hands arrive the following morning,
Ada's piano proves too heavy for them and is abandoned. Ada feels out of place
among the gossiping older women of the expatriate community. She visits a neigh-
bour, Baines, seeking help in retrieving her piano. He refuses, but when she plays the
instrument on the beach, he is watching.

Baines visits Stewart, offering to buy the piano in exchange for land and piano
lessons. Stewart agrees. Ada is angry at not being consulted, but Stewart persuades
her to give Baines lessons. It is Ada who plays, while Baines is more interested in
her than the lessons. He proposes that she should earn the piano back at the rate of
one black key for each lesson. The 'price' becomes sexual. Flora is resentful at being
excluded and watches through the keyhole as the couple make love. When Stewart
admonishes her for joining in the Maori children's suggestive games, she becomes
annoyed and blurts out what is happening. Baines has grown uncomfortable with the
deceit involved in the relationship and returns the piano. Stewart offers to arrange
for Baines to have piano lessons with somebody else, but Baines rejects the offer.
Ada has lost interest in playing and goes to Baines. He tells her to leave if she has
any feeling for him, but he cannot keep up this stance. Flora tells Stewart where Ada

has gone. He watches the couple from outside the house as they make love. Jealousy spurs him into being more demonstrative that night, but Flora interrupts the couple. The next morning, Stewart boards up the windows and doors, imprisoning Ada. She retaliates by not allowing him to touch her, though she can touch him. When Baines announces that he is moving away, Stewart removes the planks. Ada responds by sending a reluctant Flora to Baines with a love message written on a piano key. Flora gives Stewart the message instead and in his anger he attacks the piano with an axe. One of Ada's fingers is chopped off and it is this which Flora takes to Baines.

Stewart is filled with remorse and anger. When he has tended Ada, he goes to Baines's house. Flora is sleeping there. He holds a gun to Baines's head and declares that he wants Baines and Ada gone. Accompanied by Flora, the couple leave by boat. Ada insists on the piano being thrown overboard. Her foot catches on a rope attached it, dragging her into the water, but she frees herself. Baines and Ada are next seen living together, with Ada learning to talk again and giving piano lessons. Baines has made her a prosthetic finger. The final moments reprise the underwater scene, with Ada still attached to the piano.

Cultural Context

The Piano derived from an idea by Jane Campion, though Jane Mander's novel *The Story of a New Zealand River* (1920) may have been the unacknowledged source.[1] The critical success of *Angel at My Table* (NZ/Australia, 1990) gave Campion access to international funding and Hollywood stars for *The Piano*. The outlay was justified: for a budget of US$8 million, worldwide earnings amounted to US$116 million by April 1994, with US earnings rivalling those of *Crocodile Dundee* (Peter Fairman, Australia, 1986), the most popular Australian film till that date.[2] *The Piano* could be said to have launched the New Zealand film industry, which had its commercial success consolidated by Peter Jackson.

Reviews were generally positive, with aesthetic grounds being cited most often for the film's success.[3] Desson Howe of the *Washington Post* was ecstatic: '*The Piano* plays itself with such contrapuntal richness, it resonates in you forever.... There is something mystically compelling about writer/director Jane Campion's 1993 Cannes winner. On one level it's a fairy story for adults. But on others, it evokes powerful eroticism, sexual mustiness, emotional anguish and numerous other themes.'[4] Hal Hinson, writing for the same paper, was more cautious: '*The Piano* is a moody, atmospheric film that ... conveys as much through suggestion and implication as by direct statement. The performances, too, are exceptionally rich and detailed. Yet in some degree they remain mysterious, as if Campion had insisted that the characters remain half-hidden in shadow.'[5] For Geoff Brown of *The Times,* 'Campion still thinks and feels afresh, and thinks in images.... *The Piano* takes us right to the heart of sexual repression and erotic desires.'[6] Derek Malcolm in the *Guardian* had doubts about Harvey Keitel, but concluded that 'The film boldly traverses territory akin to some unwritten Brontë novel. And it does so with notable passion and conviction.'[7] Iain Johnstone of the *Sunday Times* was more equivocal: 'Beautiful, but it's hard to believe a frame of it.... You may be transported by the poetry of this strange, brave and often beautiful film or maybe not.... Somehow the signature lingers longer than the painting.'[8] Richard Alleva in *Commonweal* took a more critical line: 'The Piano, far from being a masterpiece, isn't even a good movie. It suffers from something that is lethal to dramatists and film directors: a basic lack of curiosity about what makes human beings tick.'[9] As a measure of audience responses, Web site comments are generally positive and come mainly from women. The dissenters are men.[10]

Subjective Impression

This is a film about how feelings are expressed. Ada accedes to her father's wishes, being sent abroad to a man she has never seen. She shows no strong objection to this life-changing event. Being mute, she conveys her feelings through sign language, which her daughter interprets, and through piano playing. Her new husband does not interest her. Like some D. H. Lawrence heroine, she is attracted to the rougher Baines, even if initially she is wary of him. Stewart regards his wife as a social adornment. Only when he discovers Baines's treachery does he display stronger feelings. Jealousy turns to anger, evident in his attack on the piano. Just as quickly it turns to remorse, but the damage is done.

Stewart loses most, but perhaps this is a male viewpoint. Baines's feelings are difficult to read, so it is not clear how far his affair with Ada is premeditated. Even when it becomes explicit, we are unsure of the depth of their relationship. Flora is initially close to her mother, but her loyalties shift. She feels sidelined by her mother's affair and sides with Stewart until his outburst of violence. Then she turns to Baines, accepting him as protector.

All the characters have something to learn. Ada grapples with her reawakened sexuality. Stewart has to confront the consequences of his behaviour. Baines's gruff persona is not obviously appealing, yet Ada discerns something attractive in it. Like Dean in *Black Narcissus,* he has to modify his bachelor existence, though he lacks Dean's good humour. Flora matures, moving away from her mother and towards the men. She learns the difficulties of trying to do the right thing, her petulance often overriding common sense: the film's climax is set in motion by her decision to give the piano key to Stewart instead of Baines. She discovers the consequences of betrayal as Stewart's attitude forces her to shift her allegiance to Baines.

My initial sympathies are with Ada, who is put upon by her father and taken for granted by Stewart. Her peevishness and her affair with Baines cause my sympathies to shift towards Stewart, a decent man who does not know how to deal with her. His outburst of violence and Baines's uncharacteristic gentleness towards Flora and Ada prompt me to see both men differently. Flora's behaviour seems inconsistent and exasperates me, but her youth provides an excuse.

This is a film of fluctuating emotions and changing loyalties. In this it could be said to resemble real life; my problem is the inconsistency of the characters' responses. The mute Ada who obeys her father, crossing the world to marry a man she has never seen, is not the woman who embarks on an affair. She becomes steadily less credible in her reactions. What makes her deceive Stewart is unclear, which is symptomatic of the sketchy representation of their relationship. This weakness extends to other characters: Stewart's tragedy is ignored, Flora's fierce loyalty to her mother is compromised without any response from Ada, while Baines changes from being an onlooker to a lover with little preparation for the audience. Campion's agenda seems to derive from the demands of the plot rather than the motivations of her characters, which is a flaw I find hard to forgive.

Analysis

The Piano has generated more literature than any other film of its decade. Though it has maintained its status in film guides and with the public, it has attracted criticism on three fronts: its attitude towards women, its treatment of race and the quality of the storytelling.

A film by a woman about a woman might be expected to adopt a feminist viewpoint. Campion invests Ada with a modern sensibility while setting the film in the past, an ambiguity which allows a range of feminist interpretations to be applied. Ada takes control of her life to the extent that she rebels against Stewart rather than adopting the role of compliant wife, but only to set up home with another man. A trenchant critic like bell hooks has none of this: '[Campion] does employ feminist "tropes", even as her work betrays feminist visions of female actualization, celebrates and eroticizes male domination.'[11] Stewart is castigated: 'Rather than being deterred by her love for Baines, it appears to excite Stewart's passion; he longs to possess her all the more. Unable to win her back from Baines, he expresses his rage, rooted in misogyny and sexism, by physically attacking her and chopping off her finger with an ax.'[12] Ada is perceived as a victim of gender politics. A weakness of this approach is that the historical context is ignored: a single mother in the nineteenth century had few options. The second criticism is that hooks ignores emotions: this is a tale rooted in frustrated love, passion and betrayal rather than misogyny and sexism, while domination is a loaded term. It could be argued that Ada dominates the men, playing them off against each other.

A student viewer, Allison Yanos, adopts a more moderate stance, following Foucault in acknowledging complexity in gender relations rather than inevitable conflict. Her conclusion is that Baines does not exert power over Ada but helps her to assume her gender identity.[13] Sue Gillett also discerns something more than domination in the relationships. Hollywood spectacle is absent, allowing female audiences to identify with Campion's female leads and become immersed in their lives rather than seeing them as icons. By contrast, 'The veils Campion removes from her men leave them naked and exposed, vulnerable in the face of their own desires (which ... might leave them open to rejection) and the desires of women.' The consequence is that 'Campion's narratives are driven by this will to free her lovers from the romantic merry-go-round of conflict and idealisation, letting them rest in a compassionate embrace.'[14] This helps to explain the film's appeal to women, though not men's opposition: they might prefer to identify with the higher-status Stewart and feel baffled by Ada's behaviour.

The Bluebeard legend is rendered in silhouette for the villagers' pageant, inviting comparisons between Stewart's behaviour and Bluebeard. The link is made by Peter N. Chumo II.[15] Cyndy Hendershot develops it:

> Stewart's attempt to adopt the role of Bluebeard indicates his attempt to be the traditional European husband: *The Piano* consistently argues that aligning oneself with European imperialism is tantamount to becoming pathetically monstrous. Becoming Bluebeard means for Stewart becoming the imperial master in the home: the Maoris' reaction to the production of Bluebeard indicates that they see deeper implications in the fairy tale than merely a husband's anger at his wife.[16]

This is to stretch the analogy. What distinguishes Bluebeard is that he has a succession of wives and murders them. His new bride discovers this and has to confront her likely fate. Bluebeard is hardly the traditional European husband as Hendershot asserts, while his connection with European imperialism is tenuous, the story predating the rise of empires. Nor was a European story likely to figure in a nineteenth-century New Zealand village pageant staged by British expatriates. Campion ignores authenticity in favour of making a point about gender and racial politics.

The Piano was released in the heyday of postcolonial theory, so it is not surprising that Campion's treatment of the Maoris sparked comment. Stuart Klawans uses the Bluebeard performance to examine the film's racial implications: 'A group of Maoris, alarmed at the pantomime in the ... pageant, storms the stage; though later, when a similar crisis erupts in real life, the same Maoris don't budge. People who are malleable and credulous, the film seems to argue, are likely to be undependable to boot.'[17] Mark A. Reid takes a world-weary stance: 'The film presents another recycled colonial romance in which indigenous people are displaced, like the Maori people in the film's mise-en-scène.'[18] Baines's role comes in for particular attention, his closeness to the Maoris distinguishing him from his compatriots. Like Dean in *Black Narcissus,* he belongs to neither community but functions as an intermediary. Reid asserts that Baines's adoption of Maori tattoos signifies his colonization of the Maori body; an alternative interpretation is that the Maoris are colonizing the colonizer.[19] The film's principal characters are immigrants, and the indigenous population has little to do beyond signifying the remoteness of the location in geographical and cultural terms. To give Maoris a greater role would be to tell a different story, though it is noteworthy that when Stewart collects Ada and her possessions from the beach, a Maori stands behind him, mimicking him. If the film reveals any irony, it is in the knowingness of the Maoris.

The middle-class girl who is thrust into an alien world was a mainstay of Victorian literature from Wilkie Collins to Mrs Gaskell and Sheridan Le Fanu. She fell on hard times, or struggled to make a new life among the lower classes. Sometimes she did both. *The Piano* is a variation on this story which need have no racial overtones. How far a postcolonial perspective should be applied to a film made in the 1990s and set in the 1840s is another matter. An obvious comparison is made between the settlers' Victorian prudery and the Maori's relaxed attitude towards sexuality, notably when Stewart stops Flora from participating in the Maori children's games of simulated masturbation. As Victorian notions of morality date from later in the century, and Scottish Presbyterianism is not evident in the film, Campion's point seems misplaced, particularly as none of her principal characters is a model of sexual propriety.

A number of such inconsistencies, implausibilities and omissions are enumerated by Harry Pearson, John Simon and Richard Alleva.[20] Why should Ada's commentary at the opening and closing of the film be in the voice of a child and why is a mute woman talking about herself? Why is Ada mute, and does it add anything to the story? The love triangle would exist if she could speak. What happened to Flora's father? How did Stewart find his bride and why is there no formal marriage ceremony? How does Baines come to be taking tea in Stewart's house while the women talk about Ada? If Ada has the will to stop speaking, why does she agree so meekly to her piano being abandoned on the beach? How does a piano remain usable when left below high tide level? How do the men in the film make a living? Neither Baines nor Stewart is seen farming. Crucially, why does Ada send a written message to an illiterate man? (Clare Corbett worked as assistant editor on the film and asserts that he would understand the import of the message merely by receiving the key, but Ada's gesture renders useless the piano which is her means of expression.[21]) And no pianist would use a prosthetic finger in preference to changing the fingering. With so many loose ends, the film dwindles into a string of beautiful images. Pearson is scathing: 'Those who expect a fundamental understanding of mise-en-scène will not find it here, nor will they find much in the way of internal logic, a necessity, I think, if a movie is to retain its power over time, and not to be seen as the cultural artifact of a changing and troublesome era in masculine-feminine relations.'[22]

Two aspects of the film which call for particular attention are the acting and the music. Holly Hunter has to show the developing relationship with Baines by expression and gesture. As Alleva puts it, 'we have to be gripped by the process, not the outcome.' The trouble is that 'Campion has turned the usually irrepressible Holly Hunter into something monochromatically dour, even forbidding—a white mask of ungracious chastity. That's a fine image to start from, but the actress doesn't alter it significantly as the sex duel proceeds. By the time our heroine rushes into Baines's arms, she seems guided more by the dictates of plot than by passion.'[23] This dourness extends to the men. Baines is a loner and inexpressive by nature, which makes him an unappealing figure. Keitel seems hard put to know what to do with him. Stewart's restraint is never explained, given that he sought a bride from the other side of the world. His sense of loss becomes evident in the final scenes, but, as Baines is taking Ada to something better, by this point in the story we should be sharing her exaltation. Campion seems to constrain her performers, recalling Hal Hinson's opinion that the characters never really emerge from the shadows. They might be inhibited, but they have to be believable. It is the older immigrant women who give a sense of life beyond the camera, even though Campion makes them peripheral. The other exception is Flora, who has a vitality denied to the adult leads, yet even she becomes worn down by her surroundings.

In a study of music in Campion's earlier work, Geraldine Bloustien points out that in *Two Friends* (Australian Television Corporation, 1986), music symbolizes a cultured world to which the heroine is ultimately denied access.[24] The use of music in *the Piano* is more complex. The cultured world Ada leaves behind is hardly seen, but she is distanced from it by her self-imposed silence, by having to bring up a child alone and, above all, by her exile. The importance of music in her life becomes understandable, even if Campion's use of the device is clumsy. It is impossible to divine Ada's emotions from her playing, yet this is its purpose in the film.

Michael Nyman is a composer who polarizes opinions, and his work in this film is no exception. For Matthew Hancock, 'The brilliance lies in bringing out the beauty from within the sombre tones through a rhythmic pulse that has the audience lost in the music, sucked in by the hope lying within the despair of the characters and landscapes.'[25] Simon takes the opposing view: 'Except for one piece of mauled Chopin, the score is by Michael Nyman, one of the most self-important, overrated, and, to my ears, worthless composers around; for this period piece, he has written his usual New Age claptrap.'[26] Hunter played the music herself. According to the composer, she was less good at precise rhythmic passages, which must have proved a challenge given that Nyman is stronger on repetitive, almost hypnotic rhythm than on melody or harmony.[27] The consequence of this mismatch is that Hunter gives the impression of limbering up for a performance which never comes.

Aside from the music's quality is the matter of its appropriateness. Why should a nineteenth-century woman be playing compositions so clearly belonging to a later age? The incongruity is jarring, pointing up that this is a drama for late twentieth-century audiences rather than a faithful recreation of the period. So long as audiences accept the conceit, then the music fulfils its purpose. The risk is that the film dates along with the music, losing any aspirations to universality and dwindling into Pearson's 'cultural artifact of a changing and troublesome era'.

The final minutes of the film are as problematic as any. Following Fellini's example, Campion offers two endings. In one, Ada is dragged underwater with the piano; in the other, she frees herself and is seen living with Baines and Flora. She gives piano lessons and is learning to talk again. The first ending lacks internal logic: assuming a piano could be pushed off a small boat without overturning it, why should Ada discard something which is so important to her? No musician would discard a piano so casually. For bell hooks, the piano is soiled with tainted memories, in which case why not leave it behind?[28] Barbara Quart is more speculative: 'This comes not out of any confusion on Campion's part, but rather from her openness to irrational forces resistant to neat understanding and verbalization. Perhaps the instrument is related to death because it has filled all Ada's needs and replaced other human attachments.'[29] This leaves unanswered questions. Why is a rope fastened to the piano and how does it become caught around Ada's shoe? Why should she try to commit suicide with the prospect of happiness ahead of her? Campion's happy ending might be Ada's hallucination as she drowns. Alternatively, it might be a sop to Hollywood values, but it is weak, given all that has happened, and renders the underwater sequence superfluous. Its optimism should not be taken at face value, according to Carmel Bird, for whom Ada's veil portends no happy ending.[30] Campion reprises the image of Ada being pinned underwater, suggesting to Alan A. Stone the tragedy which lies ahead: 'Caught, finally, in the ordinariness of a life without art, she dreams of the imprisoning silence of death.'[31] This invests the film with a subtlety which is hard to justify, given the contradictory nature of the final scenes. The heroine's suicide in Tolstoy's *Anna Karenina* shows how it should be done.

The combination of high production values, moody photography, sophisticated dramatic devices and high seriousness signifies that Campion intended *The Piano* to be treated as art. It aspires to resonate beyond the confines of the story, touching on what Quart terms the mythic, with its themes of love, conquest and revenge.[32] Yet despite echoes of *Bluebeard* and *Beauty and the Beast, The Piano* never rises above the level of high-class melodrama. Bird is perceptive on this point:

> The film does not have the quality of a fairy tale in which strange things can be accepted without motive, rhyme or reason. In dream we accept, but the fact of silence does not have the nature of a dream. It is such an odd and dramatic piece of behaviour, and I think a storyteller can't be allowed to shrug it off.[33]

With such devices as Ada's muteness, Nyman's out-of-period music and the seahorse drawn in the sand, *The Piano* glories in artifice (or artiness), while aspiring to realism in its settings and ethnographic detail. Campion's visual flair is not married to convincing characters or a strong dramatic sense, the consequence being that despite the visual pleasures, the narrative loses direction.

This work fits Dwight Macdonald's definition of middlebrow culture, which so irks Umberto Eco: it borrows avant-garde procedures after they are worn out and bends them to create a message understood by all; it constructs the message as a source of effects which can be sold as art and satisfies consumers by convincing them that they have experienced culture.[34] Eco decries this distaste for popularization, but, when confronted by *The Piano,* I can appreciate Macdonald's point.

–16–

Kill Bill: Volume 1 (US, 2003):
Violence as Art

Production companies: A Band Apart/Miramax Films
Producer: Lawrence Bender
Director/Screenplay: Quentin Tarantino
Photography: Robert Richardson
Production design: Yohei Taneda, David Wasco
Art Director: David Bradford
Editor: Sally Menke
Cast: Uma Thurman (the Bride), Lucy Liu (O-Ren Ishii), Vivica A. Fox (Vernita Green), Daryl Hannah (Elle Driver)

Synopsis

In a preface, Bill shoots the injured and pregnant Bride. Only his hands are seen. The Bride is next encountered visiting Vernita in American suburbia. The two women fight with anything which comes to hand, the Bride eventually killing her adversary with a knife. She crosses Vernita's name off the list of Deadly Viper Assassination Squad members who are to be killed in reprisal for what happened to her. In another flashback, the injured Bride is seen lying in an El Paso chapel, being examined by a policeman who treats her as though she is already dead.

A stylish woman walks into a hospital. This is Elle Driver. She changes into a nurse's uniform and finds the Bride unconscious and alone. As Elle is about to administer a lethal injection, Bill telephones to order that the mission be aborted. Honour demands that the Bride should not be killed in her sleep.

Four years later, the Bride awakens after a mosquito bite. She goes in search of O-Ren Ishii, the next name on the list. An animé sequence reveals O-Ren's life story. As a child, she witnessed the murder of her parents. Her revenge was to kill the paedophile boss of the gang who murdered them. By the age of twenty, she was a top assassin.

O-Ren has taken control of Japanese criminal gangs, decapitating the only gangland boss who opposes her. The Bride commissions a sword from a retired craftsman in Okinawa and stages a showdown at a busy club. She disposes of O-Ren's bodyguards. O-Ren escapes, but the Bride intercepts her in the garden and kills her. The Bride leaves Japan in her quest for Bill, unaware that her daughter is alive.

Cultural Context

Quentin Tarantino came to public attention in the early 1990s with *Reservoir Dogs* (US, 1992) and *Pulp Fiction* (US, 1994). *Jackie Brown* (US, 1997) had less commercial success. A six-year gap followed before *Kill Bill* was ready. Uniquely for a high-profile film, its length meant that it was released in two parts. Pulp crime fiction stories from *Black Mark* magazine provided the inspiration, and there were liberal borrowings from other films.[1]

The grudging admiration of Peter Bradshaw in the *Guardian* was representative of one school of critical reaction: 'The extravagant power of his infantilist genes makes objections and qualifications look obtuse. What comes to mind, frankly, is Godard's playful tribute to Nicholas Ray as the essence of cinema.... *Kill Bill* just leaves you feeling excited: pointlessly, wildly excited. How many films can do that?'[2] Something of this excitement communicated itself to Roger Ebert, who likened Tarantino to 'a virtuoso violinist racing through "The Flight of the Bumblebee"', even if the film was 'all storytelling and no story'.[3] The opposition was forthright. Documentary film-maker Nick Broomfield declared: 'If I'd made that, I'd change my name,' while for David Denby in the *New Yorker:* '*Kill Bill* is what's formally known as decadence and commonly known as crap.'[4] J. Hoberman of the *Village Voice* was equally dismissive: 'There's not much innocence in the Tarantino world—but neither is there any real consequence.... Flowing no less freely than blood, a stream of ersatz wisdom irrigates the action.'[5] Kim Newman acknowledged that Tarantino was maturing technically but found the subject matter regressive: 'This is a down-and-dirty kung-fu picture with embarrassing costumes, cobbled-together soundtracks, gushers of gore and characters who have the most primary-coloured emotional range imaginable.'[6]

The public has fewer reservations. A 2004 estimate was that the two parts of *Kill Bill* would take ten times their production costs of US$55 million. As a measure of the film's international popularity, of the US$110 million box-office takings for *Kill Bill: Volume 1,* 60 per cent came from outside of North America; according to Miramax, 60 per cent of viewers were males aged between 18 and 34.[7] In January 2008, the film ranked 119th among the top 250 films on the IMDb Web site, with males in the 18–29 age group comprising 49 per cent of the voters.[8] Fifteen months earlier, it was in fifty-third position.

Subjective Impression

The flashback structure makes events difficult to follow, yet by dividing the narrative with inter-titles which place events in a time sequence, Tarantino is indicating that the story cannot be dismissed in favour of the excitement of the moment. The Bride takes revenge on the attackers who left her for dead on her wedding day, a premise which gives scope for scenes in Japan and America as she seeks out her victims. The killing of Vernita Green establishes the pattern for the film's violence. Tarantino subverts concern for his characters by encouraging us to laugh at the film's excesses or be excited by the violence. At best, the characters arouse fleeting affection, but they cannot be mistaken for real people. The disjunction becomes acute when the animated sequence of O-Ren's childhood ends. We are confronted by actors again, but the characters they portray are no more real than the animated characters we have just seen. The nearest the film comes to a moral dilemma is when Vernita's daughter returns from school while the Bride and Vernita are fighting. The two women show a semblance of friendship, the truce continuing after the girl goes to her room. Her presence has changed the two women's relationship, and we anticipate a tentative friendship, an expectation which is dashed when fighting erupts again. The girl is drawn by the noise and finds her mother dead on the floor. The Bride tries to apologize, but she is lost for words. What can she say? Then her composure reasserts itself. She leaves without haste or apparent emotion, crossing Vernita's name off her list of victims.

Nobody in the film emerges any the wiser. The only emotion the bride displays is a desire for revenge. I am hard put to gain any insight from these one-dimensional characters. What remains is the excitement of the quest, but this transient pleasure is unlikely to survive repeated viewing in the absence of anything deeper.

Analysis

Tarantino has been more prolific in giving interviews than making films. As with Hitchcock, his pronouncements have to be treated warily, but he did say that the 'human stuff' would come in the second part of *Kill Bill* and that he intended the film to be in two parts.[9] This absolves him from introducing believable characters in the first part, but taking him at his word, each part must stand alone, whatever its blemishes. The first volume has been criticized for its violence, lack of originality and weak characterization. A related issue is how these factors relate to the film's structure.

According to Jim McLellan, '[Tarantino] likes pulp because of the way it sometimes puts bad guys centre stage, courting an audacity which can take an audience into uncharted territories, places where they don't know quite how to feel.[10] Visiting uncharted territories and putting marginal characters centre stage is challenging, especially if it jolts the audience out of stock responses, but concerns about the film's violence have overshadowed the journey. Thane Peterson's response is representative: 'But with his latest movies, the director makes virtually every scene a pretext for humiliating, brutalizing, or murdering his characters.... And coming at a time when Americans are being bombarded by real images of US servicemen and women humiliating and torturing Iraqis, that leaves me feeling very uneasy.'[11] Such sentiments echo those of Gregg Easterbrook, who gained notoriety and lost his job by questioning whether Jews like Harvey Weinstein of Miramax and Michael Eisner (head of Disney, the owners of Miramax), should be promoting such material.[12] It can be argued that Tarantino distances the violence by treating it in cartoon fashion. Comic-book violence has been a feature of the cinema since the days of slapstick comedy and Tom and Jerry cartoons. CGI has blurred the distinction between feature films and animation, creating new possibilities for stylized violence. A standard was set by Ang Lee's *Crouching Tiger, Hidden Dragon* (Taiwan/HK/US/China, 2001), which blended the mythic forms of the revenge drama and the quest, while distinguishing itself by having a woman at the centre of the action. Tarantino is less keen on computerized techniques, but in *Kill Bill* he shows a similar emphasis on the quest and the heroine's revenge by the sword. Visually he pays homage to his predecessor in the nightclub scene, when the Bride single-handedly takes on a small army. Tarantino's version is more knowing. The volume of gore and the one-dimensional characters emphasize that the film is not to be taken seriously, but A. O. Scott of the *New York Times* remains unconvinced:

> [Tarantino] undermines this argument with sequences that cross the line between jolting and sickening. While the Bride is in the hospital, a cretinous orderly named Buck rents out her unconscious body for sex; when she wakes up, she kills Buck's latest customer by chewing off part of his face, and then takes care of Buck by slamming his head in a metal door.[13]

The debate on how audiences' behaviour is influenced by the cinema has a long pedigree, the American Payne Fund studies of the 1930s being the most exhaustive examination of the topic.[14] Psychological research has proliferated since then, with no firm conclusions emerging. Nor are moral panics new: at the time of the Jack the Ripper murders in 1888, *Punch* suggested that hoardings displaying lurid murder scenes to publicize stage dramas stimulated the 'morbid imagination of unbalanced minds'.[15] Such an approach can dwindle into the distaste for the masses noted in the first chapter, the premise being that the better class of people can be exposed to salacious or violent material with impunity, while the masses cannot resist its appeal. The problem for liberals is that film can be used to instil undesirable attitudes, as in the screening of *Rambo* films to child soldiers in Sierra Leone.[16] The censorship debate is a matter of parading your values as much as wielding empirical data.

Noël Carroll suggests that art excels in imprinting and interrogating for audiences the ethos of a people, including its morality. He dismisses banal moral insights derived from art because of the absence of argument or evidence to support them.[17] His thesis is that art involves audiences in a continuous process of making moral judgements, engaging the emotions and offering an understanding of the meaningfulness of life in an age when the Church has abnegated responsibility and there are few other sources of moral guidance. Of particular interest is Carroll's contention that a work of art offers a point of view which can be evaluated morally. *Kill Bill* begins with the physical consequences of violence as the Bride is seen lying injured. With her recovery, the film adopts her viewpoint as she embarks on her quest for vengeance. Despite the growing body count, she suffers no ill effects. The conclusion must be that vengeance is acceptable and achievable, which scores badly on Carroll's moral balance sheet. In mitigation, if the characters are not meant to be taken seriously, then neither is the moral message, but this only reinforces the point that *Kill Bill* lacks a moral focus. Perhaps providing one was never Tarantino's intention, but an audience cannot sit through so many killings without taking a moral stance on the Bride's activities.

Among anecdotal opinions on the effects of film, a thoughtful contribution echoing Carroll's view comes from Harry McCallion, who grew up in working-class Glasgow and saw army service before becoming a barrister. Though he concedes that screen violence became more graphic by 1980, he concludes that 'Violence, however graphically portrayed, does not in itself promote more violence. What promotes violence is the message that it works, or is the only answer.'[18] The violence in *Kill Bill* works and no alternative is presented, which makes the film's moral position questionable. If this offers succour to the censorship lobby, another of McCallion's comments provides ammunition for libertarians: 'Some might argue that is the true function of film, to allow you to escape from reality; personally I felt … that the cinema must provoke people and make them think. You cannot do that if films are so sanitised they lose their ability to shock. In fact, I believe this actually encourages violence.'[19] Critical responses to *Kill Bill* indicate that it provokes people, though not necessarily to emulate the violence. Whether it makes them think is another matter. The consequences of violence are not shown; neither can there be empathy with figures who are patently unreal. *Monty Python and the Holy Grail* (Terry Gilliam and Terry Jones, GB, 1975) is an antecedent, but unlike *Kill Bill,* it retains its humanity by relishing the humour.

Having hooked his audience, can Tarantino offer them anything worthwhile? Richard Linklater risks presenting political and philosophical ideas in his animated vision of a dystopian future, *A Scanner Darkly* (US, 2006), but is he handicapped by his choice of a medium with a restricted emotional range which cannot convey complex ideas? In signalling that *Kill Bill* should be approached like a cartoon, Tarantino demeans his characters, leading his audiences towards film as sensation and away from the real concerns and feelings which it can explore. Sensation has its place, but if Tarantino wants to be taken seriously as a film-maker, something more is needed.

Animated film can convey humour, which makes it useful for transgressing political or cultural norms. *Kill Bill* emphasizes excitement in a series of situations which might be farcical in other hands. An example is that abrupt ending of the fight between the Bride and Vernita Green when Vernita's daughter appears. It is easy to imagine how Laurel and Hardy would respond if a relative interrupted one of their squabbles. Tarantino plays the scene straight. Elsewhere he displays touches of humour, such as when the Bride despatches O-Ren's bodyguards and chops pieces off the stick clutched by the last, the most terrified and the shortest of her opponents. Roger Moore's James Bond also links humour to violence, but the effect depends on making the audience complicit in the joke, which neither Tarantino nor Thurman attempt. Instead we have to fall back on Tarantino's jaunty knowingness.

Does *Kill Bill* reveal Tarantino's values and, if so, what are they? A supporter might argue that he hides his true values behind an implied author. The weakness of this position is that Tarantino does not offer the kind of ironic authorial voice which Robert Hamer provided in *Kind Hearts and Coronets* (GB, 1949). In the absence of an implied author, we look to the real one. Another possible defence of Tarantino is that he hides his values behind the conventions he pastiches, but such reticence is uncharacteristic. If he were to direct a children's story or a romance, it might dispel the niggling suspicion that either he relishes violence, or he views the world solely through the perspectives of his favourite films.

The second criticism of *Kill Bill* arises from this possibility: the film amounts to a collage of other people's ideas. Given that video artists sample films and musicians sample other people's recordings, this need not be a drawback unless Tarantino is setting himself up as an auteur.[20] He has built up a following, even if few demands are made on his audiences beyond strong stomachs. Any originality resides in the way he references a wide range of films and brings minority genres like animé and Hong Kong thrillers into the mainstream. The storyline of *Kill Bill* hangs together, even if it lurches from one set piece to another with little cumulative effect. *Kind Hearts and Coronets* is varied by the ingenuity of each murder; Tarantino resorts to more of the same and a succession of killings by the sword results in dwindling audience interest. It is possible to admire his eclecticism without liking *Kill Bill*. Judged by the standards of narrative cinema, it is a flawed work, but the director may have had other intentions.

The lack of believable characters has other implications. As Manohla Dargis of the *Los Angeles Times* puts it, '[Tarantino's] previous films 'have been stuffed to the gills with movie allusions. But what made those films rock weren't the salutes to Hong Kong shoot-'em-ups, it was the anguish in Tim Roth's voice as his character bled to death, the shock of John Travolta's assassin meeting his end on the can, the lyrical stillness of Pam Grier's face.'[21] Thurman is inexpressive by comparison, which is symptomatic of Tarantino's lack of interest in real people.

For Philip Hensher, the director finds stars with 'an aura of exhausted celebrity' and his relationship to them is crucial:

> For Tarantino, films are all about stars, and no one can deny that he creates a marvellous frisson in his work by the sheer verve of his casting. In many ways, he reminds me of Visconti, who had a similar genius for perceiving a quality in an unlikely actor, and extracting a performance which could never be repeated. It works for Tarantino.[22]

The questions Hensher leaves open are whether Thurman fills the role of star and whether his explanation excuses the film's haphazard structure. Marsha Kinder confronts the latter issue in writing about *Pulp Fiction.* Her viewpoint is equally applicable to *Kill Bill:* 'By constructing a violent nonlinear narrative full of ellipses, Tarantino cracks open traditional genres to show how original variations can still be generated within the gaps.'[23] Christopher Sharrett takes the opposing view, going further than Dargis in lamenting the absence of characterization:

> The endless citations of Tarantino's favorite movies have little to do with homage since there is no inflection, no attempt to expand upon ideas of past films except by way of pointless hyperbole. But inflection may be far from the point, since a snide sarcasm pervades every frame of this film. Tarantino is too unfocused to be a parodist; rather, *Kill Bill* conveys contempt for its characters, certainly for humanity and—the biggest joke on us—even the action genres that supposedly enamor the director.[24]

The only point of agreement between Sharrett and Kinder is that Tarantino references a range of genres. I find it hard to discern Kinder's 'variations within the gaps' as the body count rises. Repetition rather than variation seems the order of the day. The surprise is that a former scriptwriter like Tarantino should abandon dialogue in favour of nonstop action for its own sake.

Tarantino was the *enfant terrible* of the cinema industry, propelled into the mainstream by Miramax. With fame came greater accountability. Box-office takings suggest that audiences are enthusiastic about *Kill Bill: Volume 1.* How the *enfant* handles this responsibility is another matter. A case can be made for saying that it is incumbent upon a film-maker who reaches a wide audience to project positive values. *Kill Bill* fails by this criterion: if anyone revels in violence, it is Tarantino. The counter-argument is that a film-maker has a duty to push against societal norms. In McCallion's terms, the work should provoke. Uma Thurman used this romantic ideal as justification when promoting the second volume of *Kill Bill:* 'People have to have creative freedom and you either believe in them or you don't. I believe in Quentin as an artist.'[25] But creative freedom requires a purpose, and this is hard to discern in Tarantino's work. No statement about the human condition is apparent. Instead he seems content to enjoy playing among the movie genres. His support for feminism is limited to the principle that women can kill as efficiently as men, which hardly amounts to a critique. The irony is that in an experiment which involved viewing Tarantino's *Reservoir Dogs,* the emphasis on violence significantly reduced women's enjoyment of the film and increased their anxiety.[26]

Film-makers may conform passively to societal norms on the basis that rules are rules. This is the path taken by genre-followers. Others conform actively, though for varying reasons. It may be difficult to criticize a repressive regime without risking repercussions, so that fear created the climate of conformity in the Stalinist era. Conversely, there are film-makers like Leni Riefenstahl and John Wayne whose work buttresses the established order rather than critiquing it. Theirs is the conformity of choice. Ken Loach and Sam Peckinpah are among the rebels. These figures have an uneasy relationship with media corporations and are likely to be found on the fringes of the industry, where they struggle for funding. An exception is Charlie Kaufman, who manages to find a niche for original material within mainstream cinema. Tarantino is a maverick who came in from the cold. The pace of *Kill Bill* generates excitement—it is difficult for an efficiently made action film to do anything else—but referencing so many other works leaves little scope for anything more. *Kill Bill* is ostensibly the work of a rebel, but Tarantino's rebellion amounts to encouraging underage Australian teenagers to see his film.[27] The community is absent in his work. Instead he propounds the individualism of do-it-yourself justice which proved popular in Michael Winner's *Death Wish* series (US, 1974–85). The difference is that Winner lacked cult status; the final irony is that Tarantino may have sacrificed his advantage by making a box-office hit.

–17–

The Tarnish on the Tinsel: Great Films Reconsidered

The fourteen films encompass three-quarters of a century of cinema, with an American bias which parallels the industry itself. All the films have been judged significant; all have flaws noted by several commentators. The first twelve films belong to the old masters canon, while arguments could be made for *The Piano* and *Kill Bill: Volume 1* belonging to the popular or the eclectic canons. In terms of the time model, these two works have yet to prove themselves. *The Battleship Potemkin* and *8½* are minority interest films; the others have achieved canonic status after taking their chance in the mainstream distribution system. *Citizen Kane, It's a Wonderful Life* and *The Night of the Hunter* were box-office failures on their first release, while *The 39 Steps, The Godfather, The Piano* and *Kill Bill: Volume 1* were money-makers. Status seems to have little to do with how a film fares commercially.

Television became the cinema's arch rival, but its importance in bringing films to a new audience cannot be underestimated. *Citizen Kane* disappeared from public and critical view for over a decade until a television company bought the rights to the RKO library and the film resurfaced. *It's a Wonderful Life* had a longer wait, its rediscovery being triggered by the failure to renew copyright, which made it a cheap schedule-filler for television companies. The case of *The Night of the Hunter* is less clear. It failed to make much initial impact; whether it would still be remembered today without television screenings is debatable. The same might be said of Powell and Pressburger's films and Hitchcock's early work. Television makes older films accessible to large audiences. It may be no coincidence that its ubiquity was followed by the emergence of film studies as a discipline.

Initial press coverage can belie a film's later reputation. First impressions may not be as considered as later analyses, but they provide spontaneous responses which a film's subsequent status can eclipse. When a critic has the opportunity to reconsider a film, the difference between first thoughts and a considered opinion can be illuminating. Bosley Crowther returned to *Citizen Kane* after a matter of days, by which time doubts about the film were emerging. Roger Ebert had the luxury of looking back two decades on *Raging Bull* and he still liked it. Critics are privileged audience members, but their reviews are sometimes our only evidence about a film's initial reception. Their opinions are often quoted, but there is a paucity of research on the power of critics, their range of viewpoints and the pressures exerted upon them by movie moguls, production companies and newspaper owners.[1]

All the films except *The Godfather* and *The 39 Steps* could be described as personal projects for their directors, though the same might be said of many less elevated works. All the directors became involved in scriptwriting, the exception being David Lean, whose major contribution to scripting *Lawrence of Arabia* was to sack his first writer. A creative force like Chaplin or Welles can take on several roles. Commitment to a project may blind a director to its flaws if there is nobody to provide a balancing view. The point was made by David Raksin, a music arranger on *Modern Times:* 'Like many self-made autocrats, Chaplin demanded unquestioning obedience from his associates; years of constant deference to his point of view had persuaded him that it was the only one that mattered.'[2] An unhindered vision may result in individualistic films, but at the risk of self-indulgence. Problems like excessive length, illogicalities of plot and structural weakness may arise for other reasons. The virtue of a division of labour is that the creative tension it sets up can detect and iron out flaws, even if it risks leading to compromises.

All the films raise moral issues, though without necessarily espousing conventional morality: *Kill Bill* advocates retribution rather than adherence to the law. In general terms, the older the film, the less chance of heroes and villains being confused. Ambiguity was evident by the time of *Lawrence of Arabia,* mirroring society's uncertainty about what values to uphold. The exception among later films is *The Godfather,* but by being set in the 1940s, it is absolved from having to indulge in moral ambiguity.

Do moral issues have to be addressed if a film has claims to greatness? If art aspires to be universal or to carry a message for future generations, it must rise above culturally bound values, but what is left can be a chilly beauty. The alternative is to abandon universality and get down and dirty, taking the risk of works becoming outmoded as values change.

A film-maker can sneak moral concerns into a film; for example worries about the atomic bomb pervade Robert Aldrich's *Kiss Me Deadly* (US, 1955). Others may attribute a moral stance or amorality to films. This can be a slippery slope, for as Peter Schjeldahl cautions, moralizers take as their business not only who gets to take pleasure, but when, where and how.[3] He omits to mention that moralizers can cling to values which are becoming outmoded, as the *Lady Chatterley* trial demonstrated in 1960. The ideal is for film-makers to probe society's changing moral climate without becoming prescriptive and without being cowed by social pressures. The best film-makers achieve this, their characters becoming more than vessels for conveying ideas. Works based on ideas rather than deriving from character can be effective in the hands of George Bernard Shaw, Michael Frayn, Tom Stoppard, or, in a different way, Georges Feydeau, but too often I sense ideas swamping the fourteen films rather than being their starting point. Five weaknesses keep recurring:

1. The ideas are not always big enough. Hitchcock and Tarantino betray a narcissistic interest in film-making which excludes wider considerations.
2. Style becomes an end in itself, notably in *Citizen Kane, The Night of the Hunter, 2001: A Space Odyssey* and *The Piano.* A director's vision can become so all-pervasive that the characters never take wing.
3. The dialogue is mundane. This applies particularly to *2001: A Space Odyssey,* and Kubrick agreed. Dialogue is nonexistent for Ada in *The Piano.* Bergman performs the same trick in *Persona* (Sweden, 1966) and gives us insight into the character, where Ada remains unknowable. Two films which have believable characters are *Black Narcissus* and *8½.* In the former, the novelist had already provided them; in the latter, the director made himself the subject. The weaknesses in these films lie elsewhere.
4. Shaw, Frayn and Stoppard employ humour to put across ideas, as did directors like Lindsay Anderson and Preston Sturges. The films considered are generally light on humour. Not every film has to be a comedy, but without humour, directors can take themselves too seriously.
5. There is an absence of emotional and intellectual resolution in the films, with endings which feel arbitrarily applied rather than emerging from the narrative. This does not preclude ambiguity, as the endings of *The Piano* and *8½* demonstrate, but I contend that in these examples, ambiguity arises from directorial uncertainty rather than emotional complexity. *Modern Times, It's a Wonderful Life* and *The Night of the Hunter* become maudlin, while *Black Narcissus* lapses into melodrama. Ideological considerations dominate *The Battleship Potemkin,* while the ending of *Citizen Kane* is clever rather than moving. In each case the experience is incomplete, and I am left feeling dissatisfied rather than having my emotional world expanded. An exception is *2001: A Space Odyssey.* Here the problem is that, however powerful the ending, the rest of the film fails to live up to it.

Ray Carney makes a useful distinction between film-making which aims for surface realism and an opposing strand embracing American romanticism and the cinema of Capra and Dreyer, which explores states of feeling.[4] Carney's approach provides a way of understanding some of the criticisms levelled at the fourteen films. Their surface realism is incidental. The paradox is that the emotional approach espoused by Jenefer Robinson should lead to the criticism of films which are dependent on feeling. One solution to this conundrum is that Carney fails to distinguish between the perspectives of film-makers and audiences. The former may want to explore feelings; what matters is the clarity with which their intentions are conveyed. Once a film is released, its reception cannot be controlled. Its makers may wish to subvert the expectations of audiences and critics, but cultural norms are not lightly overturned. Part of the film-maker's skill lies in judging the moment. The makers of *Rock Around the Clock* (Fred F. Sears, US, 1956) succeeded; *Peeping Tom* is a case where the moment was misjudged. This is justification enough for seeking to understand the historical context of a film's production and reception.

'Renoir withdrew his camera from … expressive close-ups … and showed the events,' thus breaking 'the congealing melodramatic cliché of American and German cinema'.[5] In describing Renoir's achievement, David Thomson succinctly characterizes melodrama. *The 39 Steps* and *The Night of the Hunter* are melodramas in the silent film tradition, which Eisenstein refined rather than redefined in *The Battleship Potemkin.* The stilted movements and expressive close-ups might be intended to explore states of feeling, but they can be heavy going. There are strong melodramatic elements in *It's a Wonderful Life* and *Black Narcissus,* notably in the performances of Lionel Barrymore and Kathleen Byron. What matters is not the sacrifice of realism—melodrama has been defined by Steve Neale as the counterpoint to realism—but Thomson's sense of congealing cliché which drains these films of their freshness.[6] It can be argued that melodrama is outdated in an era which favours understatement and values irony. This underlines the precarious nature of the canon, with some films dwindling into historical curiosities as their tropes become outmoded. A play can be restaged and reinterpreted for each generation; a film preserves the attitudes, values and techniques of its time. The nearest it can come to emulating a theatrical revival is a remake, which at best complements rather than displaces the original. This is one reason for letting go lightly as films age. There is a case for restricting the term *classic* to films which provide a record of past performances and film-making styles, while making no presumption as to quality.

Another characteristic of melodrama is that it signals the appropriate emotional response, allowing little scope for variation. For Richard Lazarus, the basic emotions are anger, anxiety, fright, guilt, shame, sadness, envy, jealousy, disgust, happiness, pride, relief, hope, love and compassion.[7] It is arguable whether melodrama can encompass even this limited range: anxiety and fright or guilt and shame can be difficult to delineate, while Guido's sense of anomie in *8½* is unlikely to register. The consequence of this restricted emotional palate is that empathy becomes harder to achieve. This weakness can be reinforced by a dominating performance which disrupts ensemble playing. Like Boris Karloff's Frankenstein's monster or Laughton's hunchback in *The Hunchback of Notre Dame,* Robert Mitchum mesmerizes in *The Night of the Hunter,* but at the cost of restricting the interplay between characters. All he can do is wheedle and bully. The audience is invited to root for his downfall, but little else. He has no more substance than a pantomime villain. The best films offer more.

The Evolution of an Industry

Demographic and economic change and the development of alternative media will impact on the cinema industry and the canon. CGI expands the scope of action sequences and crowd scenes to the point where it can be a significant factor in the cost of a film rather than a cheap substitute for live action. If it has not yet resulted in any out-and-out masterpieces, it has prompted a reaction from directors like Tarantino and Tony Scott, who favour more traditional techniques. Its use or abuse may be a fault line in the cinema of the future.

A generation ago, the cinema was the home of big-budget films; today, they are as likely to be viewed on DVD or view-on-demand TV. This affects films like *Lawrence of Arabia* and *2001: A Space Odyssey,* which exploit scale. Immensity, whether of the desert or outer space, cannot be fully experienced on a small screen. The impact of the soundtrack is similarly diminished by not being heard in the acoustic of a large cinema, irrespective of the excellence of home sound systems. A benefit from the popularity of domestic viewing is that restoring and digitally remastering films like *Modern Times* becomes economic, though too many DVDs are still copied from substandard prints. These battle scars confer a patina of age on a film, so that for better or worse it can be treated like an historical artefact rather than a drama with contemporary relevance.

Changed viewing habits have other implications. The shift to home viewing takes away the communal experience of cinema going, which provides not only a sense of occasion and an opportunity for exchange of ideas about the film, but infects an audience with the collective emotions of fear, suspense and laughter.[8] The failure of sitcoms which transfer to the big screen points up the problem. Like horror films, they are predicated on the response of the audience, and this will vary with the medium.

Another change in the cinema industry affects the distribution of niche material. The British art house circuit of the 1960s screened foreign language films which were not seen elsewhere, perpetuating a distinction between serious films for an elite audience and entertainment films for the masses. When American independent cinema became critically and commercially successful, the distinction between serious and entertainment films broke down, while marketing minority-interest films on video led to the collapse of the art house distribution system built up since the Second World War. This was symbolized by the closure of the Paris Pullman and Academy cinemas in London. Today the situation is confused. Foreign language films are being squeezed out of specialized metropolitan cinemas by more commercial fare, while the burgeoning digital, satellite and cable television channels perceive such material as unattractive to advertisers and marginalize it. On the credit side, DVD rentals give access to a wide range of material, with animated features such as the *Wallace and Gromit* films finding an enthusiastic following and genres from the Bollywood musical to Japanese animé expanding into the Western mainstream. The proliferation of film studies courses and film festivals encourages audiences to seek out neglected works. These changes may draw more genres to the canon, but not necessarily more foreign language films.

Since *The Battleship Potemkin, Modern Times* and *The 39 Steps* were made, Bolshevism, the Depression and an impending European war have lost their relevance.

Neither *The Piano* nor *Kill Bill,* the two most recent films considered, proclaims an explicit political message, though they reveal a licence in showing sex and violence which distinguishes them from the earlier titles. Attitudes and mores are seldom absolute or consistent. Boundaries of what is acceptable move rather than disappear, with paedophilia remaining beyond the pale: Nicole Kassell's *The Woodsman* (US, 2003) is a rare and courageous attempt to challenge the boundaries. The religious sentiments in *It's a Wonderful Life* and *Black Narcissus,* which passed unnoticed in the 1940s, may prove uncomfortable for today's audiences, while bleeping out the name of Guy Gibson's dog, Nigger, in a 2001 television screening of *The Dam Busters* (Michael Anderson, GB, 1954) is indicative of changing racial sensibilities.[9] Film should provide the opportunity to experience values which differ from our own. Coming to a film with too many preconceptions is unhelpful if we are to derive anything from it, but neither is there any virtue in pretending that bias does not exist. A more productive course is to acknowledge it and to use film as a means of reassessing our beliefs.

The 39 Steps and *Lawrence of Arabia* work within existing conventions, reflecting the conservatism of their makers. This need not be construed as a defect: what matters is how the conventions are used. Neither Eisenstein's montage in *The Battleship Potemkin* nor the deep-focus photography of *Citizen Kane* were new, but these films assumed significance because the techniques were used extensively and their makers trumpeted the fact. For epithets like *great* and *best* to be applied, quality rather than innovation is important, and quality has to be argued for. Sometimes it seems as though self-publicists like Eisenstein, Welles and Tarantino make the running, which seems ironic in the rarefied world of the canon.

A Subjective Approach to Film

My four subjective criteria were outlined in the second chapter: a work must be absorbing enough to suspend time, it should offer a new way of looking at the familiar, it must linger in the memory if it is to enrich or disturb and it has to be experienced in the gut as well as the mind. None of the fourteen works considered offers me the overwhelming emotional experience which my *Lieblingsfilme* provide. *Modern Times* seems contrived to produce easy emotion; *The Battleship Potemkin* has a crude political message and indifferent acting; *Black Narcissus* and *Kill Bill: Volume 1* are slight if overwrought works by interesting filmmakers; *The 39 Steps* harks back to silent film; *The Night of the Hunter* sinks under stylistic excesses, while *Citizen Kane* and *Lawrence of Arabia* are unbalanced by overbearing central performances. *The Godfather, 2001: A Space Odyssey, Raging Bull* and *The Piano* come across as glum exercises in virtuoso direction which have left their humanity behind. *It's a Wonderful Life* has an unexpectedly bitter centre beneath the sugar coating, while Fellini's *8½* is more interesting than I expected, even if the director's self-absorption proves trying. Many will disagree with these judgements. It is easier to discuss art in the restricted terms of structure or performance styles.

Yet technical issues are not independent of emotional responses. Kendall Walton cites the example of shooting a roller-coaster ride: the effect on the viewer will depend on whether the camera is aligned with the horizontal, giving a detached viewpoint, or attached to a swaying car, which involves the viewer in the action.[10] Fashions change, albeit inconsistently: the crisp editing of *The 39 Steps* means that it still comes across as fast-paced, even if the acting style is dated. The viewer's age affects the response, with handheld camerawork and jump cuts being accepted as normal by a teenager, who may be impatient at the slowness and staginess of a film from fifty years ago which seems well paced and natural to an older person. One implication is that the viewer can become so habituated to a director's style that it ceases to be noticed. A film by Bresson or Rohmer comes across as unfolding at a realistic pace, while a recent release which strives for a sense of actuality seems contrived and self-conscious. This reinforces the conservatism of the canon, despite figures like Godard and Tarkovsky, who manage to be canonic as well as violating cinematic norms. Assimilation of styles by the audience makes a simple distinction between objective analysis and subjective response problematic. The latter involves not only Lazarus's basic emotions, but values which are internalized, allowing us to get emotional about them. *Raging Bull* will mean more to a fan of boxing than an opponent. The violence of *Kill Bill* will seem distasteful to some but pass unnoticed by fans of John Woo. What matters is whether a quasi-objective critical stance or something more open-minded is adopted. In practice, a shared culture means that there will be agreement about many values and attitudes. This becomes apparent in wartime films which promote unity in the face of a common enemy. As Susan Feagin puts it: 'We find ourselves to be the kind of people who respond negatively to villainy, treachery and injustice. This discovery, or reminder, is something which, quite justly, yields satisfaction.'[11] Such commonality of feeling may be conspicuous by its absence when a film intended for a domestic audience is screened abroad, but shared values generally ensure enough unity of response for film producers to gamble on whether a project will find an audience.[12]

Few people come to a film knowing nothing about it. The lucky dip of a film festival is the nearest we come to a state of innocence. The response to the film is itself incorporated into the stock of memories, enriching experience which can be drawn upon in the future. Nor is the role of memory passive. Aspects of film likely to loom disproportionately large are those which are pivotal, highly dramatic, or produce an emotional effect, for example the eye-slitting scene which opens *Un chien andalou*, or the Russian roulette scene in *The Deer Hunter*. The conflicting emotions produced by ambiguity can be rehearsed in tranquillity, with Antonioni's films providing examples of endings which can be endlessly reinterpreted. The film is reworked in the memory, so that each viewer is left with something unique. One purpose of art is to generate new insights by utilizing this phenomenon.

If it is accepted that the initial response to a film is emotional, then methodological difficulties do not provide sufficient reason for ignoring the implications. Nor is such an approach unique in being difficult to articulate. Psychoanalytic and auteur models offer no more precision and are based on questionable assumptions, but this has not hindered their popularity. Such methodological difficulties are not unique to film studies: university English departments went through similar upheavals when the new historicism and structuralism displaced Leavisite analysis. The academic model employed may not affect our immediate emotional response to art, but shapes how we rationalize decisions already made. First impressions are taken out of the realm of the subjective by trying to analyze them. A first step to unpicking this conundrum is to follow Jenefer Robinson in paying attention to psychological and neurophysiological studies. Echoing the procedures adopted by the Payne Fund Studies, one strategy is to observe the physiological aspects of emotion, such as sweating and heart rate. This offers a measure of precision compared with trying to second-guess mental processes using psychoanalytic methods. The second step is to consider the implications for the canon.

The Canon Re-examined

The fame of *Citizen Kane* is such that it serves as a touchstone for dissidents. Jason Solomons of the *Observer* responded to the announcement that it headed *Sight and Sound*'s 2002 list of best films: 'But why do I greet *Kane*'s hegemony with such disappointment? The film itself is far from boring, yet its very name associated ... with that Greatest title is enough to induce a big yawn.'[13] David Thomson expressed similar sentiments: 'It's not healthy for film that *Kane* goes on and on being regarded as—yeah, I think "classic" is a fusty word. The movie I saw last night ought to be the one that matters most. Or the movie I'm going to see tonight.'[14] Nick Roddick went further:

> *Citizen Kane* is a very good film, but it is not The Best Film of All Time, a status to which it has risen because its director ... was a great self-publicist, because it is full of bravura visual and narrative flourishes, and because it got trashed by the studio, partly in reaction to Welles' belief that he could get away with anything he liked and partly because of the Faust-like rumour circulating that it was The Best Film of All Time.[15]

The award for heresy goes to the academic Joel David: 'So are American porn films better than *Citizen Kane?* Almost all of them aren't, but a precious handful are ... I already found *Kane* too whiney-white-guy precocious the first time I saw it, 20-odd years ago.'[16] Such opinions highlight one risk of labelling works as classic, best, or great: there are dissenters to confront. Labelling an era holds similar dangers. It is easy to discern a 'golden age' on the basis of a few works, for example British wartime cinema, Czech films of the 1960s, or American independent films of the 1970s.

The role of critics and academics as guardians of the past is confirmed, while films which do not fit the thesis remain hidden. This situation is being challenged as academics stake out new territory. One spin-off is a renewed interest in topics like British films of the 1950s.[17] Such gains carry their own risks, with films becoming objects of study rather than keys to pleasure as they are appropriated into the curriculum.

The cinema has a short history compared with the other arts, but if twentieth-century figures like Picasso and Shostakovich can enter the hall of fame, the fast-track approach to canonization should apply equally well to film directors. This conclusion throws up several issues. First, should a film or a director's body of work be fêted? If the latter is accepted, the auteur model seems not far away. Secondly, much of cinema's history is already lost beyond retrieval. We search among the remnants and dream of what we have lost. Finally, if film embodies the values and circumstances of its creation, a work may suffer if the values become discredited or out of fashion. The neglect of the East German DEFA studios was touched on earlier. Quota quickies made for the British market between the wars are only now being reassessed, while the swinging London films of the 1960s deserve reappraisal. This raises the question whether we should keep the aesthetic and historical approaches separated, or do a better job in marrying them. The former option offers conceptual clarity. Discerning aesthetic value can wait until works are better known.

Raymond Durgnat, Ray Carney and David Thomson are high-profile writers who have responded emotionally to film. The irony is that Durgnat castigated A. L. Kennedy for her subjective response to Powell and Pressburger's *The Life and Death of Colonel Blimp* (GB, 1943).[18] Jonathan Rosenbaum and Paul Schrader favour the canon as a transparent means of upholding film quality. Rosenbaum does not offer unqualified support, seeing canon formation as an active process which is necessary because academics have not offered an alternative to the box office as a way of measuring the worth of films. His ideal is to escape the insularity of Bloom's Western canon and the aesthetic considerations which lead to a dichotomy between art and entertainment, though what goes in their place is less clear.[19] Rosenbaum reveals in his introduction to *Essential Cinema* that he was invited by the publisher to put together a collection of his writings.[20] This explains why the essays on individual films, however illuminating, fail to add up to a coherent argument in favour of canons, which are hardly mentioned after the introduction. An intriguing side issue is Rosenbaum's use of the term *canons*. This avoids the straightjacket of a single canon, but given a plethora of canons, why should one be privileged over another? One answer is that the most influential voices hold sway, including that of Rosenbaum himself.

Paul Schrader's book on the canon was never written. He was invited to write a cinematic equivalent of Bloom's *The Western Canon,* but abandoned what he came to regard as a hopeless task. He recounts his experiences in a journal article.[21] Like Rosenbaum, Schrader is unwilling to wait for the time model of greatness to do its work, and, with the market model excluded by default, this leaves the consensus model. Both authors dodge the question of who makes the selection, though

Schrader does offer his criteria. These are beauty, strangeness (originality is never completely assimilated), unity of form and subject matter, a traceable lineage (a great work builds on what has gone before), value which is still apparent after repeated viewings, viewer engagement and moral resonance (even if the morality is questionable as in *The Triumph of the Will*).[22] With the arguable exception of lineage, Schrader's criteria are subjective, which makes *Lieblingsfilme* a more appropriate term than *canon* for his own selection. He stands against the old masters canon by proclaiming his interest in films which address contemporary situations: 'Historical films interest me more as history than art.'[23] Pauline Kael made a similar point in preferring *Bonnie and Clyde* (Arthur Penn, US, 1967) to *Closely Observed Trains* (Jiri Menzel, Czechoslovakia, 1966): 'It is closer to us, it has some of the qualities of direct involvement that make us care about movies.'[24] The dangers of isolationism and of constantly seeking relevance to the parochial or the ephemeral need to be acknowledged, but what comes across in these comments is the subjective nature of the authors' responses. Supporters of the canon and commentators who favour a more personal response to film may not be so far apart.

As the internet and DVDs allow greater access to films, the power of consumers increases, challenging the authority of the consensus canon.[25] Its supporters may seek to maintain their position by promoting high art, its justification being expressed less in terms of quality than the effect on those who aspire to it. Rosenbaum considers that his proposed canon can make better citizens, while Willie van Peer waxes lyrical on what good books can offer: 'Literature takes us away from our grey everyday selves, but brings us back enriched with new sensibilities.'[26] Schrader's caveat about the two-edged nature of moral resonance is timely: those who acquire new sensibilities might favour approaches not anticipated by Rosenbaum or van Peer, such as YouTube or blogs. At least the concept of moral resonance gets away from a canon whose justification is purely aesthetic, even if the full implications of a subjective approach remain to be explored.

Rosenbaum and Schrader have stimulated debate. In reviewing Rosenbaum's book, Brian Hu makes the point that great films are worth seeing again not to confirm their greatness, but to allow us to reflect on the meaning of a classic in film culture.[27] This is to give the canon a sociological role, even if Hu dodges the central issue of what makes films great. Donato Totaro criticizes Schrader's restrictive view of the canon (the age of the films, the under-representation of Asian cinema and the espousal of high culture) and for not distinguishing between personal and evaluative statements.[28] This begs the question whether evaluation can be something more than a justification of personal likes and dislikes. Christopher Long goes full circle, echoing Janet Staiger's call for the canon to embrace previously marginalized works and for evaluative criteria to be eliminated or mitigated.[29] He finds Rosenbaum wanting in this second task. But what is left of the canon if both conditions are satisfied?

Do we need the canon? It gives film a place at the feast beside the other arts, though the argument that it provides a basis for what we should study no longer applies as academics range across the cinema geographically and historically. Nor does the canon address the role of the cinema as entertainment. Pauline Kael ventures into the lion's den: 'It's appalling to read solemn academic studies of Hitchcock and von Sternberg by people who seem to have lost sight of the primary reason for seeing films like *Notorious* or *Morocco*—which is that they were not intended solemnly, that they were playful and inventive and faintly (often deliberately) absurd.'[30] Tarantino is one contemporary director who has not lost sight of playfulness and absurdity, even if he sacrifices the inventiveness of his earlier films to parade his eclecticism in *Kill Bill*. But at least he has found an audience.

The literature on the consumers of film—the audiences—is meagre, the more so the further back we go in time.[31] It is indicative of how our approach to film has narrowed, with aesthetics, the circumstances of production and skirmishes for a place in film lineage appearing more alluring and easier to write about than reception. As audiences become sidelined in these sometimes arcane discussions, the market model offers a measure of their opinions, which might be why old-school academics like the art historian Ernst Gombrich are suspicious of it.[32] The films are there for us to enjoy. We should play the game of arguing their worth, but the canon is a straitjacket we do not need. We could do worse than adopt Howard Felperin's attitude towards literary canons: noncanonical interpretation 'goes against the grain of prevailing notions of the cultural or institutional context that work to constrain its reading ... and grafts the text into a context that might well seem at the time novel, counter-intuitive, or downright implausible, but was, at least in retrospect, always readily available.'[33] Paying more attention to our feelings democratizes responses to film, and the consequences are far-reaching. Let John Guillory have the last word:

> In a culture of such universal access, canonical works could not be expressed as they so often are, as lifeless monuments, or as proofs of class distinction.... The point is not to make judgment disappear but to reform the conditions of its practice.... Socializing the means of production and consumption would be the condition of an aestheticism unbound, not its overcoming. But, of course, this is only a thought experiment.[34]

Notes

Introduction

1. Ingmar Bergman interviewed by Marie Nyneröd in *Bergman and the Cinema* (Marie Nyneröd, Swedish Television, 2004).

1 So Who Says It's Great?

1. Pierre Bourdieu, *Distinction: A Social Critique of the Judgement of Taste,* tr. Richard Nice (London: Routledge, 1989).
2. Alan Carter, programme notes for Ballets Minerva at the Commonwealth Institute, London, W8, November 1968.
3. Michael Thompson, *Rubbish Theory: The Creation and Destruction of Value* (Oxford: Oxford University Press, 1979), p. 9. *Model* is a more appropriate term than *theory* given that what matters is the usefulness of the ideas rather than their validity.
4. Ibid., pp. 62–124.
5. Cassius Longinus, *On the Sublime,* tr. W. Rhys Roberts, ch. 7, *Peitho's Web,* n.d., http://classicpersuasion.org/pw/longinus/desub002.htm, accessed 27 December 2007.
6. J. M. Magrini, 'On the Sublime: Longinus, Burke and Kant', *Carleton University Student Journal of Philosophy,* 20/1 (2002), http://www.carleton.ca/philosophy/cusjp/v20/n1/magrini.html, accessed 27 December 2007.
7. Paul Coughlin, 'Sublime Moments', *senses of cinema,* 11 (2000–1), http://www.sensesofcinema.com/contents/00/11/sublime.html, accessed 27 December 2007.
8. Monika Fludernik, Universität Freiburg, 'Sublime', *Literary Encyclopedia,* 2001, http://www.litencyc.com/php/stopics.php?rec=true&UID=1070, accessed 27 December 2007.
9. Umberto Eco, *The Open Work,* tr. Anna Cancogni (London: Hutchinson Radius, 1989), p. 196.
10. David Cohen, 'Ambiguity and Intention', *Interdisciplines,* n.d., http://www.interdisciplines.org/artcog/papers/11, accessed 27 December 2007.
11. Fludernik, 'Sublime'.

12. Igor Yevin, 'Ambiguity and Art', *Mathematical Institute of the Serbian Academy of Sciences and Arts,* n.d., http://www.mi.sanu.ac.yu/vismath/igor/index.html, accessed 27 December 2007.

13. Herbert Read, *Art and Alienation: The Role of the Artist in Society* (London: Thames & Hudson, 1967), p. 22.

14. Fludernik, 'Sublime'.

15. C. G. Jung, *The Archetypes and the Collective Unconscious,* tr. R.F.C. Hull, vol. 9, part 1 of *Collected Works,* 2nd edn (London: Routledge & Kegan Paul, 1968), pp. 76 and 84.

16. Ibid., pp. 4–7, 21–4 and 42–53.

17. Ibid., pp. 25–32 and 54–72.

18. Ibid., p. 84.

19. Mark Twain, *Following the Equator* (1897), *The Columbia World of Quotations,* 1996, *Bartleby.com,* http://www.bartelby.com/66/47/61947.html, accessed 28 December 2007.

20. Holly Koelling, *Classic Connections: Turning Teens on to Great Literature,* (Westport, CT: Libraries Unlimited, 2004).

21. *Ex-Classics,* http://www.exclassics.com, accessed 27 December 2007.

22. Charles Augustin Sainte-Beuve, 'What Is a Classic?', *The Harvard Classics 1909–14, Bartleby.com,* 2005, http://www.bartleby.com/32/202.html, accessed 28 December 2007.

23. Julie Phillips, 'Classics Defined: Robert Osborne's Classic Film Festival Offers Another Round of Favorites', *OnLineAthens,* 23 March 2006, http://onlineathens.com/stories/032306/marquee_20060323011.shtml, accessed 28 December 2007.

24. John Guillory, *Cultural Capital: The Problem of Literary Canon Formation* (Chicago: University of Chicago Press, 1993), p. 6.

25. Harold Bloom, *The Western Canon: The Books and School of the Ages* (London: Macmillan, 1995), p. 38.

26. Ibid., p. 522.

27. Ibid., p. 553.

28. Eco, *The Open Work,* p. 194.

29. Bloom, *The Western Canon,* p. 33.

30. Read, *Art and Alienation,* p. 24.

31. Ibid.

32. Clement Greenberg, *Art and Culture* (London: Thames & Hudson, 1973), p. 15.

33. Jenefer Robinson, *Deeper Than Reason: Emotion and Its Role in Literature, Music and Art* (Oxford: Clarendon Press, Oxford University Press, 2005), pp. 105–35, 258–92. As in the case of Thompson (n. 4), *model* seems a more appropriate term than *theory.*

34. Ivan Gaskell, 'Reflections of Rembrandt's *Jeremiah*', in Michael Ann Holly and Keith Moxey (eds), *Art History, Aesthetics, Visual Studies* (Williamstown, MA: Sterling and Francine Clark Art Institute, 2002), pp. 175–86.

35. Robinson, *Deeper than Reason,* pp. 117–19.
36. See Wayne C. Booth, *The Rhetoric of Fiction* (Chicago: University of Chicago Press, 1961).
37. Robinson, *Deeper than Reason,* pp. 179–84.
38. Ibid., pp. 128–30.
39. Ibid., pp. 126–8.
40. Ibid., pp. 136–8 and 159.
41. Ibid., pp. 160–94.
42. Natalie Friedman, 'How to Make Your Students Cry: Lessons in Atrocity, Pedagogy, and Heightened Emotion', *Journal of Mundane Behavior,* 3/3 (2002), http://www.mundanebehavior.org/issues/v3n3/friedman.htm, accessed 27 December 2007.
43. Philip Fisher, 'Darkness and the Demand for Time in Art', in Holly and Moxey, (eds), *Art History, Aesthetics, Visual Studies,* pp. 87–104.

2 The Celluloid Canon

1. Janet Staiger, 'The Politics of Film Canons', *Cinema Journal,* 24/3 (1985), pp. 4–5.
2. UK Film Council, *Statistical Yearbook, 2006–07* (London: 2007), http://www.ukfilmcouncil.org.uk/media/pdf/5/8/Stats_Year_book.pdf, p. 16, accessed 23 June 2008.
3. Adrian Martin, 'Light My Fire (The Geology and Geography of Film Canons)', *senses of cinema,* 14 (2001), Pandora Archive, National Library of Australia. Currently unavailable.
4. Ava Preacher Collins, 'Loose Canons: Constructing Cultural Traditions Inside and Outside the Academy', in Jim Collins, Hilary Radner and Ava Preacher Collins, (eds), *Film Theory Goes to the Movies: Cultural Analysis of Contemporary Film* (New York: Routledge, 1993), pp. 86–102.
5. Ian Christie, 'Canon Fodder', *Sight and Sound,* 2/8 (1992), p. 33.
6. Ian Christie, 'The Rules of the Game', *Sight and Sound,* 12/9 (2002), p. 27.
7. Ibid., p. 24.
8. Ibid., pp. 28–36 and 40–50.
9. Nick James, 'Modern Times', *Sight and Sound,* 12/12 (2002), pp. 20–3.
10. Jonathan Rosenbaum, 'List-o-Mania or, How I Stopped Worrying and Learned to Love American Movies', *Chicago Reader,* 26 June 1998.
11. Ibid.
12. Jonathan Rosenbaum, *Essential Cinema: On the Necessity of Film Canons* (Baltimore, MD: Johns Hopkins University Press, 2004).
13. Kevin Lee, 'Jonathan Rosenbaum's 1000 Essential Films: Questions and Answers', *Also Like Life Productions,* n.d., http://www.alsolikelife.com/FilmDiary/rosenbaum100qa.html, accessed 28 December 2007.

14. AFI's 100 Years ... 100 Movies ... 10th Anniversary Edition, AFI, 2007, http:// connect.afi.com/PageServer?pagename=100yearsList (registration required to access site), accessed 23 June 2008.
15. 'The *Village Voice* 100 Best Films of the Century', *Village Voice,* 4 January 2000.
16. Top 250 Movies as Voted by Our Users, *IMDb,* http://imdb.com/chart/top, accessed 27 December 2007.
17. User Ratings for *The Godfather* (1972), *IMDb,* http://imdb.com/title/tt0068646/ ratings, accessed 27 December 2007.
18. Ibid.
19. See '201 Greatest Movies of All Time', *Empire,* March 2006, pp. 77–101; Tim Dirks, '*Empire* Magazine's 100 Greatest Movies of All Time' (1999 and 2003), *The Greatest Films,* http://filmsite.org/empireuk100.html, accessed 28 December 2007.
20. Kevin Maher, 'I Am Your Fantasy Father', *Times,* 21 April 2005.
21. All-Time Worldwide Box Office, *IMDb* http://imdb.com/boxoffice/alltimegros s?region=world-wide, accessed 27 December 2007.
22. Ryan Gilbey (ed.), *The Ultimate Film* (London: BFI, 2005).
23. Aaron Caldwell and Mark Caldwell, *Top 100 Movie Lists,* 2007, http://www. geocities.com/aaroncaldwell/abc1.html; Tim Dirks, 'Other Great Films Lists', *The Greatest Films,* 1996–2007, http://filmsite.org/greatlists2.html; The 1,000 Greatest Films, *They Shoot Pictures, Don't They,* 2006, http://www.they shootpictures.com/gf1000.htm; Todd M. Compton, *In Search of a Canon: Movie Polls through the Years* (Mountain View, CA: Magos Press, 2007), http://www.geocities.com/Athens/Oracle/7207/pollsTOC.htm, all accessed 23 June 2008.
24. Aaron Caldwell and Mark Caldwell, 'FIAF Centenary List' (1995), *Top 100 Movie Lists,* http://www.geocities.com/aaronbcaldwell/dimfiaf.html, accessed 28 December 2007.
25. Derek Malcolm, *Derek Malcolm's Personal Best: A Century of Films* (London: I. B. Tauris, 2000).
26. Rosenbaum, 'List-o-Mania'.
27. Tim Dirks, '100 Greatest Films: Film Selection Criteria', *The Greatest Films,* 1996–2007, http://filmsite.org/criteria.html, accessed 28 December 2007.
28. Ty Burr, 'Once upon a Classic', *Boston Globe,* 23 March 2003.
29. User Ratings for *Citizen Kane* (1941), *IMDb,* http://imdb.com/title/tt0033467/ ratings, accessed 28 December 2007.
30. Paul Fraumeni, 'What Makes a Great Film?', *University of Toronto,* [2003], http://www.new.utoronto.ca/bios/askus35.htm, accessed 23 June 2008.
31. Ibid.
32. Christie, 'The Rules of the Game', p. 24.
33. Ibid.
34. Peter Wollen, 'Films: Why Do Some Survive and Others Disappear?', *Sight and Sound,* 3/5 (1993), pp. 26–8.

35. Donato Totaro, 'The *Sight and Sound* of Canons', *Offscreen,* January 2003, http://www.horschamp.qc.ca/new_offscreen/canon.html, accessed 28 December 2007.

36. Martin, 'Light My Fire'.

37. Milan Pavlovic, '30 Lieblingsfilme (30 Favorite Films Poll)', *Jeeem's CinePad,* 1995, http://www.cinepad.com/awards/lieblingsfilme.htm, accessed 28 December 2007.

38. Christopher Hitchins interviewed by Philip Dodd, *Night Waves,* BBC Radio 3, 1 June 2005.

39. C. G. Jung, *The Archetypes and the Collective Unconscious,* tr. R.F.C. Hull, vol. 9, part 1 of *Collected Works,* 2nd edn (London: Routledge & Kegan Paul, 1968), p. 69.

3 *The Battleship Potemkin* (USSR, 1925): The Politics of the Cinema

1. D. J. Wenden, '*Battleship Potemkin:* Film and Reality', in K.R.M. Short (ed.), *Feature Film as History* (London: Croom Helm, 1981), p. 51.

2. Richard Taylor, *'The Battleship Potemkin': The Film Companion* (London: I. B. Tauris, 2000), pp. 4–10.

3. Ibid., pp. 12 and 102; Astrid Ule and Eric Hansen, '*Battleship* Resurfaces', *Hollywood Reporter,* International Edition, 8 February 2005, *EBSCO research databases;* Ronald Bergan, 'Original Potemkin Beats the Censors after 79 Years', *Guardian,* 18 February 2005. I am grateful to Keith Withall for additional information.

4. Taylor, *'The Battleship Potemkin,'* pp. 112–17; *Bronenosets Potyomkin* (1925), *IMDb,* http://imdb.com/title/tt0015648, accessed 29 December 2007.

5. Quoted in Taylor, *'The Battleship Potemkin',* p. 73.

6. Ibid., p. 84.

7. Nestor Almendros, 'Fortune and Men's Eyes', *Film Comment,* 27/4 (1991), p. 61.

8. Anna Chen, 'In Perspective: Sergei Eisenstein, Film Director, 1898–1948', *Anna Chen's Website,* 1998, http://www.annachen.co.uk/writing_eisenstein1.html, accessed 29 December 2007.

9. Taylor, '*The Battleship* Potemkin', p. 115.

10. Karin Moser, 'Introduction: 1905 GOD *(Bronenosez Potemkin)*', *COLLATE Project,* n.d., http://deutsches-filminstitut.de/collate/collate_sp/se/se_04.html, accessed 29 December 2007; Ian Christie, 'The Rules of the Game', *Sight and Sound,* 12/9 (2002), pp. 24 and 27.

11. Taylor, '*The Battleship Potemkin*', p. 65.

12. Fred Schader, 'The *Potemkin*', *Variety* (1926), in '*Bronenosets Potemkin* Cine-File', *Pacific Film Archive,* http://www.mip.berkeley.edu/cgi-bin/cine_film_detail.pl/cine_img?31, accessed 29 December 2007.

13. David Thomson, *The New Biographical Dictionary of Film*, 4th edn (London: Little, Brown, 2003), p. 266.
14. Dan Shaw, 'Sergei Eisenstein', *senses of cinema*, 30 (2004), http://www.sensesof cinema.com/contents/directors/04/eisenstein.html, accessed 29 December 2007.
15. Sergei Eisenstein, 'The Montage of Film Attractions' (1924), in *Selected Works*, vol. 1: *Writings, 1922–34*, tr. Richard Taylor (London: BFI; and Bloomington: Indiana University Press, 1988), pp. 44–5.
16. Thomson, *The New Biographical Dictionary of Film*, p. 266.
17. Eisenstein, 'The Montage of Film Attractions', p. 45.
18. Shaw, 'Sergei Eisenstein'.
19. Ibid.
20. Thomson, *The New Biographical Dictionary of Film*, p. 266.
21. Seymour Benjamin Chatman, *'Battleship Potemkin': The Odessa Steps* (Mount Vernon, NY: Macmillan Films, 1975), in *'Bronenosets Potemkin* CineFile', *Pacific Film Archive*, http://www.mip.berkeley.edu/cgi-bin/cine_film_detail.pl/cine_img?31, accessed 29 December 2007.
22. Wenden, *'Battleship Potemkin:* Film and Reality', p. 37.
23. Shaw, 'Sergei Eisenstein'.
24. Thomson, *The New Biographical Dictionary of Film*, p. 267.
25. Almendros, 'Fortune and Men's Eyes', p. 59.
26. James Goodwin, 'Eisenstein: Ideology and Intellectual Cinema', *Quarterly Review of Film Studies*, 3/2 (1978), p. 170; Stanley J. Solomon, 'Chatham Film Society Program Notes' (1964), in *'Bronenosets Potemkin* CineFile', *Pacific Film Archive*, http://www.mip.berkeley.edu/cgi-bin/cine_film_detail.pl/cine_img?31, accessed 29 December 2007.
27. Helen Grace, *'Battleship Potemkin'*, *senses of cinema*, 4 (2000), http://www.senseso fcinema.com/contents/cteq/00/4/potemkin.html, accessed 29 December 2007.
28. Quoted in Taylor, *The Battleship Potemkin*, p. 112.
29. Ule and Hansen, *'Battleship* Resurfaces'.
30. Roger Ebert, Review of *The Battleship Potemkin*, *Chicago Sun-Times*, 19 July 1978.
31. Nigel Gosling, *Paris 1900–1914: The Miraculous Years* (London: Weidenfeld and Nicholson, 1978), p. 161.
32. Annette Michelson, 'Eisenstein at 100: Recent Reception and Coming Attractions', *October*, 88 (1999), pp. 69–85.
33. Wenden, *'Battleship Potemkin:* Film and Reality', pp. 45–56.
34. Grace, *'Battleship Potemkin'*.
35. Sergei Eisenstein, *The Battleship Potemkin*, tr. Gillon R. Aitken (London: Lorrimer, 1968), p. 67; Wenden, 'Battleship *Potemkin:* Film and Reality', p. 52; Hector Currie, 'A New Look at Eisenstein's *Potemkin*', in David Platt (ed.), *Celluloid Power: Social Criticism from 'The Birth of a Nation' to 'Judgment at Nuremberg'* (Metuchen, NJ: Scarecrow Press, 1999), pp. 168–75.

36. Dr William Boehart, It Simply Blows Your Mind …, posted 17 June 2003, *Amazon,* http://www.amazon.ca/Battleship-Potemkin-Grigori-Aleksandrov/dp/customer-reviews/6305090033, accessed 29 December 2007.

4 *The 39 Steps* (GB, 1935): Romance on the Run

1. Review of *The 39 Steps, Monthly Film Bulletin,* 2/17 (1935), p. 72.
2. Review of *The 39 Steps, Times,* 6 June 1935.
3. *Daily Mirror,* 9 September 1935, quoted in Tom Ryall, *Alfred Hitchcock and the British Cinema,* 2nd edn (London: Athlone Press, 1996), p. 105; John Sedgwick, *Popular Filmgoing in 1930s Britain: A Choice of Pleasures* (Exeter: University of Exeter Press, 2000), pp. 258 and 269.
4. Mark Glancy, *The 39 Steps* (London: I. B. Tauris, 2003), pp. 87–9.
5. Andre Sennwald, 'Alfred Hitchcock's New Picture, *The Thirty-Nine Steps*', *New York Times,* 14 September 1935.
6. Nick James, 'Nul Britannia', *Sight and Sound* 12/9 (2002), p. 38.
7. Jane Sloan, *Alfred Hitchcock: A Filmography and Bibliography Updated* (Berkeley and Los Angeles: University of California Press, 1995); Andrea Sarafian King, 'Hitchcock Bibliography … Revised', *British Film Institute,* 2002, http://www.bfi.org.uk/filmtvinfo/publications/bibliographies/hitchcock.pdf, accessed 29 December 2007.
8. Robert E. Kapsis, 'Alfred Hitchcock: Auteur or Hack?', *Cineaste,* 14/3 (1986), pp. 30–5.
9. Raymond Durgnat, *The Strange Case of Alfred Hitchcock* (London: Faber and Faber, 1974).
10. Ibid., p. 129.
11. Ibid., p. 128.
12. Glancy, *The 39 Steps,* p. 18.
13. Durgnat, *The Strange Case of Alfred Hitchcock,* p. 127.
14. John Orr, *Hitchcock and 20th Century Cinema* (London: Wallflower Press, 2005), pp. 63–6.
15. Tim Dirks, '*The 39 Steps* (1935)', *Film Site,* 1996–2007, http://filmsite.org/thirt.html, accessed 31 December 2007.
16. Durgnat, *The Strange Case of Alfred Hitchcock,* p. 126.
17. Gary Johnson, review of *The 39 Steps* DVD, *Images,* 8 (2004), http://www.imagesjournal.com/issue08/reviews/39steps, accessed 31 December 2007.
18. Robin Wood ('George Kaplan'), 'Alfred Hitchcock: Lost in the Wood', *Film Comment,* 8/4 (1972), p. 47.
19. Nicholas Haeffner, *Alfred Hitchcock* (Harlow: Pearson Longman, 2005).
20. Durgnat, *The Strange Case of Alfred Hitchcock,* p. 131.
21. François Truffaut with Helen G. Scott, *Hitchcock* (London: Paladin, 1978), p. 78.

22. Alfred Hitchcock, 'Why I Make Melodramas' (1936), *'The MacGuffin' Web Page,* http://www.labyrinth.net.au/%7emuffin/melodramas_c.html, accessed 31 December 2007.

23. Recounted by Googie Withers at a talk attended by Brian McFarlane (personal communication).

24. Ken Mogg, review of Mark Glancy, *The 39 Steps, Screening the Past,* 2004, http://www.latrobe.edu.au/screeningthepast/reviews/rev_16/KMbr16a.html, accessed 31 December 2007.

25. Charles Higham, 'Hitchcock's World', *Film Quarterly,* 16/2 (1962–3), p. 4.

26. David Thomson, *The New Biographical Dictionary of Film,* 4th edn (London: Little, Brown, 2003), p. 403.

27. Charles Thomas Samuels, 'Sightings: Hitchcock', *American Scholar,* 39 (1970), p. 295, in *'The Thirty-Nine Steps* CineFile', *Pacific Film Archive,* http://www.mip.berkeley.edu/cgi-bin/cine_film_detail.pl/cine_img?21091+21091+432, accessed 31 December 2007.

28. Ibid., p. 298.

29. Dennis R. Perry, 'Imps of the Perverse: Discovering the Poe/Hitchcock Connection', *Literature/Film Quarterly,* 24/4 (1996), internet version consulted: http://www.cswnet.com/~erin/eap4.htm, accessed 31 December 2007 (currently unavailable).

30. Higham, 'Hitchcock's World', p. 3.

31. Perry, 'Imps of the Peverse'.

32. Wood, 'Hitchcock: Lost in the Wood', p. 53.

33. Robin Wood, *Hitchcock's Films Revisited,* rev. edn (New York: Columbia University Press, 2002), p. 207.

5 *Modern Times* (US, 1936): A Tramp for All Seasons

1. Charles J. Maland, *Chaplin and American Culture: The Evolution of a Star Image* (Princeton. NJ: Princeton University Press, 1989), pp. 157–8.

2. Frank S. Nugent, 'Heralding the Return, after an Undue Absence, of Charlie Chaplin in *Modern Times*', *New York Times,* 6 February 1936.

3. Graham Greene, *The Graham Greene Film Reader: Mornings in the Dark,* ed. David Parkinson (Manchester: Carcanet: 1993), pp. 73–4.

4. Ibid., p. 74.

5. 'Mr Chaplin's New Film', *Times,* 12 February 1936.

6. Review of *Modern Times, Monthly Film Bulletin,* 3/26 (1936), pp. 28–9.

7. Quoted in Alistair Cooke (ed.), *Garbo and the Night Watchmen* (London: Secker & Warburg, 1971), pp. 274–5.

8. Mick LaSalle, *'Modern Times* Keeps Up with Ours', *San Francisco Chronicle,* 26 December 2003.

9. Chris Dashiell, 'Really Modern Times', *CineScene*, 2004, http://www.cinescene. com/dash/moderntimes.htm, accessed 31 December 2007.

10. *Modern Times* (1936), *IMDb*, http://imdb.com/title/tt0027977, accessed 31 December 2007.

11. 'The Last Laugh: Your Favourite 50', *Observer*, 22 July 2007.

12. *Manchester Guardian*, 14 July 1936.

13. Cooke, *Garbo and the Night Watchmen*, pp. 255–76.

14. Ian Christie, 'The Rules of the Game', *Sight and Sound*, 12/9 (2002), p. 27.

15. Andrew Sarris, *The American Cinema: Directors and Directions, 1929–1968* (New York: E. P. Dutton, 1968), p. 39.

16. David Robinson, review of *Modern Times*, *Sight and Sound*, 41/2 (1972), p. 110.

17. David Robinson, '*Modern Times*', *Charlie Chaplin Official Website*, 2004, http://www.charliechaplin.com/en/articles/6, accessed 31 December 2007.

18. Charles Chaplin, 'Pantomime and Comedy', *New York Times*, 27 January 1931, in Donald McCaffrey (ed.), *Focus on Chaplin* (Englewood Cliffs, NJ: Prentice-Hall, 1971), p. 64.

19. Andrew Sarris, *You Ain't Heard Nothin' Yet—The American Talking Film: History and Memory, 1927–1949* (New York: Oxford University Press, 1998), p. 148.

20. Julian Smith, *Chaplin* (Boston: Twayne, 1984), p. 98.

21. Garrett Stewart, 'Modern Hard Times: Chaplin and the Cinema of Self-Reflection', *Critical Inquiry*, 3/2 (1976), p. 313.

22. Dashiell, 'Really Modern Times'.

23. Jonathan Rosenbaum, 'Rediscovering Charlie Chaplin', *Cineaste*, 29/4 (2004), p. 53.

24. Ibid.

25. Stephen M. Weissman, 'Charles Chaplin's Film Heroines', *Film History*, 8/4 (1996), pp. 439–45; Joyce Milton, *Tramp: The Life of Charlie Chaplin* (New York: Da Capo Press, 1998); Kenneth S. Lynn, *Charlie Chaplin and His Times* (New York: Simon & Schuster, 1997).

26. David Thomson, *The New Biographical Dictionary of Film*, 4th edn (London: Little, Brown, 2003), p. 151.

27. J. H. Matthews, *Surrealism and Film* (Ann Arbor: University of Michigan Press, 1971), pp. 29–36.

28. Martin F. Norden, 'The Avant-Garde Cinema of the 1920s: Connections to Futurism, Precisionism, and Suprematism', *Leonardo*, 17/2 (1984), pp. 108–12; Marcel Oms, 'Charlie Chaplin, Stranger and Brother: Shadows on the Screen', *UNESCO Courier*, October 1989, *BNET Research Center*, http://findarticles.com/ p/articles/mi_m1310/is_1989_Oct/ai_8114683, accessed 31 December 2007.

29. Maland, *Chaplin and American Culture*, p. 151.

30. Lynn, *Charlie Chaplin and His Times*, p. 375.

31. Maland, *Chaplin and American Culture*, pp. 129–30.

32. Jorn K. Bramann, '*Modern Times*', *Frostburg State University Philosophical Forum,* 2006, http://faculty.frostburg.edu/phil/forum/ModernTimes.htm, accessed 31 December 2007.

33. Maland, *Chaplin and American Culture,* pp. 153–4.

34. Stewart, 'Modern Hard Times', p. 313.

35. Ibid.

6 *Citizen Kane* (US, 1941): The Tragedy of Ambition

1. Van Nest Polglase received a credit as head of the department, but Perry Ferguson worked on the film. Orson Welles and Peter Bogdanovich, *This Is Orson Welles,* ed. Jonathan Rosenbaum (London: HarperCollins, 1993), p. 73.

2. Robert L. Carringer, 'The Script of *Citizen Kane*', in James Naremore (ed.), *Orson Welles's 'Citizen Kane': A Casebook* (New York: Oxford University Press, 2004), pp. 79–121; Simon Callow, *Orson Welles: The Road to Xanadu* (London: Cape, 1995), pp. 484–518.

3. Welles and Bogdanovich, *This Is Orson Welles,* p. 71; Callow, *Orson Welles,* p. 519.

4. Bosley Crowther, 'Orson Welles's Controversial *Citizen Kane* Proves Sensational Film at Palace', *New York Times,* 2 May 1941.

5. Bosley Crowther, 'The Ambiguous *Citizen Kane:* Orson Welles in His First Motion Picture Creates a Titanic Character', *New York Times,* 4 May 1941.

6. Richard Griffith, review of *Citizen Kane, Los Angeles Times,* 12 May 1941, in Mark Summers, 'From Sneer to Eternity', *Vanity Fair,* March 2006, p. 342, *EBSCO research databases.*

7. Review of *Citizen Kane, Times,* 13 October 1941.

8. Dilys Powell, *The Golden Screen: Fifty Years of Films,* ed. George Perry (London: Pavilion Books, 1989), p. 29.

9. Robert L. Carringer, *The Making of 'Citizen Kane'* (Berkeley and Los Angeles: University of California Press, 1985), pp. 111–17.

10. Andrew Sarris, 'Kane: For and Against', *Sight and Sound,* 1/6 (1991), p. 22; Welles and Bogdanovich, *This Is Orson Welles,* p. 87.

11. Carringer, *The Making of 'Citizen Kane'*, p. 119; Denis Seguin, 'Gold in the Vaults', *Screen International,* 20–25 April 2007, p. 11.

12. Ian Christie, 'The Rules of the Game', *Sight and Sound,* 12/9 (2002), pp. 24 and 27.

13. Roger Ebert, review of *Citizen Kane, Chicago Sun-Times,* 24 May 1998.

14. Top 250 Movies as Voted by Our Users, *IMDb,* http://imdb.com/chart/top, accessed 7 January 2008.

15. Pauline Kael, *Raising Kane: Pauline Kael on the Best Film Ever Made* (London: Methuen, 1995), pp. 93–5.

16. Peter Wollen, '*Citizen Kane*', in Naremore (ed.), *Orson Welles's 'Citizen Kane*', pp. 261–2.
17. Callow, *Orson Welles,* p. 512.
18. James Naremore, 'Style and Meaning in *Citizen Kane*', in Naremore (ed.), *Orson Welles's 'Citizen Kane*', p. 138; Callow, *Orson Welles,* pp. 512–14.
19. Callow, *Orson Welles,* p. 512; David Thomson, *The New Biographical Dictionary of Film,* 4th edn (London: Little, Brown, 2003), p. 612.
20. Bosley Crowther, review of *Citizen Kane, New York Times,* 4 May 1941.
21. See Michael Denning, 'The Problems of Magic: Orson Welles's Allegories of Anti-Fascism', in Naremore (ed), *Orson Welles's 'Citizen Kane',* pp. 185–216.
22. David Bordwell, 'Deep-Focus Photography', in David Bordwell, Janet Staiger and Kristin Thompson (eds), *The Classical Hollywood Cinema: Film Style and Mode of Production to 1960* (London: Routledge, 1985), pp. 341–52.
23. Carringer, *The Making of 'Citizen Kane',* p. 89; Callow, *Orson Welles,* p. 522.
24. Carringer, *The Making of 'Citizen Kane',* p. 62.
25. François Thomas, '*Citizen Kane:* The Sound Track', in Naremore (ed.), *Orson Welles's 'Citizen Kane',* pp. 164–7.
26. Richard Rowland, 'American Classic', *Hollywood Quarterly,* 2/3 (1947), p. 264.
27. Kael, *Raising Kane,* p. 90; Andrew Sarris, '*Citizen Kane:* the American Baroque', in Ronald Gottesman (ed.), *Focus on 'Citizen Kane'* (Englewood Cliffs, NJ: Prentice-Hall, 1971), p. 103.
28. Welles and Bogdanovich, *This is Orson Welles,* p. 51.
29. Charles Higham, 'From *The Films of Orson Welles*', in Gottesman (ed.), *Focus on 'Citizen Kane',* p. 144.
30. Welles and Bogdanovich, *This Is Orson Welles,* p. 84.
31. Susan Ohmer, *George Gallup in Hollywood* (New York: Columbia University Press, 2006), ch. 7.
32. David Thomson, *America in the Dark: Hollywood and the Gift of Unreality* (London: Hutchinson, 1978), p. 128.
33. Kael, *Raising Kane,* p. 94.
34. Sarris, '*Citizen Kane:* The American Baroque', p. 103.
35. For an alternative view see Denning, 'The Problems of Magic'.
36. Naremore, 'Style and Meaning in *Citizen Kane*', p. 157.
37. Tangye Lean, review of *Citizen Kane, Horizon,* 4 (1941), in Gottesman (ed.), *Focus on 'Citizen Kane',* p. 61.
38. Robin Bates with Scott Bates, 'Fiery Speech in a World of Shadows: Rosebud's Influence on Early Audiences', *Cinema Journal,* 26/2 (1987), p. 3. This retrospective view by Scott Bates carries the inherent dangers of distortion. See also Jonathan Rosenbaum, 'Jonathan Rosenbaum Responds to Robin Bates's "Fiery Speech in a World of Shadows: Rosebud's Influence on Early Audiences"', *Cinema Journal,* 26/4 (1987), pp. 60–4.

7 *It's a Wonderful Life* (US, 1946): Seeking the American Hero

1. Joseph McBride, *Frank Capra: The Catastrophe of Success* (London: Faber and Faber, 1992), pp. 510–19.
2. Ibid. p. 525; Donald Dewey, *James Stewart: A Biography* (London: Little, Brown, 1997), pp. 263–6.
3. Charles K. Wolfe, *Frank Capra: A Guide to References and Resources* (Boston: G. K. Hall, 1987).
4. Bosley Crowther, review of *It's a Wonderful Life, New York Times,* 23 December 1946.
5. Virginia Wright, review of *It's a Wonderful Life, New York Daily News,* 12 December 1946, in Wolfe, *Frank Capra,* p. 267.
6. Pauline Kael, *5001 Nights at the Movies* (London: Arrow Books, 1987), p. 286.
7. Review of *It's a Wonderful Life, Times,* 5 April 1947.
8. Dilys Powell, *The Golden Screen: Fifty Years of Films,* ed. George Perry (London: Pavilion Books, 1989), p. 67.
9. McBride, *Frank Capra,* pp. 529–30.
10. Davi Napoleon, '*Wonderful Life:* Broadway Bound?', *American Film,* 11/7 (1986), p. 10; David P. Hayes, 'Re *It's a Wonderful Life*', *Classic Movies: Related Articles from My Newsgroup Postings,* 22 October 1997, http://articles.dhwritings.com/c02.html; David P. Hayes, 'Re *It's a Wonderful Life*', *Classic Movies: Related Articles from My Newsgroup Pages,* 25 October 1997, http://articles.dhwritings.com/c04.html; Jon Avner, 'Can I Show *It's a Wonderful Life?*', *efilm center,* n.d., http://www.film-center.com/canishow.html, all accessed 31 December 2007.
11. John Mariani, 'The Intelligent Heart', *Film Comment,* 15/5 (1979), p. 37.
12. AFI Agrees: It's a 'Wonderful' Film, *IMDb,* 15 June 2006 (studio briefing), http://imdb.com/title/tt0038650/news; Top 250 Movies as Voted by Our Users, *IMDb,* http://imdb.com/chart/top, both accessed 31 December 2007.
13. James Martin, 'What's so Wonderful?', *America,* 20–27 December 1997, p. 22, *EBSCO research databases.*
14. Aljean Harmetz, 'Movie Classic', *American Heritage,* October 2005, internet version consulted: http://www.americanheritage.com/articles/magazine/ah/2005/5/2005_5_69.shtml, accessed 31 December 2007.
15. Ibid.
16. Elliott Stein, 'Capra Counts His Oscars', *Sight and Sound,* 41/3 (1972), p. 162.
17. Martin, 'What's so Wonderful?', p. 22.
18. Leland Poague, *Another Frank Capra* (Cambridge: Cambridge University Press, 1994), p. 196.
19. Stuart Voytilla, *Myth and the Movies: Discovering the Mythic Structure of Over 50 Unforgettable Films* (Studio City, CA: Michael Wiese Productions, 1999), pp. 8–12.

20. Glenn Erickson, '"Films Blanc" and What Dreams May Come', *DVD talk,* 1998, http://www.dvdtalk.com/dvdsavant/s58filmblanc.html, accessed 2 January 2008.

21. See Robert B. Ray, *A Certain Tendency of the Hollywood Cinema, 1930–1980* (Princeton, NJ: Princeton University Press, 1985), p. 202.

22. An example is 'Best Movies', *Reader's Digest,* May 2004, p. 68. *It's a Wonderful Life* is ranked alongside *Singin' in the Rain* and *Citizen Kane.*

23. Stein, 'Capra Counts His Oscars', p. 162.

24. Jonathan Munby, 'A Hollywood Carol's Wonderful Life', in Mark Connelly (ed.), *Christmas at the Movies: Images of Christmas in American, British and European Cinema* (London: I. B. Tauris, 2000), p. 47.

25. Ray Carney, 'Capra and the Critics, or: Ideology Is Only a Sliver of Life', *Boston University,* 2003, http://people.bu.edu/rcarney/capra/capracrit.shtml, accessed 2 January 2008.

26. Ibid.

27. Raymond Carney, *American Vision: The Films of Frank Capra* (Cambridge: Cambridge University Press, 1986), pp. 430–1.

28. Ibid., p. 379.

29. Glenn Erickson, '*It's a Wonderful Life*—or: It's a Wonderful Recut?', *DVD talk,* 1998, http://www.dvdtalk.com/dvdsavant/s55wonderful.html, accessed 2 January 2008.

30. Patrick J. Deneen, 'Awakening from the American Dream: The End of Escape in American Cinema?', *Perspectives on Political Science,* 31/2 (2002), *EBSCO research databases.*

31. Ibid.

32. Glenn Erickson, 'Films Blanc'. For an example of the interest in film noir, see Robin Wood, 'Ideology, Genre, Auteur', *Film Comment,* 13/1 (1977), pp. 46–51.

33. Bosley Crowther, 'The Spirits Move: A Comparison of Inspirations in British and Hollywood Movies', *New York Times,* 12 January 1947.

34. Stephen J. Brown, 'Theological Optimism: the Films of Frank Capra', *Theology,* 101/804 (1998), p. 439.

35. Munby, 'A Holiday Carol's Wonderful Life', pp. 41–2.

36. Vito Zagarrio, 'It is (Not) a Wonderful Life: For a Counter-Reading of Frank Capra', in Robert Sklar and Vito Zagarrio (eds), *Frank Capra: Authorship and the Studio System* (Philadelphia: Temple University Press, 1998), pp. 79–86.

37. This attitude is found elsewhere. See Anna Siomopoulos, '"I Didn't Know Anyone Could Be So Unselfish": Liberal Empathy, the Welfare State, and King Vidor's *Stella Dallas', Cinema Journal,* 38/4 (1999), pp. 3–23.

38. Erickson, 'Films Blanc'.

39. Munby, 'A Holiday Carol's Wonderful Life', pp. 42 and 55.

8 *Black Narcissus* (GB, 1947): Nuns in Exotic Places

1. Review of *Black Narcissus, Picture Show,* 24 July 1948.
2. Review of *Black Narcissus, Monthly Film Bulletin,* 14/161 (1947), p. 60.
3. *Daily Film Renter,* 16 September 1948.
4. Review of *Black Narcissus, Times,* 24 April 1947.
5. Dilys Powell, *The Golden Screen: Fifty Years of Films,* ed. George Perry (London: Pavilion Books, 1989), pp. 67–8.
6. James Agee, *Agee on Film* (London: Peter Owen, 1963), pp. 272–3.
7. Derek Elly (ed.), '*Variety' Movie Guide* (London: Hamlyn, 1991), p. 61; review of *Black Narcissus, Kinematograph Weekly,* 24 April 1947, p. 27.
8. Michael Powell, *A Life in Movies* (London: Heinemann, 1986); Michael Powell, *Million Dollar Movie* (London: Heinemann, 1992); Ian Christie, *Arrows of Desire: The Films of Michael Powell and Emeric Pressburger* (London: Faber and Faber, 1994).
9. Geoff Andrew, '*Black Narcissus*', in John Pym (ed.) *Time Out Film Guide,* 15th edn (London: Time Out, 2006), p. 118.
10. Kilmeny Fune-Saunders (ed.), *Radio Times Guide to Films,* 7th edn (London: BBC Worldwide, 2006), p. 137.
11. Mark Duguid, '*Black Narcissus*', *BFI screenonline,* 2003–6, http://www.screenonline.org.uk/film/id/438337/index.html, accessed 2 January 2008.
12. Gary Morris, 'Powell and Pressburger's *Black Narcissus* on DVD', *Bright Lights Film Journal,* 33 (2001), http://www.brightlightsfilm.com/33/blacknarcissus.html, accessed 2 January 2008.
13. Sarah Street, *Black Narcissus* (London: I. B. Tauris, 2005), pp. 64–72.
14. Dibyaduti Purkayastha, '*Black Narcissus* (1946): A "Desi" Perspective', *The Powell & Pressburger Pages,* n.d., http//www.powell-pressburger.org/Reviews/47_BN/BN06.html, accessed 2 January 2008.
15. Anh Hua, 'Primitive Spectacle in *Black Narcissus*', *Journal of Social and Political Thought,* 1/2 (2000), http://www.yorku.ca/jspot/2/ahua.htm, accessed 2 January 2008.
16. Andrew Moor, *Powell and Pressburger: A Cinema of Magic Spaces* (London: I. B. Tauris, 2005), p. 191.
17. John Huntley, *British Technicolour Film* (London: Skelton Robinson, [1949]), p. 114.
18. For tonal variations between three DVD transfers see Gary W. Tooze, review of *Black Narcissus* DVD, *DVDBeaver,* n.d., http://www.dvdbeaver.com/film/DVDReview2/blacknarcissus.htm, accessed 2 January 2008.
19. Raymond Durgnat, 'Retrospective: *Black Narcissus* … and in Theory: Towards a Superficial Structuralism', *Monthly Film Bulletin,* 51/609 (1984), p. 315.
20. David Thomson, 'A Romantic Sensibility: The Films of Michael Powell', *American Film,* 6/2 (1980), p. 51.

21. Alton Jerome McFarland, 'Madness through Music: An Analysis of Sound in *Black Narcissus*', *The Powell & Pressburger Pages,* n.d., http://www.powell-pressburger.org/Reviews/47_BN/MadnessThroughMusic.html, accessed 2 January 2008.
22. Diana Dors, *Swingin' Dors* (London: World Distributors, 1960), p. 13.
23. Obituary for Rumer Godden, *Daily Telegraph,* 14 November 1998.
24. Michael Walker, '*Black Narcissus',* Framework, 9 (1978–9), pp. 9–13.
25. Adrian Danks, 'Michael Powell & Emeric Pressburger', *senses of cinema,* 20 (2002), http://www.sensesofcinema.com/contents/directors/02/powell.html, accessed 2 January 2008.
26. Jean George Auriol, 'The British Film Abroad: A Study of Critical Reactions', in Roger Manvell (ed.), *The Year's Work in the Film, 1949* (London: Longmans Green, 1950), p. 48.

9 *The Night of the Hunter* (US, 1955): Return of the Big Bad Wolf

1. Simon Callow, *The Night of the Hunter* (London: BFI, 2000), pp. 22–3; Paul Hammond, 'Melmoth in Norman Rockwell Land … on *The Night of the Hunter'*, *Sight and Sound,* 48/2 (1979), p. 106; Tim Dirks, '*The Night of the Hunter* (1955)', *The Greatest Films,* 1996–2007, http://filmsite.org/nightof.html, accessed 2 January 2008.
2. Callow, *The Night of the Hunter,* pp. 32 and 41–2.
3. Philip T. Hartung, review of *The Night of the Hunter, Commonweal,* 7 October 1955, in Ardis Sillick and Michael McCormick (eds), *Some Like It Not: Bad Reviews of Great Movies* (London: Aurum Press, 1996), p. 35.
4. Bosley Crowther, 'Bogeyman Plus', *New York Times,* 30 September 1955.
5. Review of *The Night of the Hunter, Times,* 28 November 1955.
6. Dilys Powell, *The Golden Screen: Fifty Years of Films,* ed. George Perry (London: Pavilion Bo 1989), p. 127.
7. Roger Ebert, review of *The Night of the Hunter, Chicago Sun-Times,* 24 November 1996; Edward Guthmann, review of *The Night of the Hunter, San Francisco Chronicle,* 15 September 1995.
8. Kevin Hagopian, 'Film Notes: *The Night of the Hunter'*, *New York State Writers' Institute,* n.d., http://www.albany.edu/writers-inst/webpages4/filmnotes/fn-f00n5b.html, accessed 27 June 2008.
9. *The Night of the Hunter* (1955), *IMDb,* http://imdb.com/title/tt0048424, accessed 2 January 2008.
10. Gordon Gow, '*The Night of the Hunter'*, *Films and Filming,* February 1975, pp. 48–53.
11. Ibid., p. 52.
12. Hammond, 'Melmoth in Norman Rockwell Land …', p. 105.

13. Ibid., p. 109.
14. David Thomson, 'A Child's Demon', *Sight and Sound,* 9/4 (1999), p. 22.
15. Crowther, 'Bogeyman Plus'.
16. Callow, *The Night of the Hunter',* pp. 54–5.
17. Review of *The Night of the Hunter, Variety,* 1 January 1955.
18. Thomson, 'A Child's Demon', p. 22. Lillian Gish is the likely source of this revisionist view. George Eells, *Robert Mitchum: A Biography,* London: Robson Books, 1984), p. 187.
19. Callow, *The Night of the Hunter,* p. 65.
20. Thomson, 'A Child's Demon', p. 22.
21. Larry Gross, 'Baby, I Don't Care', *Sight and Sound,* 7/9 (1997), p. 9.
22. Jack Ravage, *'The Night of the Hunter* [On Videotape]', *Film Quarterly,* 42/1 (1988), p. 44.
23. Callow, *The Night of the Hunter,* p. 63.
24. Davis Grubb: Biographical Information, *West Virginia Wesleyan College,* n.d., http://www.wvwc.edu/lib/wv_authors/authors/a_grubb.htm, accessed 2 January 2008.
25. Paul Fraumeni, 'What Makes a Great Film?', *University of Toronto,* [2003], http://www.utoronto.ca/bios/askus35.htm, accessed 27 June 2008.

10   *Lawrence of Arabia* (GB, 1962): An Englishman in the Sun

1. Joel Hodson, 'Who Wrote *Lawrence of Arabia?:* Sam Spiegel and David Lean's Denial of Credit to a Blacklisted Screenwriter', *Cineaste,* 20/4 (1994), pp. 12–17.
2. Gary Crowdus and Alan Farrand, 'Restoring Lawrence: An Interview with Robert Harris', *Cineaste,* 17/2 (1989), pp. 22–3.
3. Review of *Lawrence of Arabia, Variety,* 19 December 1962.
4. 'Full-Length Portrait of Lawrence of the Desert', *Times,* 11 December 1962.
5. Roger Sandall, review of *Lawrence of Arabia, Film Quarterly,* 16/3 (1963), p. 56.
6. Bosley Crowther, 'A Desert Warfare Spectacle', *New York Times,* 17 December 1962.
7. Steven Ross, 'In Defense of David Lean', *Take One,* 3/12 (1972). Quotation taken from internet version, no longer available.
8. Desson Howe, review of *Lawrence of Arabia, Washington Post,* 3 February 1989.
9. Chris Dashiell, review of *Lawrence of Arabia, CineScene.com,* 2001, http://www.cinescene.com/flicks/flicks062001.html#lawrence, accessed 2 January 2008.
10. Rita Kempley, review of *Lawrence of Arabia, Washington Post,* 8 February 1989.
11. Jonathan Rosenbaum, review of *Lawrence of Arabia, Chicago Reader,* http://onfilm.chicagoreader.com/movies/capsules/5248_LAWRENCE_OF_ARABIA, accessed 2 January 2008.

12. *Lawrence of Arabia* Named Best British Film Ever, *IMDb,* 16 August 2004 (studio briefing), http://imdb.com/title/tt0056172/news, accessed 3 January 2008.
13. Review of *Lawrence of Arabia, Variety,* 19 December 1962.
14. *Lawrence of Arabia* (1962), *IMDb,* http://imdb.com/title/tt0056172, accessed 3 January 2008.
15. Kevin Brownlow, *David Lean* (London: Faber and Faber, 1992), pp. 472–3.
16. Roger Ebert, review of *Lawrence of Arabia, Chicago Sun-Times,* 2 September 2001.
17. David Thomson, *The New Biographical Dictionary of Film,* 4th edn (London: Little, Brown, 2003), p. 656.
18. Rosenbaum, review of *Lawrence of Arabia.*
19. Marco Lanzagorta, '*Lawrence of Arabia:* The Burden of the Empire', *PopMatters,* 2003, http://www.popmatters.com/pm/film/reviews/36429/lawrence-of-arabia-dvd, accessed 3 January 2008.
20. Michael Wilson, '*Lawrence of Arabia:* Elements and Facets of the Theme', *Cineaste,* 21/4 (1995), pp. 30–2.
21. Joel C. Hodson, *Lawrence of Arabia and American Culture: The Making of a Transatlantic Legend* (Westport, CT: Greenwood Press, 1995), ch. 7; Robert Bolt, 'Apologia', *Cineaste,* 21/4 (1995), pp. 33–4.
22. Gary Crowdus, '*Lawrence of Arabia:* The Cinematic (Re)Writing of History', *Cineaste,* 17/2 (1989), pp. 14–21.
23. See *T. E. Lawrence Society,* http://www.telsociety.org.uk; *Al-Bab,* http://www.al-bab.com/arab/lawrence.htm, both accessed 3 January 2008.
24. Jeffrey Richards, *Films and British National Identity: From Dickens to 'Dad's Army'* (Manchester: Manchester University Press, 1997), p. 57.
25. Andrew Kelly, Jeffrey Richards and James Pepper, *Filming T. E. Lawrence: Korda's Lost Epic* (London: I. B. Tauris, 1997); Jeffrey Richards and Jeffrey Hulbert, 'Censorship in Action: The Case of *Lawrence of Arabia*', *Journal of Contemporary History,* 19/1 (1984), pp. 153–70; Richards, *Films and British National Identity,* p. 56.
26. Damian Cannon, review of *Lawrence of Arabia, Movie Reviews UK,* 1997, http://www.film.u-net.com/Movies/Reviews/Lawrence_Arabia.html, accessed 3 January 2008.
27. Alain Silver 'David Lean', *senses of cinema,* 30 (2004), http://www.sensesof cinema.com/contents/directors/04/lean.html, accessed 3 January 2008.
28. Thomson, *The New Biographical Dictionary of Film,* p. 505.

11   *8½* (Italy/France, 1963): The Director as Superstar

1. Jacqueline Reich, '*Otto e mezzo/8½',* in Giorgio Bertellini (ed.), *The Cinema of Italy* (London: Wallflower Press, 2004), p. 144.

2. Eric Rhode, review of *8½*, *Sight and Sound*, 32/4 (1963), p. 193.
3. Powell, Dilys, *The Golden Screen: Fifty Years of Films*, ed. George Perry, London: Pavilion Books, 1989, p. 198.
4. 'Fellini's New Film in Rome', *Times*, 13 February 1963.
5. Review of *8½*, *New York Herald Tribune*, 26 June 1963, quoted in Claudio G. Fava and Aldo Vigano, *The Films of Federico Fellini*, tr. Shula Curto (Secaucus, NJ: Citadel Press, 1981), p. 118.
6. Desson Howe, review of *8½*, *Washington Post*, 26 February 1993.
7. Hal Hinson, review of *8½*, *Washington Post*, 26 February 1993.
8. Roger Ebert, review of *8½*, *Chicago Sun-Times*, 7 May 1993.
9. Terry Gilliam, 'Close-Up', BBC2, 27 November 1995, transcribed for 'Terry Gilliam's Favourite Movies', ed. Phil Stubbs, *Dreams*, http://www.smart.co.uk/dreams/tgclip.htm; Martin Scorsese, 'Premio "Fondazione Fellini" a Martin Scorsese', *Fondazione Fellini*, 2005, http://www.federicofellini.it/newsScheda.asp?end_where=news&id=401; Lars-Olaf Löthwall, 'An Interview with Ingmar Bergman', *Take One*, 2/1 (1968), internet version consulted: *Bergmanorama*, http://www.bergmanorama.com/takeone_68.htm, accessed 4 January 2008.
10. Top 250 Movies as Voted by Our Users, *IMDb*, http://imdb.com/chart/top, accessed 4 January 2008.
11. Quoted in Philip Kemp, 'Why Fellini?', *Sight and Sound*, 14/8 (2004), p. 22.
12. Pauline Kael, *5001 Nights at the Movies* (London: Arrow Books, 1987), p. 163.
13. David Lavery, 'Major Man: Fellini as an Autobiographer', *Post Script*, 6/2 (1987), internet version consulted: http://davidlavery.net/writings/Movies/Major_Man.pdf, p. 6, accessed 4 January 2008.
14. Ibid., p. 4.
15. Kemp, 'Why Fellini?', p. 22.
16. Quoted in Lavery, 'Major Man', p. 7 (internet version).
17. Ibid., p. 3.
18. J. P. Telotte, 'Definitely Falling Down: *8½*, *Falling Down* and the Death of Fantasy', *Journal of Popular Film and Television*, 24/1 (1996), internet version consulted: *HighBeam Encyclopedia*, http://www.encyclopedia.com/doc/1G1–18533920.html, accessed 27 June 2008.
19. Alan A. Stone, '*8½*: Fellini's Moment of Truth', *Boston Review*, Summer 1995, http://bostonreview.net/BR20.3/stone.html, accessed 4 January 2008.
20. Ibid.
21. Ibid.
22. Ibid.
23. Ibid.
24. Ian Christie, 'The Rules of the Game', *Sight and Sound*, 12/9 (2002), pp. 28–36 and 40–50.
25. J. Hoberman, 'The Stunt Men', *Village Voice*, 7–13 April 1999.

26. Robin Wood, 'The Question of Fellini Continued' (source and date not stated), in '*8½* CineFile', *Pacific Film Archive,* http://www.mip.berkeley.edu/cgi-bin/cine_film_detail.pl/cine_img?24275+24275, accessed 4 January 2008.

27. An exception is Mira Liehm, *Passion and Defiance: Film in Italy from 1942 to the Present* (Berkeley and Los Angeles: University of California Press, 1984), pp. 223–4.

28. Peter Bondanella, *The Cinema of Federico Fellini* (Princeton, NJ: Princeton University Press, 1992), p. 164.

29. Marilyn Fabe, '*8½: The Steambath Sequence* (Mount Vernon, NY: Macmillan Films, 1975), p. 12, in '*8½* CineFile', *Pacific Film Archive,* http://www.mip.berkeley.edu/cgi-bin/cine_film_detail.pl/cine_img?24275+24275, p. 8, accessed 4 January 2008.

30. Ted Perry, 'Ted Perry on *8½*', in Leo Braudy and Morris Dickstein (eds), *Great Film Directors: A Critical Anthology* (New York: Oxford University Press, 1978), p. 297.

31. Stone, '*8½:* Fellini's Moment of Truth'.

12 *2001: A Space Odyssey* (GB/US, 1968): The Long Voyage to Destiny

1. Renata Adler, '*2001* is Up, Up and Away: Kubrick's Odyssey in Space Begins to Run', *New York Times,* 4 April 1968.

2. Quoted in James O'Ehley, '*2001:* 30 Years On', *The Sci-Fi Movie Page,* 1997, http://www.scifimoviepage.com/2001_30.html. For further negative coverage see Tracy McCormick, '*2001* Under Fire: Early Reviewers of Film Found It Boring, Frustrating', *Obelisk,* n.d., http://www.boraski.com/obelisk/cinema/s_reviews.html, both accessed 3 January 2008.

3. Joseph Gelmis, 'Three Reviews of *2001*' (1968–9), *The Kubrick Site,* http://www.visual-memory.co.uk/amk/doc/0040.html, accessed 3 January 2008.

4. John Russell Taylor, 'Beyond the Plot Barrier', *Times,* 7 September 1968.

5. Roger Ebert, review of *2001: A Space Odyssey, Chicago Sun-Times,* 12 April 1968.

6. Roger Ebert, review of *2001: A Space Odyssey, Chicago Sun-Times,* 27 March 1997.

7. James O'Ehley, '*2001: A Space Odyssey', The Sci-Fi Movie Page,* 1997, http://www.scifimoviepage.com/2001.html, accessed 3 January 2008.

8. Stephen Hunter, 'A Space Idiocy: *2001* Revisited', *Washington Post,* 2 November 2001.

9. *2001: A Space Odyssey* (1968), *IMDb,* http://www.imdb.com/title/tt0062622, accessed 27 June 2008.

10. Alexander Walker with Sybil Taylor and Ulrich Ruchti, *Stanley Kubrick, Director: A Visual Analysis,* rev. edn (London: Weidenfeld and Nicholson, 1999), p. 172.

11. Ibid., p. 184.

12. Joseph Gelmis, 'An Interview with Stanley Kubrick' (1969), *The Kubrick Site,* http://www.visual-memory.co.uk/amk/doc/0069.html, accessed 3 January 2008.

13. Tim Hunter with Stephen Kaplan and Peter Jaszi, 'The *Harvard Crimson* Review of *2001*' [1968], *The Kubrick Site,* http://www.visual-memory.co.uk/amk/doc/0038.html, accessed 3 January 2008.

14. Morris Beja, '*2001:* Odyssey to Byzantium', *Extrapolation,* 10 (1968), pp. 67–8, in Beja, '3 Perspectives on a Film', http://www.visual-memory.co.uk/amk/doc/0041.html, accessed 3 January 2008; Alex Eisenstein, 'The Academic Overkill of *2001*', in Beja,'3 Perspectives on a Film'; Mel McKee, '*2001:* Out of the Secret Planet', *Sight and Sound,* 38/4 (1969), pp. 204–7.

15. Leonard F. Wheat, *Kubrick's 2001: A Triple Allegory* (Lanham, MD: Scarecrow Press, 2000).

16. Carl Freedman, 'Superman Among the Stars', *Science Fiction Studies,* 28/2 (2001), http://www.depauw.edu/sfs/birs/bir84.htm, accessed 3 January 2008.

17. Don Daniels, 'A Skeleton Key to *2001*', *Sight and Sound,* 40/1 (1970–1), pp. 28–33.

18. Richard I. Pope, 'In Kubrick's Crypt, a Derrida/Deleuze Monster; or An-Other Return to *2001*', *Film Philosophy,* 7/22 (2003), http://www.film-philosophy.com/vol7–2003/n22pope, accessed 3 January 2008.

19. Quoted in John Baxter, *Stanley Kubrick: A Biography* (London: HarperCollins, 1997), p. 221.

20. Ibid., p. 215.

21. Thomas Allen Nelson, *Kubrick: Inside a Film Artist's Maze,* expanded edn (Bloomington: Indiana University Press, 2000); Claudia Zimny, '*2001* and the Motif of the Voyage', *The Kubrick Site,* n.d., http://www.visual-memory.co.uk/amk/doc/0001.html, accessed 3 January 2008.

22. Daniels, 'A Skeleton Key to *2001*'; F. Anthony Macklin, 'The Comic Sense of *2001*', *Film Comment,* 5/4 (1969), pp. 10–14.

23. Jenefer Robinson, *Deeper Than Reason: Emotion and Its Role in Literature, Music and Art* (Oxford: Clarendon Press, Oxford University Press, 2005), pp. 293–414.

24. Ibid., pp. 351–3.

25. Ibid., pp. 369–76. See also Daniel J. Levitin, *This Is Your Brain on Music: The Science of a Human Obsession* (New York: Dutton Books, 2006); and David Huron, *Sweet Anticipation: Music and the Psychology of Expectation* (Cambridge, MA: MIT Press, 2006).

26. Ebert, review of *2001: A Space Odyssey,* 1997.

27. Timothy E. Scheurer, 'The Score for *2001: A Space Odyssey,*' *Journal of Popular Film and Television,* 25/4 (1998), internet version consulted: *HighBeam Encyclopedia,* http://www.encyclopedia.com/doc/1G1–20573310.html, accessed 27 June 2008.

28. Ibid.
29. Quoted in James O'Ehley, '*2001:* 30 years on'.
30. Adam Dobson, '*2001: A Space Odyssey*. Stargazers, Navelgazers: The Search for an Answer Makes Monkeys of Us All', *Metaphilm,* 2005, http://www.metaphilm.com/index.php.detail/2001_a_space_ody.ssey, accessed 27 June 2008.
31. Walker, *Stanley Kubrick, Director,* p. 162; Baxter, *Stanley Kubrick,* p. 209.
32. Dariusz Roberte, '*2001: A Space Odyssey:* A Critical Analysis of the Film Score', *The Kubrick Site,* n.d., http://www.visual-memory.co.uk/amk/doc/0108.html, accessed 3 January 2008.

13 *The Godfather* (US, 1972): Keeping It in the Family

1. Michael Schumacher, *Francis Ford Coppola: A Filmmaker's Life* (London: Bloomsbury, 2000), p. 92.
2. Carlos Clarens, *Crime Movies: From Griffiths to 'The Godfather' and Beyond* (London: Secker & Warburg, 1980), p. 280.
3. Top 250 Movies as Voted by Our Users, IMDb, http://imdb.com/chart/top, accessed 3 January 2008.
4. Quoted in Peter Cowie, *The Godfather Book* (London: Faber and Faber, 1997), pp. 69–70.
5. John Russell Taylor, 'A Heritage and Its History', *Times,* 22 August 1972.
6. A. D. Murphy, review of *The Godfather, Variety,* 15 March 1972.
7. Vincent Canby, review of *The Godfather, New York Times,* 16 March 1972.
8. WGA Names Greatest Screenplays of All Time, *IMDb,* 7 April 2006 (studio briefing), http://imdb.com/title/tt0068646/news, accessed 3 January 2008.
9. Desson Howe, '*Godfather:* Offer Accepted', *Washington Post,* 21 March 1997.
10. Jack Shadoian, *Dreams and Dead Ends: The American Gangster/Crime Film* (Cambridge, MA: MIT Press, 1977), pp. 326–7.
11. Ibid., p. 326.
12. Naomi Greene, 'Family Ceremonies: Or, Opera in *The Godfather* Trilogy', in Nick Browne (ed.), *Francis Ford Coppola's 'The Godfather' Trilogy* (Cambridge: Cambridge University Press, 2000), pp. 133–55.
13. Shadoian, *Dreams and Dead Ends,* p. 327.
14. Schumacher, *Francis Ford Coppola,* pp. 116–17.
15. Naomi Greene, 'Coppola, Cimino: The Operatics of History', *Film Quarterly,* 38/2 (1984–5), p. 32.
16. David Thomson, 'The Discreet Charm of the Godfather', *Sight and Sound,* 47/2 (1978), p. 77.
17. Clarens, *Crime Movies,* p. 277.
18. Shadoian, *Dreams and Dead Ends,* p. 328.
19. Thomson, 'The Discreet Charm of the Godfather', p. 80.

20. Clarens, *Crime Movies,* p. 277.
21. Roger Corman, *'The Godfather'*, *Sight and Sound,* 12/9 (2002), p. 35; Steve Erickson, 'Founding Fathers', *Los Angeles Magazine,* December 2001, p. 134, *EBSCO research databases.*
22. Schumacher, *Francis Ford Coppola,* p. 104.
23. Alessandro Camon, *'The Godfather* and the Mythology of Mafia', in Nick Browne (ed.), *Francis Ford Coppola's 'The Godfather' Trilogy,* pp. 57–75.
24. David Ray Papke, 'Myth and Meaning: Francis Ford Coppola and Popular Responses to the Godfather Trilogy', in John Denvir (ed.), *Legal Reelism: Movies as Legal Texts* (Urbana: University of Illinois Press: 1996), pp. 1–22.
25. User Ratings for *The Godfather* (1972) *IMDb,* http://imdb.com/title/tt0068646/ratings, accessed 3 January 2008.
26. Camille Paglia, 'The Italian Way of Death', *Salon,* 1996, http://www.salon.com/weekly/paglia960805.html, accessed 4 January 2008.
27. Clarens, *Crime Movies,* p. 289.
28. Charles T. Gregory, 'Good Guys and Bad Guys', *Film Heritage,* 8/3 (1973), p. 4.
29. David Thomson, *The New Biographical Dictionary of Film,* 4th edn (London: Little, Brown, 2003), p. 176.
30. Greene, 'Coppola, Cimino: The Operatics of History', p. 37.

14 *Raging Bull* (US, 1980): The Drama of the Fight

1. Pauline Kael, *Taking It All In* (New York: Holt, Rinehart and Winston, 1987), pp. 107 and 109.
2. Roger Ebert, review of *Raging Bull, Chicago Sun-Times,* 1 January 1980.
3. Joseph McBride, review of *Raging Bull, Variety,* 12 November 1980.
4. Philip Oakes, 'Portrait of a Fighter in a Mean Street', *Sunday Times,* 22 February 1981.
5. Tom Pulleine, 'A Fair Knockout for the Aesthetes', *Guardian,* 19 February 1981.
6. Roger Ebert, review of *Raging Bull, Chicago Sun-Times,* 10 May 1998.
7. Amy Taubin, 'Primal Scream', *Village Voice,* 2–8 August 2000.
8. Ty Burr, review of *Raging Bull, Boston Globe,* 11 March 2005.
9. AFI's 100 Years … 100 Movies … 10th Anniversary Edition, *AFI,* 2007, http://connect.afi.com/site/PageServer?pagename=100yearsList *(registration required)*; *Raging Bull* (1980), *IMDb* http://imdb.com/title/tt0081398, both accessed 28 June 2008.
10. Dan Georgakas, review of *Raging Bull, Cineaste,* 11/1 (1980–1), pp. 28–30; David Thomson, 'The Director as *Raging Bull:* Why Can't a Woman Be More Like a Photograph', 1981 review reprinted in *Film Comment,* 34/3 (1998), pp. 52–63.
11. Georgakas, review of *Raging Bull,* p. 28.

12. Ibid., p. 29.
13. Thomson, 'The Director as *Raging Bull*', p. 56.
14. Ibid., p. 59.
15. Ibid.
16. Francesco Caviglia, 'Looking for Italian Male Adulthood, Old Style', *Point of View,* 12 (2001), http://pov.imv.au.dk/Issue_12/section_1/artc4A.html, accessed 4 January 2008.
17. Michael Bliss, *Martin Scorsese and Michael Cimino* (Metuchen, NJ: Scarecrow Press, 1985), p. 124.
18. Robin Wood, '*Raging Bull:* The Homosexual Subtext', *Movie,* 31–2 (1986), pp. 108–14.
19. Ibid., p. 110.
20. Richard A. Blake, 'Redeemed in Blood: The Sacramental Universe of Martin Scorsese', *Journal of Popular Film and Television,* 24/1 (1996), pp. 2–9, internet version consulted: *HighBeam Encyclopedia.* http://www.encyclopedia.com/doc/1g1–18533918.html, accessed 3 January 2008.
21. Ibid.
22. Thomson, 'The Director as *Raging Bull*', p. 56.
23. David Thomson, 'Animal Instinct', *Guardian,* 10 August 2007.
24. Georgakas, review of *Raging Bull,* p. 29.

15 *The Piano* (Australia/NZ/France, 1993): Love in a Rough Place

1. Diane Long Hoeveler, 'Silence, Sex, and Feminism: An Examination of *The Piano*'s Unacknowledged Sources', *Literature/Film Quarterly,* 26/2 (1998), pp. 109–16.
2. Stephen Crofts, 'Foreign Tunes? Gender and Nationality in Four Countries' Reception of *The Piano*', in Harriet Margolis (ed.), *Jane Campion's 'The Piano'* (Cambridge: Cambridge University Press, 2000), pp. 135–6.
3. Ibid., p. 149.
4. Desson Howe, review of *The Piano, Washington Post,* 19 November 1993.
5. Hal Hinson, review of *The Piano, Washington Post,* 19 November 1993.
6. Geoff Brown, 'Campion Finds an Epic Voice', *Times,* 28 October 1993.
7. Derek Malcolm, 'Keynote in the Silence', *Guardian ,* 28 October 1993.
8. Iain Johnstone, 'Silent Plight', *Sunday Times,* 31 October 1993.
9. Richard Alleva, 'A Word of Dissent: This Piano Is Out of Tune', *Commonweal,* 14 January 1994, internet version consulted: http://www.thefreelibrary.com/The+Piano.-a014979701, accessed 4 January 2008.
10. IMDb User Comments for *The Piano* (1993), *IMDb,* http://imdb.com/title/tt0107822/usercomments; *The Piano:* Movie Opinion, *Universitetet I Oslo,* http://www.fys.uio.no/~magnushj/Piano/opinion.html, both accessed 4 January 2008.

11. bell hooks, 'Sexism and Misogyny: Who Takes the Rap? Misogyny, Gangsta Rap, and *The Piano*', *Z Magazine,* February 1994, http://www.westga.edu/ ~gfraser/bell%20hooks.doc, accessed 4 January 2008.
12. Ibid.
13. Allison R. Yanos, 'The Piano as a Point of Resistance', *Fresh Writing,* 1 (2001– 02), http://www.nd.edu/~frswrite/issues/2001–2002/Yanos.shtml, accessed 4 January 2008.
14. Sue Gillett (Sue Gillet), 'A Pleasure to Watch: Jane Campion's Narrative Cinema', *Screening the Past,* 12 (2001), http://www.latrobe.edu.au/screeningthepast/ firstrelease/fr0301/sgfr12a.htm, accessed 4 January 2008 (currently unavailable).
15. Peter N. Chumo II, 'Keys to the Imagination: Jane Campion's *The Piano*', *Literature/Film Quarterly,* 25/3 (1997), pp. 173–6.
16. Cyndy Hendershot, '(Re)Visioning the Gothic: Jane Campion's *The Piano*', *Literature/Film Quarterly,* 26/2 (1998), internet version consulted: *BNET Research Center,* http://findarticles.com/p/articles/mi_qa3768/is_199801/ai_n8764512/ pg_3, accessed 4 January 2008.
17. Stuart Klawans, review of *The Piano, Nation,* 6 December 1993, p. 704, *EBSCO research databases.*
18. Mark A. Reid, 'A Few Black Keys and Maori Tattoos: Re-Reading Jane Campion's *The Piano* in Post Negritude Time', *Quarterly Review of Film and Video,* 17/2 (2000), p. 107.
19. Ibid.
20. Harry Pearson, review of *The Piano, Films in Review,* 45/3–4 (1994), pp. 56– 7; John Simon, 'Praise Jack, Shoot *The Piano*', *National Review,* 27 December 1993, pp. 65–7, internet version consulted: *BNET Research Center,* http:// findarticles.com/p/articles/mi_m1282/is_n25_v45/ai_14779808, accessed 4 January 2008; Alleva, 'A Word of Dissent'.
21. Clare Corbett, 'Cutting It Free: Notes on *The Piano* in the Editing Room', in Felicity Coombs and Suzanne Gemmell (eds), *Approaches to 'The Piano'* (Sydney: John Libby, 1999), p. 171.
22. Pearson, review of *The Piano,* p. 56.
23. Alleva, 'A Word of Dissent'.
24. Geraldine Bloustien, 'Jane Campion: Memory, Motif and Music', *Continuum: The Australian Journal of Media & Culture,* 5/2 (1990), http://wwwmcc. murdoch.edu.au/ReadingRoom/5.2/Bloust.html, accessed 4 January 2008.
25. Michael Hancock, review of *The Piano, Metro,* 148 (2006), p. 171, *EBSCO research databases.*
26. Simon, 'Praise Jack, Shoot *The Piano*'.
27. Claudia Gorbman, 'Music in *The Piano*', in Margolis, *Jane Campion's 'The Piano',* p. 47.
28. hooks, 'Sexism and Misogyny'.
29. Barbara Quart, review of *The Piano, Cineaste,* 20/3 (1994), p. 56.

30. Carmel Bird, '*The Piano:* An Essay on Jane Campion's Film, Part 2', *The Home Page of Carmel Bird,* n.d., http://www.carmelbird.com/piano02.html, accessed 4 January 2008.

31. Alan A. Stone, '*The Piano*', *Boston Review,* n.d., http://bostonreview.net/BR19.1/stone.html, accessed 4 January 2008.

32. Quart, review of *The Piano,* p. 56.

33. Carmel Bird, '*The Piano:* An Essay on Jane Campion's Film, Part 1', *The Home Page of Carmel Bird,* n.d., http://www.carmelbird.com/piano01.html, accessed 4 January 2008.

34. Eco, *The Open Book,* p. 192.

16 *Kill Bill: Volume 1* (US, 2003): Violence as Art

1. For a comprehensive list of borrowings see D. K. Holm, *Kill Bill: An Unofficial Casebook* (London: Glitterbooks, 2004).

2. Peter Bradshaw, 'Bride of Blood. Film of the Week: *Kill Bill: Volume 1*', *Guardian,* 10 October 2003.

3. Roger Ebert, review of *Kill Bill: Volume 1, Chicago Sun-Times,* 10 October 2003.

4. Nick Broomfield, '*Kill Bill* Should Never Have Left the Lab', *Guardian,* 2 July 2004; David Denby, 'Dead Reckoning', *New Yorker,* 13 October 2003.

5. J. Hoberman, 'Enter the Lady Dragon', *Village Voice,* 8–14 October 2003.

6. Kim Newman, review of *Kill Bill: Volume 1, Sight and Sound,* 13/12 (2003), p. 42.

7. Thane Peterson, 'Too Much Kill in the Kill Bills', *Business Week Online,* 5 May 2004, http://www.businessweek.com/bwdaily/dnflash/may2004/nf2004055_4548_db028.htm, accessed 5 January 2008.

8. User Ratings for *Kill Bill: Vol. 1* (2003), *IMDb,* http://imdb.com/title/tt0266697/ratings, accessed 5 January 2008.

9. Angela Baldassarre, 'Sans Quentin', *Access,* April–May 2004, http://www.accessmag.com/Archives/69-Quentin.html, accessed 5 January 2008.

10. Jim McLellan, 'Tarantino on the Run', in Paul A. Woods (ed.), *Quentin Tarantino: The Film Geek Files* (London: Plexus, 2005), p. 57.

11. Thane Peterson, 'Too Much Kill in the Kill Bills'.

12. Douglas McCollam, 'A Fall from Grace', *Columbia Journalism Review,* 1 (2004), http://cjrarchives.org/issues/2004/1/easterbrook-mccollam.asp, accessed 5 January 2008.

13. A. O. Scott, 'Blood Bath & Beyond', *New York Times,* 10 October 2003.

14. See Garth Jowett, Ian C. Jarvie and Kathryn H. Fuller, *Children at the Movies: Media Influence and the Payne Fund Controversy* (Cambridge: Cambridge University Press, 1996).

15. Colin Wilson and Robin Odell, *Jack the Ripper: Summing Up and Verdict* (London: Corgi, 1987), p. 53.

16. Ishmael Beah, *A Long Way Gone: Memoirs of a Boy Soldier* (London: Fourth Estate, 2007), p. 121.
17. Noël Carroll, 'Art and the Moral Realm', in Peter Kivy (ed.), *The Blackwell Guide to Aesthetics* (Malden, MA: Blackwell, 2004), pp. 127–9, 131–3 and 141.
18. Harry McCallion, 'The Movies, Me and Violence', in Karl French (ed.), *Screen Violence* (London: Bloomsbury, 1996), p. 210.
19. Ibid., p. 208.
20. For a defence of Tarantino's film sampling see Nicholas Rombes, '*Kill Bill* Unplugged: How Reshaping Reality May Haunt Us Yet', *Solpix,* n.d., http://www.webdelsol.com/SolPix/sp-nickkillbill.htm, accessed 5 January 2008.
21. Manohla Dargis, 'If the Gore in *Kill Bill: Vol. 1* Doesn't Overwhelm, the Film References Might,' *Los Angeles Times,* 10 October 2003.
22. Philip Hensher, 'Our Films Should Be for Us, Not Tarantino', *Independent,* 14 May 2004.
23. Marsha Kinder, 'Violence American Style: The Narrative Orchestration of Violent Attractions', in J. David Slocum (ed.), *Violence and American Cinema* (New York: Routledge, 2001), p. 81.
24. Christopher Sharrett, review of *Kill Bill: Volume 1, Cineaste,* 29/2 (2004), p. 96.
25. Neil Smith, 'Stars Defend *Kill Bill* Violence', *BBC News Online,* 21 April 2004, http://news.bbc.co.uk/1/hi/entertainment/film/3644281.stm, accessed 5 January 2008.
26. Mike Berry, Ed Donnerstein and Tim Gray, 'Cutting Film Violence: Effects on Perceptions, Enjoyment, and Arousal', *Journal of Social Psychology,* 139/5 (1999), pp. 567–82.
27. Garry Maddox, 'Tarantino Accused of Urging Teenagers to Break Censorship Law', *Sydney Morning Herald Online,* 17 October 2003, http://www.smh.com.au/articles/2003/10/16/1065917555109.html, accessed 5 January 2008.

17   The Tarnish on the Tinsel: Great Films Reconsidered

1. For national differences see Stephen Crofts, 'Foreign Tunes? Gender and Nationality in Four Countries' Reception of *The Piano*', in Harriet Margolis (ed.), *Jane Campion's 'The Piano'* (Cambridge: Cambridge University Press, 2000).
2. Kenneth S. Lynn, *Charlie Chaplin and His Times* (London: Aurum Press, 1997), p. 382.
3. Peter Schjeldahl, 'Notes on Beauty', in Bill Beckley with David Shapiro (eds), *Uncontrollable Beauty* (New York: Allworth Press, 1998), p. 56.
4. Raymond Carney, *American Vision: The Films of Frank Capra* (Cambridge: Cambridge University Press, 1986), pp. 5–7.

5. David Thomson, *The New Biographical Dictionary of Film,* 4th edn (London: Little, Brown, 2003), p. 729.

6. Steve Neale, 'Melo Talk: On the Meaning and Use of the Term "Melodrama" in the American Trade Press', *Velvet Light Trap,* 22 (1993), p. 66.

7. Jenefer Robinson, *Deeper Than Reason: Emotion and Its Role in Literature, Music and Art* (Oxford: Clarendon Press, Oxford University Press, 2005), p. 13.

8. Annette Kuhn, *An Everyday Magic: Cinema and Cultural Memory* (London: I. B. Tauris, 2002).

9. Is Removing the 'N' Word Censorship?, *IMDb,* 11 June 2001 (studio briefing), http://imdb.com/title/tt0046889/news, accessed 5 January 2008.

10. Kendall J. Walton, 'Make-Believe in the Arts', in Susan Feagin and Patrick Maynard (eds), *Aesthetics* (Oxford: Oxford University Press, 1997), pp. 293–4.

11. Susan L. Feagin, 'The Pleasure of Tragedy', in Feagin and Maynard (eds), *Aesthetics,* p. 307.

12. For an example of getting it wrong, see Ian C. Jarvie, 'Fanning the Flames: Anti-American Reaction to *Operation Burma* (1945)', *Historical Journal of Film, Radio and Television,* 1/2 (1981), pp. 117–37.

13. Jason Solomons, 'There's More to Film than *Citizen Kane', Observer,* 11 August 2002.

14. David Birnbaum, 'Birnbaum v David Thomson', *The Morning News,* 15 March 2005, http://www.themorningnews.org/archives/personalities/birnbaum_v_david_thomson.php, accessed 5 January 2008.

15. Nick Roddick, 'Twisted Little Masterpieces', *Sight and Sound,* 17/2 (2007), p. 10.

16. Christie, Ian, 'The Rules of the Game', *Sight and Sound,* 12/9 (2002), p. 29.

17. Ian MacKillop and Neil Sinyard (eds), *British Cinema of the 1950s: A Celebration* (Manchester: Manchester University Press, 2003).

18. A. L. Kennedy, *The Life and Death of Colonel Blimp* (London: BFI, 1997); Raymond Durgnat, 'The Powell and Pressburger Mystery', *Cineaste,* 23/2 (1997), pp. 18–19.

19. Jonathan Rosenbaum, *Essential Cinema: On the Necessity of Film Canons* (Baltimore, MD: Johns Hopkins University Press, 2004), pp. xiv and xvi.

20. Ibid. p. xiii.

21. Paul Schrader, 'The Film Canon', *Film Comment,* 42/1 (2006), pp. 33–49.

22. Ibid., pp. 44–6.

23. Ibid., p. 35.

24. Pauline Kael, 'Trash, Art, and the Movies' (1969), in Pauline Kael, *Going Steady* (Boston: Little, Brown, 1970), p. 105.

25. For a discussion of this trend in the context of nineteenth-century literature, see Lucy Newlyn, *Reading, Writing and Romanticism: The Anxiety of Reception* (Oxford: Oxford University Press, 2000), p. 297.

26. Rosenbaum, *Essential Cinema,* p. xiv; Willie van Peer, 'Towards a Poetics of Emotion', in Mette Hjort and Sue Laver (eds), *Emotion and the Arts* (New York: Oxford University Press, 1997), p. 223.

27. Brian Hu, 'Taking Film Studies to the Streets (and Back Again): On the Necessity of Criticism', *Mediascape,* 1/1 (2005), http://www.tft.ucla.edu/mediascape/Spring05_TakingFilmStudiesToTheStreets.html, accessed 28 June 2008.

28. Donato Totaro, 'The Rules of His Game: Schrader's Canon', *Offscreen,* 10/12 (2006), http://www.offscreen.com/biblio/phile/essays/schraders_canon, accessed 5 January 2008.

29. Christopher Long, 'Revising the Film Canon: Jonathan Rosenbaum's *Movie Mutations* and *Essential Cinema*', *New Review of Film and Television Studies,* 4/1 (2006), pp. 17–35.

30. Kael, 'Trash, Art, and the Movies', p. 113.

31. Exceptions include Mark Jancovich, Lucy Faire and Sarah Stubbings, *The Place of the Audience: Cultural Geographies of Film Consumption* (London: BFI, 2003); Eric Smoodin, *Regarding Frank Capra: Audience, Celebrity, and American Film Studies, 1930–1960* (Durham, NC: Duke University Press, 2004).

32. E. H. Gombrich and Quentin Bell, 'Canons and Values in the Visual Arts: A Correspondence', *Critical Inquiry,* 2/3 (1976), pp. 395–410.

33. Howard Felperin, *The Uses of the Canon: Elizabethan Literature and Contemporary Theory* (Oxford: Clarendon Press, Oxford University Press, 1990), p. 98.

34. John Guillory, *Culture as Capital: The Problem of Literary Canon Formation,* Chicago: University of Chicago Press, 1993, p. 340.

Further Reading

1 So Who Says It's Great?

J. M. Bernstein, *The Fate of Art: Aesthetic Alienation from Kant to Derrida and Adorno*. Includes a discussion on the concept of the sublime.

John Carey, *What Good Are the Arts?* An argument against absolute values, though Carey provides criteria for assessing literature, which he views as the supreme art.

Nick Cox, 'Kenneth Branagh: Shakespearean Film, Cultural Capital and Star Status'. Bourdieu's approach applied to film.

Critical Inquiry, 10/1 (1983). An issue devoted to canons, including essays by Charles Altieri on the use of the canon to help us judge personal and social values, and Richard Ohmann on the social groups involved in canon formation and the significance of marketing.

Antonio R. Damasio, *Looking for Spinoza: Joy, Sorrow and the Feeling Brain.* The third of Damasio's books relating neurobiology to philosophy. All are worth reading.

Peter Goldie, *The Emotions: A Philosophical Exploration.* A complement to Jenefer Robinson's work, emphasizing the philosophical implications of emotions and how we perceive them in ourselves and others.

David Pugmire, *Sound Sentiments: Integrity in the Emotions.* Examines academics' discomfort with emotions. Distinguishes between sentimentality and emotionalism.

2 The Celluloid Canon

David Bordwell and Nöel Carroll (eds), *Post-Theory: Reconstructing Film Studies.* The essays by Carroll and Alex Neill are pertinent. The latter presents arguments against an empathic approach.

Amy Coplan, 'Catching Characters' Emotions: Emotional Contagion Responses to Narrative Fiction Film'. The empathic approach as it applies to film.

Raymond Durgnat, *Films and Feelings.* The iconoclast of writing on film argues against over-interpretation and in favour of uncertainty in films.

Christopher Hauke and Ian Alister (eds), *Jung and Film: Post-Jungian Takes on the Moving Image.* The relevance of ideas such as the anima and the archetype to film. John Izod writes on *2001: A Space Odyssey.*

Frank McConnell, *Storytelling and Mythmaking: Images from Film and Literature.* A readable survey of changing images of the hero.

3 *The Battleship Potemkin* (USSR, 1925): The Politics of the Cinema

Laura Bezerra, 'The Affair Potemkin in Germany'. How the film suffered at the hands of the German censors.

David Bordwell, *The Cinema of Eisenstein.* Places the film in the context of Eisenstein's work and theorizing.

Jason Lindop, 'Eisenstein: Intellectual Montage, Poststructuralism, and Ideology'. An assessment of how Eisenstein's writings fare in the postmodern age.

Sam Rohdie, *Montage.* A clear exposition with a chapter devoted to *The Battleship Potemkin.*

Gregg Severson, 'Historical Narrative in *The Battleship Potemkin*'. Another perspective on the real events of 1905.

4 *The 39 Steps* (GB, 1935): Romance on the Run

Richard Allen and S. Ishii-Gonzalès (eds), *Alfred Hitchcock: Centenary Essays.* A range of perspectives on Hitchcock, including how the comedies of Preston Sturges influenced his work.

Robert E. Kapsis, *Alfred Hitchcock: The Making of a Reputation.* A sociologist's view of how Hitchcock's image developed. An extended version of the essay by Capsis.

Dave Kehr, 'Hitchcock's Riddle'. Is Hitchcock an artist?

Michael Walker, *Hitchcock's Motifs.* Walker identifies some forty motifs which thread through Hitchcock's work, including food, handcuffs, blondes and trains.

Robert J. Yanal, *Hitchcock as Philosopher.* Though Yanal concentrates on the American films, he considers such issues as Hitchcock's use of myth.

5 *Modern Times* (US, 1936): A Tramp for All Seasons

David A. Gerstein, '*Modern Times* and the Question of Technology'. The use of iconography in *Modern Times.*

John Kimber, *The Art of Charlie Chaplin.* Useful in revealing the influences on Chaplin, with some pertinent criticisms of *Modern Times.*

Joan Mellen, *Modern Times.* Mellen argues for the political nature of the film.

Janet Sayers and Nanette Monin, 'Comedy, Pain and Nonsense at the Red Moon Cafe: The Little Tramp's Death by Service Work in *Modern Times*'. A detailed and favourable analysis of the penultimate scene.

University of Virginia, 'The Method'. A discussion of Chaplin's major films of the 1920s and 30s and his development as a film-maker.

6 *Citizen Kane* (US, 1941): The Tragedy of Ambition

Rick Altman, 'Deep-Focus Sound: *Citizen Kane* and the Radio Aesthetic'. A discussion of such radio techniques as audio bookends to scenes, their relationship to deep-focus photography and their effect on the viewer.

Jorn K. Bramann, *'Citizen Kane'.* How Kane's life is related to Socratic ideals. Kane as exemplar of American values.

David P. Hayes, '*Citizen Kane*'s Borrowings: Techniques Attributed to *Citizen Kane* Which Appeared in Earlier Films'. A comprehensive listing of techniques previously used in other films, though without analysis.

Clinton Heylin, *Despite the System: Orson Welles Versus the Hollywood Studios.* How the script for Citizen Kane came into being.

Leonard J. Leff, 'Reading *Kane*'. An exercise in making use of subjective responses in reading the film, with applicability to the implied author.

7 *It's a Wonderful Life* (US, 1946): Seeking the American Hero

Morris Dickstein, 'It's a Wonderful Life, but …'. Capra's film as myth.

Daniel Green, 'In Defense of *It's a Wonderful Life*'. Green dismisses the charge of sentimentalism and sees George Bailey as victim of an existential crisis.

Annalee Newitz, 'It's Fun … But It Takes Courage: Remembering Frank Capra's America'. Capra's contribution to American national identity.

Gilbert Sorrentino, 'Things Aren't What They Seem: Frank Capra's *It's a Wonderful Life*'. The film's message is 'Money is everything.'

William Swislow, 'It's a Pretty Grim Life, Actually: All Is Not So Rosey in *It's a Wonderful Life*'. Capra's view of small-town life reappraised.

George Toles, *A House Made of Light: Essays on the Art of Film.* Toles argues that Capra transcends convention without undermining it and that George's accommodation to circumstances is not synonymous with dull acquiescence.

8 *Black Narcissus* (GB, 1947): Nuns in Exotic Places

Alaknanda Bagchi, 'Of Nuns and Palaces: Rumer Godden's *Black Narcissus*'. A Christian perspective on the novel.

Kelly Davidson and John Hill, ' "Under Control?" *Black Narcissus* and the Imagining of India'. The way paternalistic attitudes cannot be shrugged off and how the film plays with irony and hysteria.

Priya Jaikumar, 'Place and the Modernist Redemption of Empire in *Black Narcissus* (1947)'. Jaikumar argues for the centrality of the colonial setting in overcoming narrative collapse.

Douglas McVay, 'Michael Powell: Three Neglected Films'. *Black Narcissus* as part of a triptych with *Gone to Earth* and *Peeping Tom*. Considers links with other films.

Henry Sheehan, '*Black Narcissus* (1947)'. Sheehan's triptych includes *A Matter of Life and Death* and *I Know Where I'm Going!* He considers the self-conscious depiction of reality lurking imaginatively beneath analysis.

9 *The Night of the Hunter* (US, 1955): Return of the Big Bad Wolf

Robert Gitt, 'The Hidden Hunter', *Guardian,* 6 June 2003. How the rushes were discovered and what they reveal about the film.

Ian Johnston, *'The Night of the Hunter'*. Johnston sees the film as a contrast of opposites and examines how this is played out on a symbolic level.

Preston Neal Jones, *Heaven and Hell to Play With: The Filming of 'The Night of the Hunter'*. An exhaustive account of the film's genesis.

Kristian Moen, ' "About as Shapeless as the Man in the Moon": The Representation of Desire and Transition in Six Films of Charles Laughton'. Places *The Night of the Hunter* in the context of Laughton's work as an actor, particularly his interest in non-naturalistic presentation.

Vicente Rodriguez-Ortega, 'Fear Factor'. The influence of *The Night of the Hunter* on later films and our attraction to Mitchum's character: 'A love we despise but one we cannot easily run away from.'

10 *Lawrence of Arabia* (GB, 1962): An Englishman in the Sun

Michael A. Anderegg, *David Lean.* Offers a more analytical account of the film and Lawrence's character than might be expected from a biography.

Steven C. Caton, *'Lawrence of Arabia': A Film's Anthropology.* The genesis of the film.

Laurence Raw, 'T. E. Lawrence, the Turks, and the Arab Revolt in the Cinema: Anglo-American and Turkish Representations'. Examines representations of the Arab and Turkish worlds in film.

Jack G. Shaheen, *Reel Bad Arabs: How Hollywood Vilifies a People.* Explores the stereotyping of Arabs. The proprietorial attitude towards wells shown in the film is inaccurate.

Jeremy Wilson, 'Lawrence of Arabia or Smith in the Desert?', *T. E. Lawrence Studies.* Historical errors in the film and their significance.

11 *8½* (Italy/France, 1963): The Director as Superstar

Albert Edward Benderson, 'Critical Approaches to Federico Fellini's *8½*'. Benderson favours a psychoanalytic approach, but gives comprehensive coverage to other models. How the Pinocchio motif appears in the film.

Edward Branigan, 'Subjectivity under Siege: From Fellini's *8½* to Oshima's *The Story of a Man Who Left his Will on Film'*. A psychological approach to *8½*, with an examination of Christian Metz's analysis of the ending. This essay is critiqued in the same issue by Paul Willeman.

Frank Burke, *Fellini's Films: From Postwar to Postmodern*. Looks at the films from the viewpoints of individualism and the shift from realist cinema to something more self-conscious.

Norman N. Holland, '*8½* and Me: The Thirty-Two Year Difference'. A reflection on a review of the film written by psychoanalyst Norman Holland thirty-two years earlier. He has come to favour a more subjective view of film, his conclusion being that we should not judge, or look for themes, but accept film as it is.

Gerry Manacsa, 'Federico Fellini, Images and Archetypes: A Personal Perspective'. Looking for archetypal images of the man, the whore and the wife in five Fellini films.

12 *2001: A Space Odyssey* (GB/US, 1968): The Long Voyage to Destiny

David Austin, *'2001: A Space Odyssey'*. The reception of the film as a personal experience with theological overtones.

Luis M. Garcia Mainar, *Narrative and Stylistic Patterns in the Films of Stanley Kubrick*. Kubrick's use of ambiguity.

Mark Crispin Miller, '*2001:* A Cold Descent'. A downbeat assessment of how the film has fared over time.

David W. Patterson, 'Music, Structure and Metaphor in Stanley Kubrick's *2001: A Space Odyssey'*. Kubrick's use of music to convey the film's visionary qualities.

Philip Strick, review of *2001: A Space Odyssey*. A closely-argued and negative review of the film from 1968. By 2002, it had joined Strick's list of the ten best films in *Sight and Sound*.

13 *The Godfather* (US, 1972): Keeping It in the Family

Jeffrey Chown, *Hollywood Auteur: Francis Coppola*. Compares Puzo's nonjudgemental approach to the Corleone family with what Chown sees as Coppola's unsympathetic view.

196 · *Further Reading*

Robert C. Cumbow, 'Altman and Coppola in the Seventies: Power and the People'. Coppola's absence of heroes distinguishes him from Altman. The attitude of both men to capitalism is discussed.

Stephen Farber, 'Coppola and *The Godfather*'. An analysis of the film's themes and the possible reasons for its success.

Phoebe Poon, 'The Corleone Chronicles: Revisiting *The Godfather* Films as Trilogy'. Places *The Godfather* in the context of the trilogy.

Jeff Reichert, 'I Couldn't Refuse'. Another latecomer to the film gives his assessment. An illustration of how a film's reputation and its length can seem daunting.

14 *Raging Bull* (US, 1980): The Drama of the Fight

Kevin J. Hayes (ed.), *Martin Scorsese's 'Raging Bull'*. Key essays on *Raging Bull*, including Todd Berliner on Scorsese's use of intellectual montage.

Marc Raymond, 'Martin Scorsese'. A survey of Scorsese's work with bibliography.

Lesley Stern, *The Scorsese Connection*. Thematic connections between *Raging Bull* and Powell and Pressburger's *The Red Shoes*.

Thomas Weiner, 'Martin Scorsese Fights Back'. An interview with Scorsese, who discusses his aims in making *Raging Bull*.

Robin Wood, *Hollywood from Vietnam to Reagan*. Detailed coverage of key films including *Raging Bull*.

15 *The Piano* (Australia/NZ/France, 1993): Love in a Rough Place

Greg Bentley, 'Mothers, Daughters, and (Absent) Fathers in Jane Campion's *The Piano*'. A study of familial relationships and shifting alliances in the film.

Annie Goldson, 'Piano Rental'. The nature of the film's appeal and its reception by audiences.

Betty Jay, ' "All Imperfect Things": Motherhood and the Aesthetics of Ambivalence in *The Piano*'. The mother-daughter relationship in the film.

Diana Saco, 'Feminist Film Criticism: *The Piano* and "the Female Gaze" '. The applicability of Laura Mulvey's essay 'Visual Pleasure and Narrative Cinema' to *The Piano*.

Screen, 'The Piano Debate', *Screen*, 36/3 (1995). Contributions by Stella Bruzzi, Lynda Dyson and Sue Gillett.

16 *Kill Bill: Volume 1* (US, 2003): Violence as Art

Theresa Duncan, 'Twin Bills: Theresa Duncan on Women and the Man in Two Recent Films'. Compares Tarantino's work with that of Sophia Coppola and makes a case for Tarantino's empathy with women.

Marty Jones, 'Quentin Tarantino's Playful Violence and High Body Count'. *Kill Bill* as part of a closed system, with Tarantino recycling film sources.

Dror Poleg, 'The Unbearable Lightness of Being Cool: Appropriation and Prospects of Subversion in the Works of Quentin Tarantino'. Poleg calls *Kill Bill* 'a sombre ballad about the artistic agency of an auteur in a postmodern world'. Examines the proposition that the film is about the director, not the Bride.

J. David Slocum, 'Film Violence and the Institutionalization of the Cinema'. Screen violence as a manifestation of how popular cinema balances the forces of social change and control. An open-minded approach with a comprehensive bibliography.

Chuck Stephens, 'The Whole She-Bang: The Incredible Two-Headed Tarantino and the Last of His Double Bills'. A defence of Tarantino's artistic aims.

17 The Tarnish on the Tinsel: Great Films Reconsidered

James S. Ackerman, 'On Judging Art without Absolutes'. Value judgements as a tool which the scientific method represses, but which should be the generators of interpretation.

Robert Audi, *The Good and the Right: A Theory of Intuition and Intrinsic Value*. A philosophical approach to whether moral values can be intrinsic.

Ray Carney, 'Art as Experience: The Fallacy of Viewing Art as a Form of Knowledge'. A rallying call similar to that of Howard Felperin, but specific to film.

Christine Gledhill and Linda Williams (eds), *Reinventing Film Studies*. A range of approaches to film studies, including Noël Carroll's essay on film evaluation.

Nicholas Tredell (ed.), *Cinemas of the Mind: A Critical History of Film Theory.* How film theory has developed. Torban Grodal's contribution on how film might inhibit empathy is relevant.

Bibliography

Many newspaper and internet reviews can accessed from *International Movie Database (IMDb),* http://imdb.com; *Metacritic,* http://www.metacritic.com; *Movie Review Query Engine,* http://www.mrqe.com; *rotten tomatoes,* http://www.rottentomatoes.com; *Top Ten Reviews,* http://movies.toptenreviews.com; *Yahoo! Movies,* http://movies.yahoo.com and *EBSCO research databases.*

Literary Web sites

Al-Bab, http://www.al-bab.com; *Ex-Classics,* http://www.exclassics.com; *T. E. Lawrence Society,* http://www.telsociety.org.uk.

Web sites providing short film reviews, film lists, or audience feedback

Amazon, http://www.amazon.co.uk; *American Film Institute,* http://afi.com; *Cine Scene.com,* http://www.cinescene.com; *DVDBeaver,* http://www.dvdbeaver.com; *Greatest Films,* http://filmsite.org; *Movie Reviews UK,* http://www.film.u-net.com; *Universitetet I Oslo,* http://www.fys.uio.no/~magnushj/Piano/opinion.html; *They Shoot Pictures Don't They,* http://www.theyshootpictures.com.

Radio and Television Programmes

Bergman and the Cinema, Marie Nyreröd, Sveriges Television, 2004.
Night Waves, BBC Radio 3, 1 June 2005.

Books, Monographs, Periodical Newspaper and Web site articles

Ackerman, James S., 'On Judging Art without Absolutes', *Critical Inquiry,* 5/3 (1979), pp. 441–69.
Adler, Renata, '*2001* is Up, Up and Away: Kubrick's Odyssey in Space Begins to Run', *New York Times,* 4 April 1968.
Agee, James, *Agee on Film,* London: Peter Owen, 1963.

Allen, Richard and Ishii-Gonzalès, S. (eds), *Alfred Hitchcock: Centenary Essays,* London: BFI, 1999.

Alleva, Richard, 'A Word of Dissent: This Piano Is Out of Tune', *Commonweal,* 14 January 1994, internet version consulted: http://www.thefreelibrary.com/ The+Piano.-a014979701, accessed 4 January 2008.

Almendros, Nestor, 'Fortune and Men's Eyes', *Film Comment,* 27/4 (1991), pp. 58–61.

Altman, Rick, 'Deep-Focus Sound: *Citizen Kane* and the Radio Aesthetic', *Quarterly Review of Film and Video,* 15/3 (1994), pp. 1–33.

Anderegg, Michael A., *David Lean,* Boston: Twayne, 1984.

Andrew, Geoff, '*Black Narcissus*', in John Pym (ed.), *Time Out Film Guide,* 15th edn, London: Time Out, 2006, p. 118.

Audi, Robert, *The Good and the Right: A Theory of Intuition and Intrinsic Value,* Princeton, NJ: Princeton University Press, 2004.

Auriol, Jean George, 'The British Film Abroad: A Study of Critical Reactions', in Roger Manvell (ed.), *The Year's Work in the Film, 1949,* London: Longmans Green, 1950, pp. 46–54.

Austin, David, '*2001: A Space Odyssey*', *Films and Filming,* July 1968, pp. 24–7.

Bagchi, Alaknanda, 'Of Nuns and Palaces: Rumer Godden's *Black Narcissus*', *Christianity and Literature,* 45/1 (1995), pp. 53–66.

Baldassarre, Angela, 'Sans Quentin', *Access,* April-May 2004, http://www.access mag.com/Archives/69-Quentin.html, accessed 11 August 2007.

Bates, Robin, with Bates, Scott, 'Fiery Speech in a World of Shadows: Rosebud's Influence on Early Audiences', *Cinema Journal,* 26/2 (1987), pp. 3–26.

Baxter, John, *Stanley Kubrick: A Biography,* London: HarperCollins, 1997.

Beah, Ishmael, *A Long Way Gone: Memoirs of a Boy Soldier,* London: Fourth Estate, 2007.

Beja, Morris, '*2001:* Odyssey to Byzantium', *Extrapolation,* 10 (1968), pp. 67–8, in Beja, '3 Perspectives on a Film'.

Beja, Morris, '3 Perspectives on a Film', *The Kubrick Site,* http://www.visual-memory.co.uk/amk/doc/0041.html, accessed 3 January 2008.

Benderson, Albert Edward, *Critical Approaches to Federico Fellini's 8½,* New York: Arno Press, 1974.

Bentley, Greg, 'Mothers, Daughters, and (Absent) Fathers in Jane Campion's *The Piano*', *Literature/Film Quarterly,* 30/1 (2002), pp. 46–58.

Bergan, Ronald, 'Original Potemkin Beats the Censors after 79 Years', *Guardian,* 18 February 2005.

Bernstein, J. M., *The Fate of Art: Aesthetic Alienation from Kant to Derrida and Adorno,* Cambridge: Polity Press, 1992.

Berry, Mike, Donnerstein, Ed and Gray, Tim, 'Cutting Film Violence: Effects on Perceptions, Enjoyment, and Arousal', *Journal of Social Psychology,* 139/5 (1999), pp. 567–82.

Bezerra, Laura, 'The Affair Potemkin in Germany', *COLLATE Project,* n.d., http://deutsches-filminstitut.de/collate/collate_sp/se/se_04a04b.html, accessed 29 December 2007.

Bird, Carmel, '*The Piano:* An Essay on Jane Campion's Film', *The Home Page of Carmel Bird,* n.d., http://www.carmelbird.com/piano01.html, accessed 4 January 2008.

Birnbaum, David, 'Birnbaum v David Thomson', *The Morning News,* 15 March 2005, http://www.themorningnews.org/archives/personalities/birnbaum_v_david_thomson.php, accessed 5 January 2008.

Blake, Richard A., 'Redeemed in Blood: The Sacramental Universe of Martin Scorsese', *Journal of Popular Film and Television,* 24/1 (1996), pp. 2–9, *HighBeam Encyclopedia,* http://www.encyclopedia.com/doc/1g1–18533918.html, accessed 3 January 2008.

Bliss, Michael, *Martin Scorsese and Michael Cimino,* Metuchen, NJ: Scarecrow Press, 1985.

Bloom, Harold, *The Western Canon: The Books and School of the Ages,* London: Macmillan, 1995.

Bloustien, Geraldine, 'Jane Campion: Memory, Motif and Music', *Continuum: The Australian Journal of Media & Culture,* 5/2 (1990), http://wwwmcc.murdoch.edu.au/ReadingRoom/5.2/Bloust.html, accessed 4 January 2008.

Bolt, Robert, 'Apologia', *Cineaste* 21/4 (1995), pp. 33–4.

Bondanella, Peter, *The Cinema of Federico Fellini,* Princeton, NJ: Princeton University Press, 1992.

Booth, Wayne C., *The Rhetoric of Fiction,* Chicago: University of Chicago Press, 1961.

Bordwell, David, *The Cinema of Eisenstein,* Cambridge, MA: Harvard University Press, 1993.

Bordwell, David, 'Deep-Focus Photography', in David Bordwell, Janet Staiger and Kristin Thompson (eds), *The Classical Hollywood Cinema: Film Style and Mode of Production to 1960,* London: Routledge, 1985, pp. 341–52.

Bordwell, David, and Carroll, Nöel (eds), *Post-Theory: Reconstructing Film Studies,* Madison: University of Wisconsin Press, 1996.

Bourdieu, Pierre, *Distinction: A Social Critique of the Judgement of Taste,* tr. Richard Nice, London: Routledge, 1989.

Bradshaw, Peter, 'Bride of Blood. Film of the Week: *Kill Bill: Volume 1',* *Guardian,* 10 October 2003.

Bramann, Jorn K., '*Citizen Kane*', *Frostburg State University Philosophical Forum,* 2004, http://faculty.frostburg.edu/phil/forum/Kane.htm, accessed 31 December 2007.

Bramann, Jorn K., '*Modern Times*', *Frostburg State University Philosophical Forum,* 2006, http://faculty.frostburg.edu/phil/forum/ModernTimes.htm, accessed 31 December 2007.

Branigan, Edward, 'Subjectivity under Siege: From Fellini's *8½* to Oshima's *The Story of a Man Who Left His Will on Film'*, *Screen,* 19/1 (1978), pp. 7–40.

Broomfield, Nick, '*Kill Bill* Should Never Have Left the Lab', *Guardian,* 2 July 2004.

Brown, Geoff, 'Campion Finds an Epic Voice', *Times,* 28 October 1993.

Brown, Stephen J., 'Theological Optimism: The Films of Frank Capra', *Theology,* 101/804 (1998), pp. 437–44.

Browne, Nick (ed.), *Francis Ford Coppola's 'The Godfather' Trilogy,* Cambridge: Cambridge University Press, 2000.

Brownlow, Kevin, *David Lean,* London: Faber and Faber, 1992.

Burke, Frank, *Fellini's Films: From Postwar to Postmodern,* New York: Twayne, 1996.

Burr, Ty, 'Once upon a Classic', *Boston Globe,* 23 March 2003.

Burr, Ty, review of *Raging Bull, Boston Globe,* 11 March 2005.

Caldwell, Aaron, and Mark Caldwell, 'FIAF Centenary List' (1995), *Top 100 Movie Lists,* http://www.geocities.com/aaronbcaldwell/dimfiaf.html, accessed 28 December 2007.

Callow, Simon, *The Night of the Hunter,* London: BFI, 2000.

Callow, Simon, *Orson Welles: The Road to Xanadu,* London: Cape, 1995.

Camon, Alessandro, '*The Godfather* and the Mythology of Mafia', in Browne (ed.), *Francis Ford Coppola's 'The Godfather' Trilogy,* pp. 57–75.

Canby, Vincent, review of *The Godfather, New York Times,* 16 March 1972.

Cannon, Damian, review of *Lawrence of Arabia, Movie Reviews UK,* 1997, http://www.film.u-net.com/Movies/Reviews/Lawrence_Arabia.html, accessed 3 January 2008.

Carey, John, *What Good Are the Arts?,* London: Faber and Faber, 2005.

Carney, Raymond, *American Vision: The Films of Frank Capra,* Cambridge: Cambridge University Press, 1986.

Carney, Raymond, 'Art as Experience: The Fallacy of Viewing Art as a Form of Knowledge', *Boston University,* 2003, http://people.bu.edu/rcarney/acad/metaphoric.shtml, accessed 2 January 2008.

Carney, Raymond, 'Capra and the Critics, or: Ideology Is Only a Sliver of Life', *Boston University,* 2003, http://people.bu.edu/rcarney/capra/capracrit.shtml, accessed 2 January 2008.

Carringer, Robert L., *The Making of 'Citizen Kane'*, Berkeley and Los Angeles: University of California Press, 1985.

Carringer, Robert L., 'The Script of *Citizen Kane'*, in Naremore (ed.), *Orson Welles's 'Citizen Kane',* pp. 79–121.

Carroll, Noël, 'Art and the Moral Realm', in Peter Kivy (ed.), *The Blackwell Guide to Aesthetics,* Malden, MA: Blackwell, 2004, pp. 126–51.

Caton, Steven C., *'Lawrence of Arabia': A Film's Anthropology,* Berkeley and Los Angeles: University of California Press, 1999.

Caviglia, Francesco, 'Looking for Male Italian Adulthood, Old Style', *Point of View,* 12 (2001), http://pov.imv.au.dk/Issue_12/section_1/artc4A.html, accessed 4 January 2008.

Chatman, Seymour Benjamin, *'Battleship Potemkin': The Odessa Steps,* Mount Vernon, NY: Macmillan Films, 1975, in *'Bronenosets Potemkin* CineFile', *Pacific Film Archive,* http://www.mip.berkeley.edu/cgi-bin/cine_film_detail.pl/cine_img?31, accessed 29 December 2007.

Chen, Anna, 'In Perspective: Sergei Eisenstein, Film Director, 1898–1948', *Anna Chen's Website,* 1998, http://www.annachen.co.uk/writing_eisenstein1.html, accessed 29 December 2007.

Chown, Jeffrey, *Hollywood Auteur: Francis Coppola,* New York: Praeger, 1988.

Christie, Ian, *Arrows of Desire: The Films of Michael Powell and Emeric Pressburger,* London: Faber and Faber, 1994.

Christie, Ian, 'Canon Fodder', *Sight and Sound,* 2/8 (1992), pp. 31–3.

Christie, Ian, 'The Rules of the Game', *Sight and Sound,* 12/9 (2002), pp. 24–50.

Chumo, Peter N. II, 'Keys to the Imagination: Jane Campion's *The Piano*', *Literature/Film Quarterly,* 25/3 (1997), pp. 173–6.

Clarens, Carlos, *Crime Movies: From Griffiths to 'The Godfather' and Beyond,* London: Secker & Warburg, 1980.

Cohen, David, 'Ambiguity and Intention', *Interdisciplines,* n.d., http://www.interdisciplines.org/artcog/papers/11, accessed 27 December 2007.

Collins, Ava Preacher, 'Loose Canons: Constructing Cultural Traditions Inside and Outside the Academy', in Jim Collins, Hilary Radner and Ava Preacher Collins (eds), *Film Theory Goes to the Movies: Cultural Analysis of Contemporary Film,* New York: Routledge, 1993, pp. 86–102.

Compton, Todd M., *In Search of a Canon: Movie Polls through the Years,* Mountain View, CA: Magos Press, 2007, http://www.geocities.com/Athens/Oracle/7207/pollsTOC.htm, accessed 28 December 2007.

Cooke, Alistair (ed.), *Garbo and the Night Watchmen,* London: Secker & Warburg, 1971.

Coplan, Amy, 'Catching Characters' Emotions: Emotional Contagion Responses to Narrative Fiction Film', *Film Studies,* 8 (2006), pp. 26–38.

Corbett, Clare, 'Cutting It Free: Notes on *The Piano* in the Editing Room', in Felicity Coombs and Suzanne Gemmell (eds), *Approaches to 'The Piano',* Sydney: John Libby, 1999, pp. 163–75.

Corman, Roger, '*The Godfather*', *Sight and Sound,* 12/9 (2002), p. 35.

Coughlin, Paul, 'Sublime Moments', *senses of cinema,* 11 (2000–1), http://www.sensesofcinema.com/contents/00/11/sublime.html, accessed 27 December 2007.

Cowie, Peter, *The Godfather Book,* London: Faber and Faber, 1997.

Cox, Nick, 'Kenneth Branagh: Shakespearean Film, Cultural Capital and Star Status', in Andy Willis (ed.), *Film Stars: Hollywood and Beyond,* Manchester: Manchester University Press, 2004.

Critical Inquiry, 10/1 (1983).

Crofts, Stephen, 'Foreign Tunes? Gender and Nationality in Four Countries' Reception of *The Piano*', in Margolis (ed.), *Jane Campion's 'The Piano'*, pp. 135–62.

Crowdus, Gary, '*Lawrence of Arabia:* The Cinematic (Re)Writing of History', *Cineaste,* 17/2 (1989), pp. 14–21.

Crowdus, Gary, and Farrand, Alan, 'Restoring Lawrence: An Interview with Robert Harris', *Cineaste,* 17/2 (1989), pp. 22–3.

Crowther, Bosley, 'The Ambiguous *Citizen Kane:* Orson Welles in His First Motion Picture Creates a Titanic Character', *New York Times,* 4 May 1941.

Crowther, Bosley, 'Bogeyman Plus', *New York Times,* 30 September 1955.

Crowther, Bosley, 'A Desert Warfare Spectacle', *New York Times,* 17 December 1962.

Crowther, Bosley, 'Orson Welles's Controversial *Citizen Kane* Proves Sensational Film at Palace', *New York Times,* 2 May 1941.

Crowther, Bosley, review of *Citizen Kane, New York Times,* 4 May 1941.

Crowther, Bosley, review of *It's a Wonderful Life, New York Times,* 23 December 1946.

Crowther, Bosley, 'The Spirits Move: A Comparison of Inspirations in British and Hollywood Movies', *New York Times,* 12 January 1947.

Cumbow, Robert C., 'Altman and Coppola in the Seventies: Power and the People', *24 Lies a Second,* 2005, http://www.24liesasecond.com/site2/index.php?page=2, accessed 3 January 2008.

Currie, Hector, 'A New Look at Eisenstein's *Potemkin*', in David Platt (ed.), *Celluloid Power: Social Criticism from 'The Birth of a Nation' to 'Judgment at Nuremberg',* Metuchen, NJ: Scarecrow Press, 1999, pp. 168–75.

Damasio, Antonio R., *Looking for Spinoza: Joy, Sorrow and the Feeling Brain,* London: Heinemann, 2003.

Daniels, Don, 'A Skeleton Key to *2001*', *Sight and Sound,* 40/1 (1970–1), pp. 28–33.

Danks, Adrian, 'Michael Powell & Emeric Pressburger', *senses of cinema,* 20 (2002), http://www.sensesofcinema.com/contents/directors/02/powell.html, accessed 2 January 2008.

Dargis, Manohla, 'If the Gore in *Kill Bill: Vol. 1* Doesn't Overwhelm, the Film References Might,' *Los Angeles Times,* 10 October 2003.

Dashiell, Chris, 'Really Modern Times', *CineScene,* 2004, http://www.cinescene.com/dash/moderntimes.htm, accessed 31 December 2007.

Dashiell, Chris, review of *Lawrence of Arabia, CineScene.com,* 2001, http://www.cinescene.com/flicks/flicks062001.html#lawrence, accessed 2 January 2008.

Davidson, Kelly, and Hill, John, ' "Under Control?" *Black Narcissus* and the Imagining of India', *Film Studies,* 6 (2005), pp. 1–12.

Deneen, Patrick J., 'Awakening from the American Dream: The End of Escape in American Cinema?', *Perspectives on Political Science,* 31/2 (2002), pp. 96–103, *EBSCO research databases.*

Denning, Michael, 'The Problems of Magic: Orson Welles's Allegories of Anti-Fascism', in Naremore (ed.), *Orson Welles's 'Citizen Kane'*, pp. 185–216.

Dewey, Donald, *James Stewart: A Biography,* London: Little, Brown, 1997.

Dickstein, Morris, 'It's a Wonderful Life, but …', *American Film,* 5/7 (1980), pp. 42–7.

Dirks, Tim, '*Empire* Magazine's 100 Greatest Movies of All Time' (1999 and 2003), *The Greatest Films,* http://filmsite.org/empireuk100.html, accessed 28 December 2007.

Dirks, Tim, '*The* Night *of the Hunter* (1955)', *The Greatest Films,* 1996–2007, http://filmsite.org/nightof.html, accessed 2 January 2008.

Dirks, Tim, '100 Greatest Films: Film Selection Criteria', *The Greatest Films,* 1996–2007, http://filmsite.org/criteria.html, accessed 28 December 2007.

Dirks, Tim, 'Other Great Films Lists', *The Greatest Films,* 1996–2007, http://filmsite.org/greatlists2.html.

Dirks, Tim, 'The *39 Steps* (1935)', *Film Site,* 1996–2007, http://filmsite.org/thirt.html, accessed 31 December 2007.

Dobson, Adam, '*2001: A Space Odyssey.* Stargazers, Navelgazers: The Search for an Answer Makes Monkeys of Us All', *Metaphilm,* 2005, http://www.metaphilm.com/index.php/detail/2001_a_space_odyssey, accessed 30 June 2008.

Dors, Diana, *Swingin' Dors,* London: World Distributors, 1960.

Duguid, Mark, '*Black Narcissus*', *BFI screenonline,* n.d., http://www.screenonline.org.uk/film/id/438337.html, accessed 2 January 2008.

Duncan, Theresa, 'Twin Bills: Theresa Duncan on Women and the Man in Two Recent Films', *ArtForum,* [42/6] (2004), *BNET Research Center,* http://findarticles.com/p/articles/mi_m0268/is_6_42/ai_113389497, accessed 5 January 2008.

Durgnat, Raymond, *Films and Feelings,* London: Faber and Faber, 1967.

Durgnat, Raymond, 'The Powell and Pressburger Mystery', *Cineaste,* 23/2 (1997), pp. 16–19.

Durgnat, Raymond, 'Retrospective: *Black Narcissus* … and in Theory: Towards a Superficial Structuralism', *Monthly Film Bulletin,* 51/609 (1984), pp. 314–16.

Durgnat, Raymond, *The Strange Case of Alfred Hitchcock,* London: Faber and Faber, 1974.

Ebert, Roger, review of *Citizen Kane, Chicago Sun-Times,* 24 May 1998.

Ebert, Roger, review of *8½, Chicago Sun-Times,* 7 May 1993.

Ebert, Roger, review of *Kill Bill: Volume 1, Chicago Sun-Times,* 10 October 2003.

Ebert, Roger, review of *Lawrence of Arabia, Chicago Sun-Times,* 2 September 2001.

Ebert, Roger, review of *Raging Bull, Chicago Sun-Times,* 1 January 1980.

Ebert, Roger, review of *Raging Bull, Chicago Sun-Times,* 10 May 1998.

Ebert, Roger, review of *The Battleship Potemkin, Chicago Sun-Times,* 19 July 1978.

Ebert, Roger, review of *The Night of the Hunter, Chicago Sun-Times,* 24 November 1996.

Ebert, Roger, review of *2001: A Space Odyssey, Chicago Sun-Times,* 12 April 1968.

Ebert, Roger, review of *2001: A Space Odyssey, Chicago Sun-Times,* 27 March 1997.

Eco, Umberto, *The Open Work,* tr. Anna Cancogni, London: Hutchinson Radius, 1989.

Eells, George, *Robert Mitchum: A Biography,* London: Robson Books: 1984.

Eisenstein, Alex, 'The Academic Overkill of *2001*', in Beja, '3 Perspectives on a Film'.

Eisenstein, Sergei, *The Battleship Potemkin,* tr. Gillon R. Aitken, London: Lorrimer, 1968.

Eisenstein, Sergei, 'The Montage of Film Attractions' (1924), in *Selected Works,* vol. 1: *Writings, 1922–34,* tr. Richard Taylor, London: BFI and Bloomington: Indiana University Press, 1988, pp. 39–58.

Elley, Derek (ed.), *'Variety' Movie Guide,* London: Hamlyn, 1991.

Erickson, Glenn, ' "Films Blanc" and What Dreams May Come', *DVD talk,* 1998, http://www.dvdtalk.com/dvdsavant/s58filmblanc.html, accessed 12 January 2008.

Erickson, Glenn, *'It's a Wonderful Life*—or: It's a Wonderful Recut?', *DVD talk,* 1998, http://www.dvdtalk.com/dvdsavant/s55wonderful.html, accessed 2 January 2008.

Erickson, Steve, 'Founding Fathers', *Los Angeles Magazine,* December 2001, p. 134, *EBSCO research databases.*

Fabe, Marilyn, *'8½': The Steambath Sequence,* Mount Vernon, NY: Macmillan Films, 1975, in '8½ CineFile', *Pacific Film Archive,* http://www.mip.berkeley.edu/cgi-bin/cine_film_detail.pl/cine_img?24275+24275, accessed 4 January 2008.

Farber, Stephen, 'Coppola and *The Godfather*', *Sight and Sound,* 41/4 (1972), pp. 217–23.

Fava, Claudio G., and Vigano, Aldo, *The Films of Federico Fellini,* tr. Shula Curto, Secaucus, NJ: Citadel Press, 1981.

Feagin, Susan L., 'The Pleasure of Tragedy', in Feagin and Maynard (eds), *Aesthetics,* pp. 305–13.

Feagin, Susan L., and Maynard, Patrick (eds), *Aesthetics,* Oxford: Oxford University Press, 1997.

Felperin, Howard, *The Uses of the Canon: Elizabethan Literature and Contemporary Theory,* Oxford: Clarendon Press, Oxford University Press, 1990.

Fisher, Philip, 'Darkness and the Demand for Time in Art', in Holly and Moxey (eds), *Art History, Aesthetics, Visual Studies,* pp. 87–104.

Fludernik, Monika, Universität Freiburg, 'Sublime', *Literary Encyclopedia,* 2001, http://www.litencyc.com/php/stopics.php?rec=true&UID=1070, accessed 27 December 2007.

Fraumeni, Paul, 'What Makes a Great Film?', *University of Toronto,* [2003], http://www.news.utoronto.ca/bios/askus35.htm, accessed 23 June 2008.

Freedman, Carl, 'Superman Among the Stars', *Science Fiction Studies,* 28/2 (2001), http://www.depauw.edu/sfs/birs/bir84.htm, accessed 3 January 2008.

Friedman, Natalie, 'How to Make Your Students Cry: Lessons in Atrocity, Pedagogy, and Heightened Emotion', *Journal of Mundane Behavior,* 3/3 (2002), http://www.mundanebehavior.org/issues/v3n3/friedman.htm, accessed 27 December 2007.

Fune-Saunders, Kilmeny (ed.), *Radio Times Guide to Films,* 7th edn, London: BBC Worldwide, 2006.

Gaskell, Ivan, 'Reflections of Rembrandt's *Jeremiah*', in Holly and Moxey (eds), *Art History, Aesthetics, Visual Studies,* pp. 175–86.

Gelmis, Joseph, 'An Interview with Stanley Kubrick' (1969), *The Kubrick Site,* http://www.visual-memory.co.uk/amk/doc/0069.html, accessed 3 January 2008.

Gelmis, Joseph, 'Three Reviews of *2001* (1968–9)', *The Kubrick Site,* http://www.visual-memory.co.uk/amk/doc/0040.html, accessed 3 January 2008.

Georgakas, Dan, review of *Raging Bull, Cineaste,* 11/1 (1980–1), pp. 28–30.

Gerstein, David A., '*Modern Times* and the Question of Technology', *Charlie Chaplin: A World Wide Web Celebration,* 1995, http://www.cartoonresearch.com/gerstein/chaplin/machines.html, accessed 31 December 2007.

Gilbey, Ryan (ed.), *The Ultimate Film,* London: BFI, 2005.

Gillet, *see* Gillett.

Gillett, Sue (Sue Gillet), 'A Pleasure to Watch: Jane Campion's Narrative Cinema', *Screening the Past,* 12 (2001), http://www.latrobe.edu.au/screeningthepast/firstrelease/fr0301/sgfr12a.htm, accessed 4 January 2008 (currently unavailable).

Gilliam, Terry, 'Close-Up', BBC2, 27 November 1995, transcribed for 'Terry Gilliam's Favourite Movies', ed. Phil Stubbs, *Dreams,* http://www.smart.co.uk/dreams/tgclip.htm, accessed 4 January 2008.

Gitt, Robert, 'The Hidden Hunter', *Guardian,* 6 June 2003.

Glancy, Mark, *The 39 Steps,* London: I. B. Tauris, 2003.

Gledhill, Christine and Williams, Linda (eds), *Reinventing Film Studies,* London: Arnold, 2000.

Goldie, Peter, *The Emotions: A Philosophical Exploration,* Oxford: Clarendon Press, Oxford University Press, 2000.

Goldson, Annie, 'Piano Rental', *Screen,* 38/3 (1987), pp. 275–81.

Gombrich, E. H., and Bell, Quentin, 'Canons and Values in the Visual Arts: A Correspondence', *Critical Inquiry,* 2/3 (1976), pp. 395–410.

Goodwin, James, 'Eisenstein: Ideology and Intellectual Cinema', *Quarterly Review of Film Studies,* 3/2 (1978), pp. 169–92.

Gorbman, Claudia, 'Music in *The Piano',* in Margolis (ed.), *Jane Campion's 'The Piano',* pp. 42–58.

Gosling, Nigel, *Paris 1900–1914: The Miraculous Years,* London: Weidenfeld and Nicholson, 1978.

Gottesman, Ronald (ed.), *Focus on 'Citizen Kane',* Englewood Cliffs, NJ: Prentice-Hall, 1971.

Gow, Gordon, '*The Night of the Hunter*', *Films and Filming,* February 1975, pp. 48–53.

Grace, Helen, '*Battleship Potemkin*', *senses of cinema,* 4 (2000), http://www.sensesofcinema.com/contents/cteq/00/4/potemkin.html, accessed 29 December 2007.

Green, Daniel, 'In Defense of *It's a Wonderful Life*', *The Reading Experience,* 2004, http://noggs.typepad.com/the_reading_experience/2004/12/in_defense_of_e.html, accessed 2 January 2008.

Greenberg, Clement, *Art and Culture,* London: Thames & Hudson, 1973.

Greene, Graham, *The Graham Greene Film Reader: Mornings in the Dark,* ed. David Parkinson, Manchester: Carcanet, 1993.

Greene, Naomi, 'Coppola, Cimino: The Operatics of History', *Film Quarterly,* 38/2 (1984–5), pp. 28–37.

Greene, Naomi, 'Family Ceremonies: Or, Opera in *The 'Godfather* trilogy', in Browne (ed), *Francis Ford Coppola's 'The Godfather' Trilogy,* pp. 133–55.

Gregory, Charles T., 'Good Guys and Bad Guys', *Film Heritage,* 8/3 (1973), pp. 1–9.

Gross, Larry, 'Baby, I Don't Care', *Sight and Sound,* 7/9 (1997), pp. 6–9.

Guillory, John, *Culture as Capital: The Problem of Literary Canon Formation,* Chicago: University of Chicago Press, 1993.

Guthmann, Edward, review of *The Night of the Hunter, San Francisco Chronicle,* 15 September 1995.

Haeffner, Nicholas, *Alfred Hitchcock,* Harlow, UK: Pearson Longman, 2005.

Hagopian, Kevin, 'Film Notes: *The Night of the Hunter*', *New York State Writers Institute,* n.d., http://www.albany.edu/writers-inst/webpages/filmnotes/fnf00n5b.html, accessed 27 June 2008.

Hammond, Paul, 'Melmoth in Norman Rockwell Land … On *The Night of the Hunter*', *Sight and Sound,* 48/2 (1979), pp. 105–9.

Hancock, Michael, review of *The Piano, Metro,* 148 (2006), p. 171, *EBSCO research databases.*

Harmetz, Aljean, 'Movie Classic', *American Heritage,* October 2005, internet version consulted: http://www.americanheritage.com/articles/magazine/ah/2005/5/2005_5_69.shtml, accessed 31 December 2007.

Hauke, Christopher, and Alister, Ian (eds), *Jung and Film: Post-Jungian Takes on the Moving Image,* Hove, East Sussex, UK: Brunner-Routledge, 2001.

Hayes, David P., '*Citizen Kane*'s Borrowings: Techniques Attributed to *Citizen Kane* which Appeared in Earlier Films', *Classic Movies: Related Articles from My Newsgroup Postings,* 9 March 1998, http://articles.dhwritings.com/a01.html, accessed 31 December 2007.

Hayes, Kevin J. (ed.), *Martin Scorsese's 'Raging Bull',* Cambridge: Cambridge University Press, 2004.

Hendershot, Cyndy, '(Re)Visioning the Gothic: Jane Campion's *The Piano*', *Literature/Film Quarterly,* 26/2 (1998), pp. 97–108, *BNET Research Center,* http://findarticles.com/p/articles/mi_qa3768/is_199801/ai_n8764512, accessed 4 January 2008.

Hensher, Philip, 'Our Films Should Be for Us, Not Tarantino', *Independent,* 14 May 2004.

Heylin, Clinton, *Despite the System: Orson Welles Versus the Hollywood Studios,* Edinburgh: Canongate, 2005.

Higham, Charles, 'From *The Films of Orson Welles*', in Gottesman (ed.), *Focus on 'Citizen Kane',* pp. 137–45.

Higham, Charles, 'Hitchcock's World', *Film Quarterly,* 16/2 (1962–3), pp. 3–16.

Hinson, Hal, review of *8½, Washington Post,* 26 February 1993.

Hinson, Hal, review of *The Piano, Washington Post,* 19 November 1993.

Hitchcock, Alfred, 'Why I Make Melodramas' (1936), *'The MacGuffin' Web Page,* http://www.labyrinth.net.au/%7emuffin/melodramas_c.html, accessed 31 December 2007.

Hoberman, J., 'Enter the Lady Dragon', *Village Voice,* 8–14 October 2003.

Hoberman, J., 'The Stunt Men', *Village Voice,* 7–13 April 1999.

Hodson, Joel C., *Lawrence of Arabia and American Culture: The Making of a Transatlantic Legend,* Westport, CT: Greenwood Press, 1995.

Hodson, Joel C., 'Who Wrote *Lawrence of Arabia?:* Sam Spiegel and David Lean's Denial of Credit to a Blacklisted Screenwriter', *Cineaste,* 20/4 (1994), pp. 12–17.

Hoeveler, Diane Long, 'Silence, Sex, and Feminism: An Examination of *The Piano*'s Unacknowledged Sources', *Literature/Film Quarterly,* 26/2 (1998), pp. 109–16.

Holland, Norman N., '*8½* and Me: The Thirty-Two Year Difference', *Journal of Aging and Identity,* 1/2 (1996), pp. 125–41, http://www.psychomedia.it/pm/culture/cinema/holland.htm, accessed 4 January 2008.

Holly, Michael Ann, and Moxey, Keith (eds), *Art History, Aesthetics, Visual Studies,* Williamstown, MA: Sterling and Francine Clark Art Institute, 2002.

Holm, D. K., *Kill Bill: An Unofficial Casebook,* London: Glitterbooks, 2004.

hooks, bell, 'Sexism and Misogyny: Who Takes the Rap? Misogyny, Gangsta Rap, and *The Piano*'', *Z Magazine,* February 1994, http://www.westga.edu/~gfraser/bell%20hooks.doc, accessed 4 January 2008.

Howe, Desson, '*Godfather:* Offer Accepted', *Washington Post,* 21 March 1997.

Howe, Desson, review of *8½, Washington Post,* 26 February 1993.

Howe, Desson, review of *Lawrence of Arabia, Washington Post,* 3 February 1989.

Howe, Desson, review of *The Piano, Washington Post,* 19 November 1993.

Hu, Brian, 'Taking Film Studies to the Streets (and Back Again): On the Necessity of Criticism', *Mediascape,* 1/1 (2005), http://www.tft.ucla.edu/mediascape/Spring05_TakingFilmsStudiesToTheStreets.html, accessed 28 June 2008

Hua, Anh, 'Primitive Spectacle in *Black Narcissus*', *Journal of Social and Political Thought,* 1/2 (2000), http://www.yorku.ca/jspot/2/ahua.htm, accessed 2 January 2008.

Hunter, Stephen, 'A Space Idiocy: *2001* Revisited', *Washington Post,* 2 November 2001.

Hunter, Tim, with Kaplan, Stephen, and Jaszi, Peter, 'The *Harvard Crimson* Review of *2001*' [1968], *The* Kubrick *Site,* http://www.visual-memory.co.uk/amk/doc/0038.html, accessed 3 January 2008.

Huntley, John, *British Technicolour Film,* London: Skelton Robinson, [1949].

Huron, David, *Sweet Anticipation: Music and the Psychology of Expectation,* Cambridge, MA: MIT Press, 2006.

Jaikumar, Priya, 'Place and the Modernist Redemption of Empire in *Black Narcissus* (1947)', *Cinema Journal,* 40/2 (2001), pp. 57–77.

James, Nick, 'Modern Times', *Sight and Sound,* 12/12 (2002), pp. 20–3.

James, Nick, 'Nul Britannia', *Sight and Sound,* 12/9 (2002), p. 38.

Jancovich, Mark, Faire, Lucy, and Stubbings, Sarah, *The Place of the Audience: Cultural Geographies of Film Consumption,* London: BFI, 2003.

Jarvie, Ian C., 'Fanning the Flames: Anti-American Reaction to *Operation Burma* (1945)', *Historical Journal of Film, Radio and Television,* 1/2 (1981), pp. 117–37.

Jay, Betty, ' "All Imperfect Things": Motherhood and the Aesthetics of Ambivalence in *The Piano*', *Scope,* 4 (2006), http://www.scope.nottingham.ac.uk/article.php?issue=4&id=125, accessed 4 January 2008.

Johnson, Gary, review of *The 39 Steps* DVD, *Images,* 8 (2004), http://www.imagesjournal.com/issue08/reviews/39steps, accessed 31 December 2007.

Johnston, Ian, *'The Night of the Hunter', not coming to a theater near you,* 2005, http://www.notcoming.com/reviews.php?id=489, accessed 2 January 2008.

Johnstone, Iain, 'Silent Plight', *Sunday Times,* 31 October 1993.

Jones, Marty, 'Quentin Tarantino's Playful Violence and High Body Count', *World Socialist Web Site,* 2003, http://www.wsws.org/articles/2003/nov2003/kill-n11.shtml, accessed 5 January 2008.

Jones, Preston Neal, *Heaven and Hell to Play With: The Filming of 'The Night of the Hunter'*, New York: Limelight Editions, 2002.

Jowett, Garth, Jarvie, Ian C., and Fuller, Kathryn H., *Children at the Movies: Media Influence and the Payne Fund Controversy,* Cambridge: Cambridge University Press, 1996.

Jung, C. G., *The Archetypes and the Collective Unconscious,* tr. R. F. C. Hull, vol. 9, part 1 of *Collected Works,* 2nd edn, London: Routledge & Kegan Paul, 1969.

Kael, Pauline, *5001 Nights at the Movies,* London: Arrow Books, 1987.

Kael, Pauline, *Raising Kane: Pauline Kael on the Best Film Ever Made,* London: Methuen, 1995.

Kael, Pauline, *Taking It All In,* New York: Holt, Rinehart and Winston, 1987.

Kael, Pauline, 'Trash, Art, and the Movies' (1969), in Pauline Kael, *Going Steady,* Boston: Little, Brown, 1970, pp. 86–129.

Kaplan, *see* Wood.

Kapsis, Robert E., *Alfred Hitchcock: The Making of a Reputation,* Chicago: University of Chicago Press, 1992.

Kapsis, Robert E., 'Alfred Hitchcock: Auteur or Hack?', *Cineaste,* 14/3 (1986), pp. 30–5.

Kehr, Dave, 'Hitchcock's Riddle', *Film Comment,* 20/3 (1984), pp. 9–18.

Kelly, Andrew, Richards, Jeffrey, and Pepper, Jane, *Filming T. E. Lawrence: Korda's Lost Epic,* London: I. B. Tauris, 1997.

Kemp, Philip, 'Why Fellini?', *Sight and Sound,* 14/8 (2004), pp. 20–3.

Kempley, Rita, review of *Lawrence of Arabia, Washington Post,* 8 February 1989.

Kennedy, A. L., *The Life and Death of Colonel Blimp,* London: BFI, 1997.

Kimber, John, *The Art of Charlie Chaplin,* London: Sheffield Academic Press, 2000.

Kinder, Marsha, 'Violence American Style: The Narrative Orchestration of Violent Attractions', in J. David Slocum (ed.), *Violence and American Cinema,* New York: Routledge, 2001, pp. 63–102.

King, Andrea Sarafian, 'Hitchcock Bibliography ... Revised', *British Film Institute,* 2002, http://www.bfi.org.uk/filmtvinfo/publications/bibliographies/hitchcock.pdf, accessed 29 December 2007.

Klwans, Stuart, review of *The Piano, Nation,* 6 December 1993, p. 704, *EBSCO research databases.*

Koelling, Holly, *Classic Connections: Turning Teens on to Great Literature,* Westport, CT: Libraries Unlimited, 2004.

Kuhn, Annette, *An Everyday Magic: Cinema and Cultural Memory,* London: I. B. Tauris, 2002.

Lanzagorta, Marco, '*Lawrence of Arabia:* The Burden of the Empire', *PopMatters,* 2003, http://www.popmatters.com/pm/film/reviews/36429/lawrence-of-arabia-dvd, accessed 3 January 2008.

LaSalle, Mick, 'Modern *Times* Keeps Up with Ours', *San Francisco Chronicle,* 26 December 2003.

Lavery, David, 'Major Man: Fellini as an Autobiographer', *Post Script,* 6/2 (1987), pp. 14–28, http://davidlavery.net/writings/Movies/Major_Man.pdf, accessed 4 January 2008.

Lean, Tangye, 'Review of *Citizen Kane', Horizon,* 4 (1941), in Gottesman (ed.), *Focus on 'Citizen Kane',* pp. 59–65.

Lee, Kevin, 'Jonathan Rosenbaum's 1000 Essential Films: Questions and Answers', *Also Like Life Productions,* n.d., http://www.alsolikelife.com/FilmDiary/rosenbaum100qa.html, accessed 28 December 2007.

Leff, Leonard J., 'Reading *Kane', Film Quarterly,* 39/1 (1985), pp. 10–21.

Levitin, Daniel, *This Is Your Brain on Music: The Science of a Human Obsession,* New York: Dutton Books, 2006.

Liehm, Mira, *Passion and Defiance: Film in Italy from 1942 to the Present,* Berkeley and Los Angeles: University of California Press, 1984.

Lindop, Jason, 'Eisenstein: Intellectual Montage, Poststructuralism, and Ideology', *Offscreen,* 11/2 (2007), http://www.offscreen.com/biblio/phile/essays/eisenstein_

intellectual_montage_poststructuralism_and_ideology/, accessed 29 December 2007.

Long, Christopher, 'Revising the Film Canon: Jonathan Rosenbaum's *Movie Mutations* and *Essential Cinema*', *New Review of Film and Television Studies*, 4/1 (2006), pp. 17–35.

Longinus, Cassius, *On the Sublime*, tr. W. Rhys Roberts, *Peitho's Web*, n.d., http://classicpersuasion.org/pw/longinus/desub002.htm, accessed 27 December 2007.

Löthwall, Lars-Olaf, 'An Interview with Ingmar Bergman', *Take One*, 2/1 (1968), pp. 16–18, *Bergmanorama*, http://www.bergmanorama.com/takeone_68.htm, accessed 4 January 2008.

Lynn, Kenneth S., *Charlie Chaplin and His Times*, London: Aurum Press, 1997; New York: Simon & Schuster, 1997.

MacKillop, Ian, and Sinyard, Neil (eds), *British Cinema of the 1950s: A Celebration*, Manchester: Manchester University Press, 2003.

Macklin, F. Anthony, 'The Comic Sense of *2001*', *Film Comment*, 5/4 (1969), pp. 10–14.

Maddox, Garry, 'Tarantino Accused of Urging Teenagers to Break Censorship Law', *Sydney Morning Herald Online*, 17 October 2003, http://www.smh.com.au/articles/2003/10/16/1065917555109.html, accessed 5 January 2008.

Magrini, J. M., 'On the Sublime: Longinus, Burke and Kant', *Carleton University Student Journal of Philosophy*, 20/1 (2002), Carleton University, http://www.carleton.ca/philosophy/cusjp/v20/n1/magrini.html, accessed 27 December 2007.

Maher, Kevin, 'I Am Your Fantasy Father', *Times*, 21 April 2005.

Mainar, Luis M. Garcia, *Narrative and Stylistic Patterns in the Films of Stanley Kubrick*, Rochester, NY and Woodbridge, Suffolk, UK: Camden House, 1999.

Maland, Charles J., *Chaplin and American Culture: The Evolution of a Star Image*, Princeton, NJ: Princeton University Press, 1989.

Malcolm, Derek, *Derek Malcolm's Personal Best: A Century of Films*, London: I. B. Tauris, 2000.

Malcolm, Derek, 'Keynote in the Silence', *Guardian*, 28 October 1993.

Manacsa, Gerry, 'Federico Fellini, Images and Archetypes: A Personal Perspective', *Out of Balance*, 2002, http://www.outofbalance.org/fellini, accessed 4 January 2008.

Margolis, Harriet (ed.), *Jane Campion's 'The Piano'*, Cambridge: Cambridge University Press, 2000.

Mariani, John, 'The Intelligent Heart', *Film Comment*, 15/5 (1979), pp. 34–9.

Martin, Adrian, 'Light My Fire (The Geology and Geography of Film Canons)', *senses of cinema*, 14 (2001), Pandora Archive, National Library of Australia. Currently unavailable.

Martin, James, 'What's so Wonderful?', *America*, 20–27 December 1997, p. 22, *EBSCO research databases*.

Matthews, J. H., *Surrealism and Film*, Ann Arbor: University of Michigan Press, 1971.

McBride, Joseph, *Frank Capra: The Catastrophe of Success,* London: Faber and Faber, 1992.

McBride, Joseph, review of *Raging Bull, Variety,* 12 November 1980.

McCaffrey, Donald (ed.), *Focus on Chaplin,* Englewood Cliffs, NJ: Prentice-Hall, 1971.

McCallion, Harry, 'The Movies, Me and Violence', in Karl French (ed.), *Screen Violence,* London: Bloomsbury, 1996, pp. 205–13.

McCollam, Douglas, 'A Fall from Grace', *Columbia Journalism Review,* 1 (2004), http://cjrarchives.org/issues/2004/1/easterbrook-mccollam.asp, accessed 5 January 2008.

McConnell, Frank, *Storytelling and Mythmaking: Images from Film and Literature,* New York: Oxford University Press, 1979.

McCormick, Tracy, '*2001* Under Fire: Early Reviewers of Film Found It Boring, Frustrating', *Obelisk,* n.d., http://www.boraski.com/obelisk/cinema/s_reviews.html, accessed 3 January 2008.

McFarland, Alton Jerome, 'Madness through Music: An Analysis of Sound in *Black Narcissus*', *Powell & Pressburger Pages,* n.d., http://www.powell-pressburger.org/Reviews/47_BN/MadnessThroughMusic.html, accessed 2 January 2008.

McKee, Mel, '*2001:* Out of the Secret Planet', *Sight and Sound,* 38/4 (1969), pp. 204–7.

McLellan, Jim, 'Tarantino on the Run', in Paul A. Woods (ed.), *Quentin Tarantino: The Film Geek Files,* London: Plexus, 2005, pp. 53–60.

McVay, Douglas, 'Michael Powell: Three Neglected Films', *Films and Filming,* January 1982, pp. 18–25.

Mellen, Joan, *Modern Times,* London: BFI, 2006.

Michelson, Annette, 'Eisenstein at 100: Recent Reception and Coming Attractions', *October,* 88 (1999), pp. 69–85.

Miller, Mark Crispin, '*2001:* A Cold Descent', *Sight and Sound,* 4/1 (1994), pp. 18–25.

Milton, Joyce, *Tramp: The Life of Charlie Chaplin,* New York: Da Capo Press, 1998.

Moen, Kristian, ' "About as Shapeless as the Man in the Moon": The Representation of Desire and Transition in Six Films of Charles Laughton', MA thesis, Concordia University, Montreal, 2001, http://www.collectionscanada.ca/obj/s4/f2/dsk3/ftp04/MQ59351.pdf, accessed 2 January 2008.

Mogg, Ken, review of Mark Glancy, *The 39 Steps, Screening the Past,* 2004, http://www.latrobe.edu.au/screeningthepast/reviews/rev_16/KMbr16a.html, accessed 31 December 2007.

Monthly Film Bulletin, review of *Black Narcissus,* 14/161 (1947), p. 60.

Monthly Film Bulletin, review of *Modern Times,* 3/26 (1936), pp. 28–9.

Monthly Film Bulletin, review of *The 39 Steps,* 2/17 (1935), p. 72.

Moor, Andrew, *Powell and Pressburger: A Cinema of Magic Spaces,* London: I. B. Tauris, 2005.

Morris, Gary, 'Powell and Pressburger's *Black Narcissus* on DVD', *Bright Lights Film Journal,* 33 (2001), http://www.brightlightsfilm.com/33/blacknarcissus. html, accessed 2 January 2008.

Moser, Karin, 'Introduction: 1905 GOD *(Bronenosez Potemkin)*', *COLLATE Project,* n.d., http://deutsches-filminstitut.de/collate/collate_sp/se/se_04.html, accessed 29 December 2007.

Munby, Jonathan, 'A Hollywood Carol's Wonderful Life', in Mark Connelly (ed.), *Christmas at the Movies: Images of Christmas in American, British and European Cinema,* London: I. B. Tauris: 2000, pp. 39–57.

Murphy, A. D., review of *The Godfather, Variety,* 15 March 1972.

Napoleon, Davi, 'Wonderful Life: Broadway Bound?', *American Film,* 11/7 (1986), p. 10.

Naremore, James, 'Style and Meaning in *Citizen Kane*', in Naremore (ed.), *Orson Welles's 'Citizen Kane',* pp. 123–59.

Naremore, James (ed.), *Orson Welles's 'Citizen Kane': A Casebook,* New York: Oxford University Press, 2004.

Neale, Steve, 'Melo Talk: On the Meaning and Use of the Term "Melodrama" in the American Trade Press', *Velvet Light Trap,* 22 (1993), pp. 66–81.

Nelson, Thomas Allen, *Kubrick: Inside a Film Artist's Maze,* expanded edn, Bloomington: Indiana University Press, 2000.

Newitz, Annalee, 'It's Fun … But It Takes Courage: Remembering Frank Capra's America', *Bad Subjects,* 11 (1994), http://eserver.org/bs/11/Newitz.html, accessed 2 January 2008.

Newlyn, Lucy, *Reading, Writing and Romanticism: The Anxiety of Reception,* Oxford: Oxford University Press, 2000.

Newman, Kim, review of *Kill Bill: Volume 1, Sight and Sound,* 13/12 (2003), pp. 39–42.

Norden, Martin F., 'The Avant-Garde Cinema of the 1920s: Connections to Futurism, Precisionism, and Suprematism', *Leonardo,* 17/2 (1984), pp. 108–12.

Nugent, Frank S., 'Heralding the Return, after an Undue Absence, of Charlie Chaplin in *Modern Times',* *New York Times,* 6 February 1936.

Oakes, Philip, 'Portrait of a Fighter in a Mean Street', *Sunday Times,* 22 February 1981.

O'Ehley, James, *'2001: A Space Odyssey', The Sci-Fi Movie Page,* 1997, http://www.scifimoviepage.com/2001.html, accessed 3 January 2008.

O'Ehley, James, *'2001:* 30 Years On', *The Sci-Fi Movie Page,* 1997, http://www.scifimoviepage.com/2001_30.html, accessed 3 January 2008.

Ohmer, Susan, *George Gallup in Hollywood,* New York: Columbia University Press, 2006.

Oms, Marcel, 'Charlie Chaplin, Stranger and Brother: Shadows on the Screen', *UNESCO Courier,* October 1989, *BNET Research Center,* http://findarticles.com/p/articles/mi_m1310/is_1989_Oct/ai_8114683, accessed 31 December 2007.

Orr, John, *Hitchcock and 20th Century Cinema,* London: Wallflower Press, 2005.

Paglia, Camille, 'The Italian Way of Death', *Salon,* 1996, http://www.salon.com/weekly/paglia960805.html, accessed 3 January 2008.

Papke, David Ray, 'Myth and Meaning: Francis Ford Coppola and Popular Responses to the Godfather Trilogy', in John Denvir (ed.), *Legal Reelism: Movies as Legal Texts,* Urbana: University of Illinois Press, 1996, pp. 1–22.

Patterson, David W., 'Music, Structure and Metaphor in Stanley Kubrick's *2001: A Space Odyssey*', *American Music,* 22/3 (2004), pp. 444–74.

Pavlovic, Milan, '30 Lieblingsfilme (30 favorite films poll)', *Jeeem's CinePad,* 1995, http://www.cinepad.com/awards/lieblingsfilme.htm, accessed 28 December 2007.

Pearson, Harry, review of *The Piano, Films in Review,* 45/3–4 (1994), pp. 56–7.

Perry, Dennis R., 'Imps of the Perverse: Discovering the Poe/Hitchcock Connection', *Literature/Film Quarterly,* 24/4 (1996), pp. 393–9.

Perry, Ted, 'Ted Perry on *8½*', in Leo Braudy and Morris Dickstein (eds), *Great Film Directors: A Critical Anthology,* New York: Oxford University Press, 1978, pp. 290–8.

Peterson, Thane, 'Too Much Kill in the Kill Bills', *Business Week Online,* 5 May 2004, http://www.businessweek.com/bwdaily/dnflash/may2004/nf2004055_4548_db028.htm, accessed 5 January 2008.

Phillips, Julie, 'Classics Defined: Robert Osborne's Classic Film Festival Offers Another Round of Favorites', *OnLineAthens,* 23 March 2006, http://onlineathens.com/stories/032306/marquee_20060323011.shtml, accessed 28 December 2007.

'The Piano Debate', *Screen,* 36/3 (1995). pp. 257–86.

Poague, Leland, *Another Frank Capra,* Cambridge: Cambridge University Press, 1994.

Poleg, Dror, 'The Unbearable Lightness of Being Cool: Appropriation and Prospects of Subversion in the Works of Quentin Tarantino', *Bright Lights Film Journal,* 45 (2004), http://www.brightlightsfilm.com/45/toilets.htm, accessed 5 January 2008.

Poon, Phoebe, 'The Corleone Chronicles: Revisiting *The Godfather* Films as Trilogy', *Journal of Popular Film and Television,* 33/4 (2006), pp. 187–95.

Pope, Richard I., 'In Kubrick's Crypt, a Derrida/Deleuze Monster; or An-Other Return to *2001*', *Film Philosophy,* 7/22, (2003), http://www.film-philosophy.com/vol7–2003/n22pope, accessed 3 January 2008.

Powell, Dilys, *The Golden Screen: Fifty Years of Films,* ed. George Perry, London: Pavilion Books, 1989.

Powell, Michael, *A Life in Movies,* London: Heinemann, 1986.

Powell, Michael, *Million Dollar Movie,* London: Heinemann, 1992.

Pugmire, David, *Sound Sentiments: Integrity in the Emotions,* Oxford: Clarendon Press, Oxford University Press, 2005.

Pulleine, Tom, 'A Fair Knockout for the Aesthetes', *Guardian,* 19 February 1981.

Purkayastha, Dibyaduti, '*Black Narcissus* (1946): A "Desi" Perspective', *The Powell & Pressburger Pages,* n.d., http//www.powell-pressburger.org/Reviews/47_BN/BN06.html, accessed 2 January 2008.

Quart, Barbara, review of *The Piano, Cineaste,* 20/3 (1994), pp. 54–6.

Ravage, Jack, '*The Night of the Hunter* [On Videotape]', *Film Quarterly,* 42/1 (1988), pp. 43–6.

Raw, Laurence, 'T. E. Lawrence, the Turks, and the Arab Revolt in the Cinema: Anglo-American and Turkish Representations', *Literature/Film Quarterly,* 33/4 (2005), pp. 252–61.

Ray, Robert B., *A Certain Tendency of the Hollywood Cinema, 1930–1980,* Princeton, NJ: Princeton University Press, 1985.

Raymond, Marc, 'Martin Scorsese', *senses of cinema,* 10 (2002), http://www.sensesofcinema.com/contents/directors/02/scorsese.html, accessed 3 January 2008.

Read, Herbert, *Art and Alienation: The Role of the Artist in Society,* London: Thames & Hudson, 1967.

Reich, Jacqueline, '*Otto e mezzo/8½*', in Giorgio Bertellini (ed.), *The Cinema of Italy,* London: Wallflower Press, 2004, pp. 143–51.

Reichert, Jeff, 'I Couldn't Refuse', *reverse shot online,* Autumn 2005, http://www.reverseshot.com/legacy/autumn05/symposium/godfather.html, accessed 3 January 2008.

Reid, Mark A., 'A Few Black Keys and Maori Tattoos: Re-Reading Jane Campion's *The Piano* in Post Negritude Time', *Quarterly Review of Film and Video,* 17/2 (2000), pp. 107–16.

Rhode, Eric, review of *8½, Sight and Sound,* 32/4 (1963), p. 193.

Richards, Jeffrey, *Films and British National Identity: From Dickens to 'Dad's Army',* Manchester: Manchester University Press, 1997.

Richards, Jeffrey, and Hulbert, Jeffrey, 'Censorship in Action: The Case of *Lawrence of Arabia*', *Journal of Contemporary History,* 19/1 (1984), pp. 153–70.

Roberte, Dariusz, '*2001: A Space Odyssey:* A Critical Analysis of the Film Score', *The Kubrick Site,* n.d. http://www.visual-memory.co.uk/amk/doc/0108.html, accessed 3 January 2008.

Robinson, David, '*Modern Times*', *Charlie Chaplin Official Website,* 2004, http://www.charliechaplin.com/en/articles/6, accessed 31 December 2007.

Robinson, David, review of *Modern Times, Sight and Sound,* 41/2 (1972), pp. 109–10.

Robinson, Jenefer, *Deeper than Reason: Emotion and Its Role in Literature, Music and Art,* Oxford: Clarendon Press, Oxford University Press, 2005.

Rodriguez-Ortega, Vicente, 'Fear Factor', *Reverse Shot Online,* Autumn 2005, http://www.reverseshot.com/legacy/autumn05/symposium/night.html, accessed 2 January 2008.

Roddick, Nick, 'Twisted Little Masterpieces', *Sight and Sound,* 17/2 (2007), p. 10.

Rohdie, Sam, *Montage,* Manchester: Manchester University Press, 2006.

Rombes, Nicholas, '*Kill Bill* Unplugged: How Reshaping Reality May Haunt Us Yet', *Solpix,* n.d., http://www.webdelsol.com/SolPix/sp-nickkillbill.htm, accessed 5 January 2008.

Rosenbaum, Jonathan, *Essential Cinema: On the Necessity of Film Canons,* Baltimore, MD: Johns Hopkins University Press, 2004.

Rosenbaum, Jonathan, 'Jonathan Rosenbaum Responds to Robin Bates's "Fiery Speech in a World of Shadows: Rosebud's Influence on Early Audiences"', *Cinema Journal,* 26/4 (1987), pp. 60–4.

Rosenbaum, Jonathan, 'Rediscovering Charlie Chaplin', *Cineaste,* 29/4 (2004), pp. 52–6.

Rosenbaum, Jonathan, review of *Lawrence of Arabia, Chicago Reader,* http://onfilm. chicagoreader.com/movies/capsules/5248_LAWRENCE_OF_ARABIA.

Ross, Steven, 'In Defense of David Lean', *Take One,* 3/12 (1972), pp. 10–18.

Rowland, Richard, 'American Classic', *Hollywood Quarterly,* 2/3 (1947), pp. 264–9.

Ryall, Tom, *Alfred Hitchcock and the British Cinema,* 2nd edn, London: Athlone Press, 1996.

Saco, Diana, 'Feminist Film Criticism: *The Piano* and '"the Female Gaze"', *Diana Saco,* 1994, http://diana.saco.name/Female_Gaze.htm, accessed 4 January 2008.

Sainte-Beuve, Charles Augustin, 'What Is a Classic?', *The Harvard Classics 1909–14, Bartleby.com,* 2005, http://www.bartleby.com/32/202.html, accessed 28 December 2007.

Samuels, Charles Thomas, 'Sightings: Hitchcock', *American Scholar,* 39 (1970), p. 295, in *'The Thirty-Nine Steps* CineFile', *Pacific Film Archive,* http://www.mip.berkeley.edu/cgi-bin/cine_film_detail.pl/cine_img?21091+21091+432, accessed 31 December 2007.

Sandall, Roger, review of *Lawrence of Arabia, Film Quarterly,* 16/3 (1963), pp. 56–7.

Sarris, Andrew, *The American Cinema: Directors and Directions, 1929–1968,* New York: E. P. Dutton, 1968.

Sarris, Andrew, *'Citizen Kane:* The American Baroque', in Gottesman (ed.), *Focus on 'Citizen Kane',* pp. 102–7.

Sarris, Andrew, 'Kane: For and Against', *Sight and Sound,* 1/6 (1991), pp. 20–3.

Sarris, Andrew, *You Ain't Heard Nothin' Yet—The American Talking Film: History and Memory, 1927–1949,* New York: Oxford University Press, 1998.

Sayers, Janet, and Monin, Nanette, 'Comedy, Pain and Nonsense at the Red Moon Cafe: The Little Tramp's Death by Service Work in *Modern Times',* paper presented at the 2nd Art of Management Conference, Paris, 2004, http://www. aacorn.net/members_all/sayers_janet/comedypainnonsense.pdf, accessed 31 December 2007.

Schader, Fred, 'The *Potemkin', Variety* (1926), in *'Bronenosets Potemkin* CineFile', *Pacific Film Archive,* http://www.mip.berkeley.edu/cgi-bin/cine_film_detail.pl/cine_img?31, accessed 29 December 2007.

Scheurer, Timothy E., 'The Score for *2001: A Space Odyssey', Journal of Popular Film and Television,* 25/4 (1998), pp. 172–83, *HighBeam Encyclopedia,* http://www.encyclopedia.com/doc/1G1-20573310.html, accessed 27 June 2008.

Schjeldahl, Peter, 'Notes on Beauty', in Bill Beckley with David Shapiro (eds), *Uncontrollable Beauty,* New York: Allworth Press, 1998, pp. 53–9.

Schrader, Paul, 'The Film Canon', *Film Comment,* 42/1 (2006), pp. 33–49.

Schumacher, Michael, *Francis Ford Coppola: A Filmmaker's Life,* London: Bloomsbury, 2000.

Scorsese, Martin, 'Premio "Fondazione Fellini" a Martin Scorsese', *Fondazione Fellini,* 2005, http://www.federicofellini.it/newsScheda.asp?end_where=news&id=401, accessed 4 January 2008.

Screen, 'The Piano Debate', *Screen,* 36/3 (1995), pp. 257–86.

Scott, A. O., 'Blood Bath & Beyond', *New York Times,* 10 October 2003.

Sedgwick, John, *Popular Filmgoing in 1930s Britain: A Choice of Pleasures,* Exeter: University of Exeter Press, 2000.

Seguin, Denis, 'Gold in the Vaults', *Screen International,* 20–25 April 2007, p. 11.

Sennwald, Andre, 'Alfred Hitchcock's New Picture, *The Thirty-Nine Steps',* *New York Times,* 14 September 1935.

Severson, Gregg, 'Historical Narrative in *The Battleship Potemkin',* *Carleton University,* 1998, http://www.carleton.edu/curricular/MEDA/classes/media110/Severson/essay.htm, accessed 29 December 2007.

Shadoian, Jack, *Dreams and Dead Ends: The American Gangster/Crime Film,* Cambridge, MA: MIT Press, 1977.

Shaheen, Jack G., *Reel Bad Arabs: How Hollywood Vilifies a People,* New York: Olive Branch Press, 2001.

Sharrett, Christopher, review of *Kill Bill, Volume 1, Cineaste,* 29/2 (2004), p. 96.

Shaw, Dan, 'Sergei Eisenstein', *senses of cinema,* 30 (2004), http://www.sensesofcinema.com/contents/directors/04/eisenstein.html, accessed 29 December 2007.

Sheehan, Henry, '*Black Narcissus* (1947)', *Film Comment,* 26/3 (1990), pp. 37–9.

Sillick, Ardis and McCormick, Michael (eds), *Some Like It Not: Bad Reviews of Great Movies,* London: Aurum Press, 1996.

Silver, Alain, 'David Lean', *senses of cinema,* 30 (2004), http://www.sensesofcinema.com/contents/directors/04/lean.html, accessed 3 January 2008.

Simon, John, 'Praise Jack, Shoot *The Piano'*, *National Review,* 27 December 1993, pp. 65–7, internet version consulted: *BNET Research Center,* http://findarticles.com/p/articles/mi_m1282/is_n25_v45/ai_14779808, accessed 4 January 2008.

Siomopoulos, Anna, ' "I Didn't Know Anyone Could Be So Unselfish": Liberal Empathy, the Welfare State, and King Vidor's *Stella Dallas',* *Cinema Journal,* 38/4 (1999), pp. 3–23.

Sloan, Jane, *Alfred Hitchcock: A Filmography and Bibliography,* Berkeley and Los Angeles: University of California Press, 1995.

Slocum, J. David, 'Film Violence and the Institutionalization of the Cinema', *Social Research,* 67/3 (2000), pp. 649–81.

Smith, Julian, *Chaplin,* Boston: Twayne, 1984.

Smith, Neil, 'Stars Defend *Kill Bill* Violence', *BBC News Online,* 21 April 2004, http://news.bbc.co.uk/1/hi/entertainment/film/3644281.stm, accessed 5 January 2008.

Smoodin, Eric, *Regarding Frank Capra: Audience, Celebrity, and American Film Studies, 1930–1960,* Durham, NC: Duke University Press, 2004.

Solomon, Stanley J., 'Chatham Film Society Program Notes', in '*Bronenosets Potemkin* CineFile' (1964), *Pacific Film Archive,* http://www.mip.berkeley.edu/cgi-bin/cine_film_detail.pl/cine_img?31, accessed 29 December 2007.

Solomons, Jason, 'There's More to Film than *Citizen Kane', Observer,* 11 August 2002.

Sorrentino, Gilbert, 'Things Aren't What They Seem: Frank Capra's *It's a Wonderful Life*', *Context,* 2 (2000), http://www.dalketarchive.com/article/show/144, accessed 30 June 2008.

Staiger, Janet, 'The Politics of Film Canons', *Cinema Journal,* 24/3 (1985), pp. 4–23.

Stein, Elliott, 'Capra Counts His Oscars', *Sight and Sound,* 41/3 (1972), pp. 162–4.

Stephens, Chuck, 'The Whole She-Bang: The Incredible Two-Headed Tarantino and the Last of His Double Bills', *Film Comment,* July–August 2004, pp. 44–7.

Stern, Lesley, *The Scorsese Connection,* Bloomington: Indiana University Press; and London: BFI, 1995.

Stewart, Garrett, 'Modern Hard Times: Chaplin and the Cinema of Self-Reflection', *Critical Inquiry,* 3/2 (1976), pp. 295–314.

Stone, Alan A., '*8½:* Fellini's Moment of Truth', *Boston Review,* Summer 1995, http://bostonreview.net/BR20.3/stone.html, accessed 4 January 2008.

Stone, Alan A., '*The Piano', Boston Review,* n.d., http://bostonreview.net/BR19.1/stone.html, accessed 4 January 2008.

Street, Sarah, *Black Narcissus,* London: I. B. Tauris, 2005.

Strick, Philip, Review of *2001: A Space Odyssey, Sight and Sound,* 37/2 (1968) pp.153–4.

Summers, Mark, 'From Sneer to Eternity', *Vanity Fair,* March 2006, p. 342, *EBSCO research databases.*

Swislow, William, 'It's a Pretty Grim Life, Actually: All Is Not So Rosey in *It's a Wonderful Life', Interesting Ideas,* n.d., http://www.interestingideas.com/ii/capra.htm, accessed 2 January 2008.

Taubin, Amy, 'Primal Scream', *Village Voice,* 2–8 August 2000.

Taylor, John Russell, 'Beyond the Plot Barrier', *Times,* 7 September 1968.

Taylor, John Russell, 'A Heritage and Its History', *Times,* 22 August 1972.

Taylor, Richard, '*The Battleship Potemkin': The Film Companion,* London: I. B. Tauris, 2000.

Telotte, J. P., 'Definitely Falling Down: *8½, Falling Down* and the Death of Fantasy', *Journal of Popular Film and Television,* 24/1 (1996), pp. 19–25, *HighBeam Encyclopedia,* http://www.encyclopedia.com/doc/1G1–18533920.html, accessed 27 June 2008.

Thomas, François, '*Citizen Kane:* The Sound Track', in Naremore (ed.), *Orson Welles's 'Citizen Kane'*, pp. 161–83.

Thompson, Michael, *Rubbish Theory: The Creation and Destruction of Value,* Oxford: Oxford University Press, 1979.

Thomson, David, *America in the Dark: Hollywood and the Gift of Unreality,* London: Hutchinson, 1978.

Thomson, David, 'A Child's Demon', *Sight and Sound,* 9/4 (1999), pp. 20–2.

Thomson, David, 'Animal Instinct', *Guardian,* 10 August 2007.

Thomson, David, 'The Director as *Raging Bull:* Why Can't a Woman be More Like a Photograph?', *Film Comment,* 34/3 (1998), pp. 52–63.

Thomson, David, 'The Discreet Charm of the Godfather', *Sight and Sound,* 47/2 (1978), pp. 76–80.

Thomson, David, *The New Biographical Dictionary of Film,* 4th edn, London: Little, Brown, 2003.

Thomson, David, 'A Romantic Sensibility: The Films of Michael Powell', *American Film,* 6/2 (1980), pp. 47–52.

Toles, George, *A House Made of Light: Essays on the Art of Film,* Detroit, MI: Wayne State University Press, 2001.

Totaro, Donato, 'The Rules of His Game: Schrader's Canon', *Offscreen,* 10/12 (2006), http://www.offscreen.com/biblio/phile/essays/schraders_canon, accessed 5 January 2008.

Totaro, Donato, 'The *Sight and Sound* of Canons', *Offscreen,* January 2003, http://www.horschamp.qc.ca/new_offscreen/canon.html, accessed 28 December 2007.

Tredell, Nicholas (ed.), *Cinemas of the Mind: A Critical History of Film Theory,* Cambridge: Icon Books, 2002.

Truffaut, François, with Scott, Helen G., *Hitchcock,* London: Paladin, 1978.

Twain, Mark, *Following the Equator* (1897), *The Columbia World of Quotations,* 1996, *Bartleby.com,* http://www.bartelby.com/66/47/61947.html, accessed 28 December 2007.

'201 Greatest Movies of All Time', *Empire,* March 2006, pp. 77–101.

UK Film Council, 'Statistical Yearbook, 2006–07', London: 2007, http://www.ukfilmcouncil.org.uk/media/pdf/5/8/Starts_Year_book.pdf, accessed 23 June 2008.

Ule, Astrid, and Hansen, Eric, '*Battleship* Resurfaces', *Hollywood Reporter,* International Edition, 8 February 2005, *EBSCO research databases.*

University of Virginia, 'The Method', *America in the 1930s,* 1998, http://xroads.virginia.edu/~1930s/FILM/chaplin/meth1.html, accessed 31 December 2007.

van Peer, Willie, 'Towards a Doctrine of Poetics', in Mette Hjort and Sue Laver (eds), *Emotion and the Arts,* New York: Oxford University Press, 1997, pp. 215–24.

'The *Village Voice* 100 Best Films of the Century', *Village Voice,* 4 January 2000.

Voytilla, Stuart, *Myth and the Movies: Discovering the Mythic Structure of Over 50 Unforgettable Films,* Studio City, CA: Michael Wiese Productions, 1999.

Walker, Alexander, with Taylor, Sybil, and Ruchti, Ulrich, *Stanley Kubrick, Director: A Visual Analysis,* rev. edn, London: Weidenfeld and Nicholson, 1999.

Walker, Michael, *'Black Narcissus', Framework,* 9 (1978–9), pp. 9–13.

Walker, Michael, *Hitchcock's Motifs,* Amsterdam: Amsterdam University Press, 2005.

Walton, Kendall J., 'Make-Believe in the Arts', in Feagin and Maynard (eds), *Aesthetics,* pp. 288–300.

Weiner, Thomas, 'Martin Scorsese Fights Back', *American Film,* 6/2 (1980), pp. 31–4.

Weissman, Stephen M., 'Charles Chaplin's Film Heroines', *Film History,* 8/4 (1996), pp. 439–45.

Welles, Orson, and Bogdanowich, Peter, *This Is Orson Welles,* ed. Jonathan Rosenbaum, London, HarperCollins, 1993.

Wenden, D. J., *'Battleship Potemkin:* Film and Reality', in K.R.M. Short (ed.), *Feature Film as History,* London: Croom Helm, 1981, pp. 37–61.

Wheat, Leonard F., *Kubrick's '2001': A Triple Allegory,* Lanham, MD: Scarecrow Press, 2000.

Wilson, Colin, and Odell, Robin, *Jack the Ripper: Summing Up and Verdict,* London: Corgi, 1987.

Wilson, Jeremy, 'Lawrence of Arabia or Smith in the Desert?', *T. E. Lawrence Studies,* 2006, http://telawrence.info/telawrenceinfo/legacy3/film/film1.htm, accessed 3 January 2008.

Wilson, Michael, *'Lawrence of Arabia:* Elements and Facets of the Theme', *Cineaste,* 21/4 (1995), pp. 30–2.

Wolfe, Charles K., *Frank Capra: A Guide to References and Resources,* Boston: G. K. Hall, 1987.

Wollen, Peter, *'Citizen Kane',* in Naremore (ed.), *Orson Welles's 'Citizen Kane',* pp. 249–62.

Wollen, Peter, 'Films: Why Do Some Survive and Others Disappear?', *Sight and Sound,* 3/5 (1993), pp. 26–8.

Wood, Robin ('George Kaplan'), 'Alfred Hitchcock: Lost in the Wood', *Film Comment,* 8/4 (1972), pp. 46–53.

Wood, Robin, *Hitchcock's Films Revisited,* rev. edn, New York: Columbia University Press, 2002.

Wood, Robin, *Hollywood from Vietnam to Reagan,* New York: Columbia University Press, 1986.

Wood, Robin, 'Ideology, Genre, Auteur', *Film Comment,* 13/1 (1977), pp. 46–51.

Wood, Robin, 'The Question of Fellini Continued' (source and date not given), in '8½ CineFile', *Pacific Film Archive,* http://www.mip.berkeley.edu/cgi-bin/cine_film_detail.pl/cine_img?24275+24275, accessed 4 January 2008.

Wood, Robin, *'Raging Bull:* The Homosexual Subtext', *Movie,* 31–2 (1986), pp. 108–14.

Yanal, Robert J., *Hitchcock as Philosopher,* Jefferson, NC: McFarland, 2005.

Yanos, Allison R., 'The Piano as a Point of Resistance', *Fresh Writing,* 1 (2001–02), http://www.nd.edu/~frswrite/issues/2001–2002/Yanos.shtml, accessed 4 January 2008.

Yevin, Igor, 'Ambiguity and Art', *Mathematical Institute of the Serbian Academy of Sciences and Arts,* n.d., http://www.mi.sanu.ac.yu/vismath/igor/index.html, accessed 27 December 2007.

Zagarrio, Vito, 'It Is (Not) a Wonderful Life: For a Counter-Reading of Frank Capra', in Robert Sklar and Vito Zagarrio (eds), *Frank Capra: Authorship and the Studio System,* Philadelphia: Temple University Press, 1998, pp. 64–94.

Zimny, Claudia, '*2001* and the Motif of the Voyage', *The Kubrick Site,* n.d., http://www.visual-memory.co.uk/amk/doc/0001.html, accessed 3 January 2008.

Index